D1190952

HOW TO MAKE YOUR OWN

SEWING PATTERNS

HOW TO MAKE YOUR OWN

SEWING PATTERNS

DONALD H. McCUNN

GALAHAD BOOKS • NEW YORK CITY

To Dr. Paul D. Reinhardt whose inspiration is the cornerstone of this book and to my wife whose assistance in many capacities has made possible the completion of this project.

Library of Congress Catalog Card Number: 74-16562
ISBN 0-88365-260-9
Published by arrangement with Hart Publishing Co., Inc.
Manufactured in the United States of America

Table of Contents

INTRODUCTION

PATTERN drafting for either street clothes or stage costumes may seem like a complex and mystifying art, but basically it is a simple process. Fundamentally, a two-dimensional piece of material is shaped and altered so that it will cover a three-dimensional body.

The first step in the drafting process is to take accurate measurements of the body to be covered. These measurements are then converted into basic patterns which fit the body closely. The basic patterns may then be adjusted, adapted, and altered to achieve different designs. Finally, subtle variations in the cut of a pattern may be made to give distinctive qualities to the finished shape.

Pattern drafting is only one part of the larger process of the design and construction of garments, whether for street clothes or for stage costumes. The overall process for creating both types of garments will be described here so that the specific role of pattern drafting may be better understood.

CLOTHING DESIGN

THE CONCEPTION OF THE DESIGN is the initial phase in clothing construction. The procedures for designing street clothes and stage costumes are quite different, so they will be described separately.

STREET CLOTHES

The first consideration in designing contemporary street clothes is to determine how they are to be used—for formal occasions, for normal everyday wear, for work or for play.

With the purpose of the garment in mind, the specific design can be developed. The idea for the design may come from a style that was seen on the street, a garment viewed in the store window, a sketch seen in a clothes catalog, or from the imagination of the designer.

This idea should then be converted into a sketch. This is an important step, because with a sketch the designer can evaluate his ideas. He can, for example, see if a particular style of collar is appropriate with a particular style of sleeve. Frequently adjustments are made at this stage which greatly enhance the finished garment.*

Once the idea has been converted into a sketch, individual touches may be added. These individual touches may be used to compensate for any special qualities in the shape of the individual wearer, so that the garment will be as flattering as possible. Or they may be used to increase the originality of the design.

The designer will now buy the appropriate material. In some instances a specific garment may be designed for material that has already been purchased. In this case, the design should be adjusted to the nature of the material.

Stage Costumes

The process of designing stage costumes is more complex than the process of designing street clothes. The design concept must encompass a series of garments, not just one, and this concept must also be related to the particular style of the play being produced.

The first step in designing stage costumes is to read the script and come to an understanding of it. The costume designer then consults with the director and the set designer to see how the specific production is to be mounted.

There are many important aspects of the staging that must be clarified during these consultations. The period in history for the production must be established. Socio-economic factors must be determined. And the overall style of the production must be set in terms of the types of realistic and/or theatrical conventions that are to be

* Line drawings of the basic outline for a woman's body and a man's body have been included in the front of the book. (See pages 18 and 19).

employed. All of these factors are established in addition to clarifying the interpretation of plot, character, and thought.

By now an image of the design has been formulated in the designer's mind. An abstract painting, collage, or drawing is frequently rendered to express this image. After this, specific costumes are developed.

The individual qualities of the characters can be greatly enhanced by conscientious and creative costume design. The first factor to consider when approaching a specific character's costume, is the requirements of the script. Sometimes a script will specify the color or the cut of the clothes, or it may call for a change of costume. For example, if a character walks out on stage in the third act and one of the other characters says, "What a lovely new dress," the credibility of the audience will be strained if it is the same dress the character was wearing in the first act.

With the requirements of the script in mind the design is developed to express the character's personality and mood through the line, color, mass, and texture of the costumes. A costume with jagged edges can express distraction; black—mourning; a nubby texture—provinciality; and a lightweight costume—frilliness. Appropriate costuming can tell the audience much about the character merely by its presence on stage.

After the design has been thought through for each of the characters in terms of all of these factors, it is time to make sketches of the costumes. These drawings will be used in many important ways. First of all, the designer may use the sketches to determine whether he has maintained a proper unity for the overall design. If the conception of one character's costume is too different from the rest it is easy to change it at this point. Secondly, the sketches are used to show the director how the production is to be costumed. The director will then determine if the design is appropriate to his interpretation. And third, the sketches will show the costume construction crew what they are to make.

As a final part of the initial design process the material for the costumes will be purchased.

PATTERN DRAFTING

Pattern drafting is the first step in the process of turning a design conception into a reality. The pattern-drafting procedure is essentially the same for street clothes and stage costumes.

There are three basic elements to work with during the drafting: first, the sketch or sketches which show what must be achieved; secondly, the material which has been purchased; and finally, the measurements of the person or people who will wear the clothes.

Before the drafting is started, such things as seam and dart placements, types of openings for the garment (i.e. lacings, buttons, hooks and eyes, zippers, etc.) and, in the case of stage costumes, any boning or stiffening that is to be done, should be determined. After this the material to be used must be examined for its properties of draping, weight, and flexibility. With these considerations in mind the actual drafting may be started.

The patterns should first be drafted onto paper. These patterns may then be cut out. Normally, if a pattern is for a close-fitting garment or a complex design it is best to cut it out of some inexpensive material such as muslin or lining material. In the case of stage costumes, the patterns, regardless of complexity, are frequently cut from muslin first. In this way expensive mistakes and corrections in the finished material are avoided. In either case, whether muslin or the final material is used, sufficiently wide seam allowances should be left for alterations during the fitting process. The garment should then be pinned together for a trial fitting. When the adjustments of the trial fitting are completed, the fabric should be machine basted and then tried on again for a final fitting.

FITTING, CUTTING, AND CONSTRUCTION

The fitting process should be viewed as the second phase of the drafting process. Drafting establishes the basic location of the seams and the darts. The fitting establishes their exact location and makes it possible to compensate for the individual contours of the body being clothed. The fitting session may also provide an opportunity to devise subtle variations in the shape of the seams and the darts which will further enhance the design. Frequently it is only during the actual fitting that the ideas for such refinements occur to the designer.

The trial garment can then be taken apart. The seam allowances are cut to conventional size, and the garment can be adjusted so that it is symmetrical where desired.

If a trial muslin copy was used, it will now act as a corrected pattern for the final garment. Where stage costumes are being made this muslin copy is frequently used as an interlining.

The garment is now ready to be sewn together in its final form. In the case of stage costumes there is normally a crew of workers who will sew the costumes together. This crew should be supervised by the pattern drafter, because he is the one who best understands the details of how the costumes are to go together.

COSTUME PARADES AND DRESS REHEARSALS

Stage costumes now have an additional testing period to undergo. When the costumes have been finished, the actors try them on for a Costume Parade. Each actor goes on stage and practices the motions he is required to perform in the production. This tests the costume for strength, durability, and correctness of fit.

The Costume Parade is also the designer's first opportunity to see the costumes in the setting and under the lighting that will be used in the performance. Alterations to some of the costumes may be necessary.

There are then two or more dress rehearsals in which the costumes are tried out under the normal production circumstances. During this time the actors have the opportunity to get used to their costumes and to practice any costume changes they may be required to perform. If the costumes have been well designed and carefully constructed they should serve to spark the imaginations of the actors and help them to develop their characterizations. The dress-rehearsal period is the final opportunity for adjustments to be made to the costumes.

Briefly then, this is how garments for both the street and stage are conceived and constructed.

HOW TO USE THIS BOOK

PATTERN DRAFTING can be very difficult or fundamentally simple. To make it difficult all that is needed is a long series of steps that must be followed by rote but which require neither intelligence nor understanding on the part of the drafter. On the other hand, pattern drafting can be easy if each step in the process is clearly related to the final outcome and if the drafter visualizes what he is doing. This book utilizes the second approach not only because it is easier, but because only by understanding what he is doing can the pattern drafter achieve real skill and creativity.

The main idea behind this book is that virtually any pattern may be drafted by making alterations to a few basic patterns. These basic patterns are the bodice, the sleeve, the skirt, and the pants.

The basic bodice, for instance, can be made into different dress styles (princess, fitted, shirtwaist, evening gown, and others), various blouse or shirt styles, jackets, coats, or robes. The designs may be varied by adding pleats or gathers, yokes, different styles of collars or necklines, wrap-around closures, button closures, or zipper closures in the front or back.

The same is true of skirts, pants, collars and sleeves. Fullness can be added in the form of gathers or pleats, widths altered, or flare added. Garments may be changed from long to short, tight-fitting to loose, to produce virtually any desired variation in style.

The book will present the basic patterns first, then show how the different variations may be achieved. We will first explain how to take measurements and how to make the basic patterns, then explain the alteration techniques which are basic to pattern variation. Section Four is a series of demonstration-lessons illustrating the application of these principles. Section Five describes how historic costumes can be drafted and points out the value of consulting authentic source material. Section Six is a discussion of fabrics. Section Seven presents a method of analyzing designs so that they may be easily interpreted into patterns. Basic sources for design ideas are described and a number of possible pattern variations are included in a checklist in this section.

To benefit the most from this book, it is suggested that the reader follow each step by actually trying it out. This means that when the measurements are being described, the reader should try taking them. Similarly, the basic patterns should be drafted from the measurements and they should be fitted. Also the alteration techniques should be practiced.

No direction, however, should be followed without an understanding of the reason behind it since it is only through this procedure that the process of learning how to draft original patterns may be mastered.

It is assumed that the reader already has some competence in the basic sewing skills such as operating a sewing machine, sewing different types of seams, making buttonholes, mounting zippers, and doing various hand stitches, as well as some experience in putting garments together. General construction information is given where necessary, but detailed descriptions of sewing and construction techniques are not included. They are available in many good books, one of which is listed in the bibliography provided at the end of this book.

Pattern drafting is a fascinating and gratifying skill, both practically useful and creatively stimulating. It is hoped that the reader will not only learn the necessary techniques but will also find the process enjoyable and rewarding.

BODY SILHOUETTES

AN IMPORTANT ASPECT of the pattern-drafting process is to have a picture or sketch of the garment to be made.

The basic outline figures of a woman (Figure 1) and a man (Figure 2) have been included here to encourage people who are unsure of their drawing abilities to create original designs.

To use the silhouettes, place tracing paper over them and sketch the design idea onto the tracing paper.

The pictures below appear in full size on the next two pages.

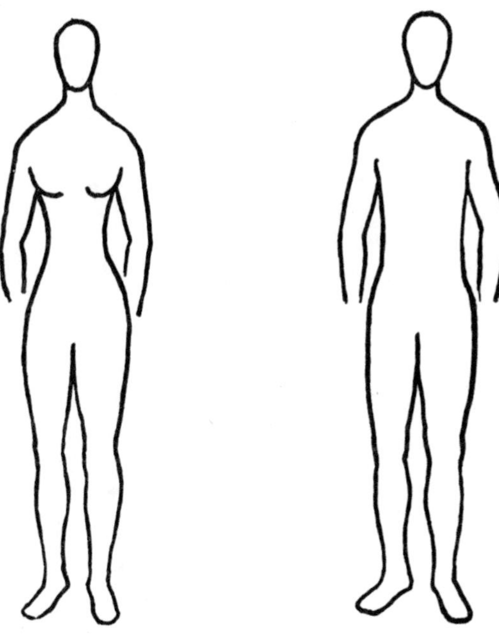

FEMALE SILHOUETTE

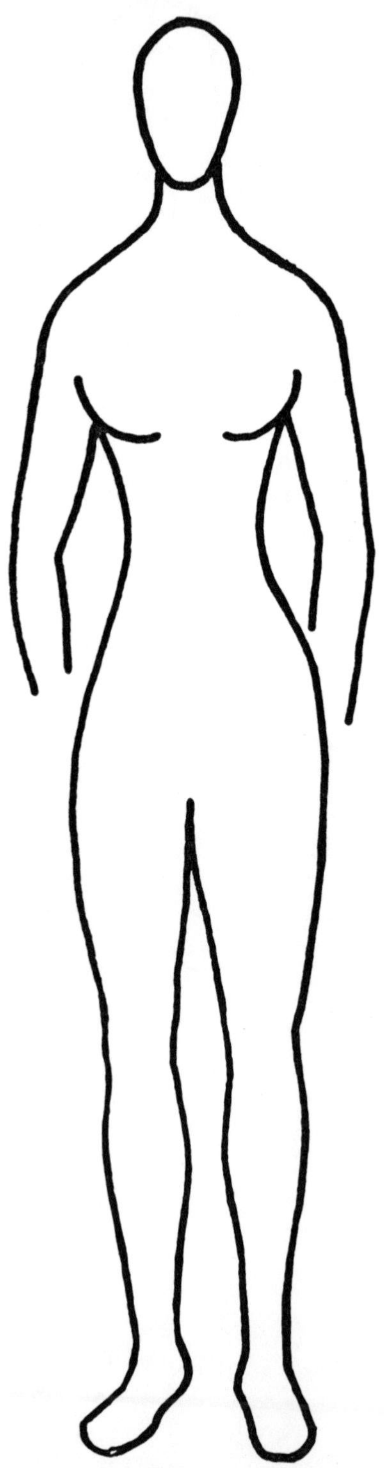

Figure 1

MALE SILHOUETTE

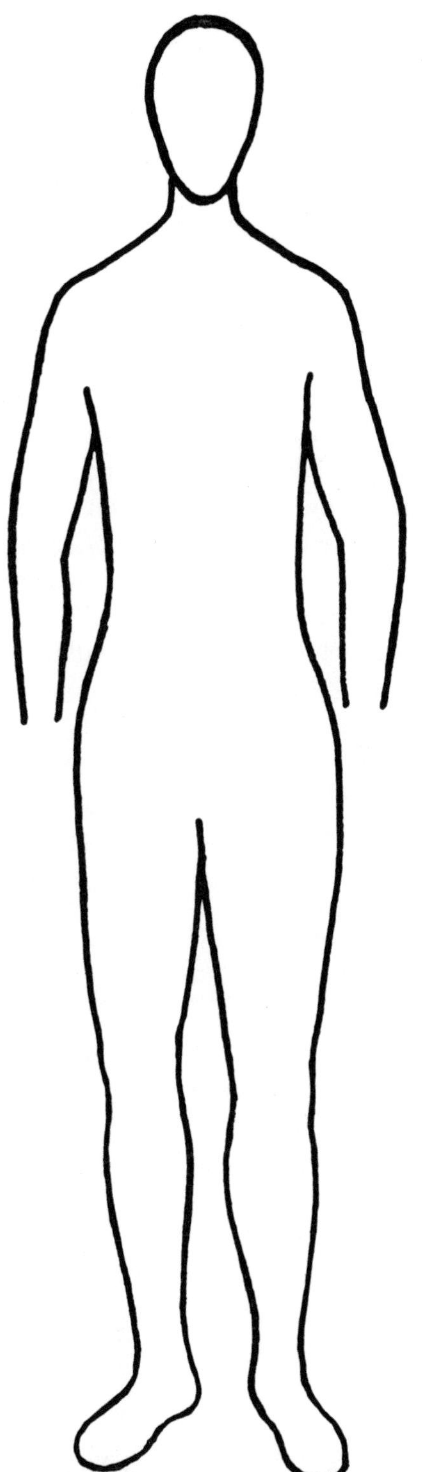

Figure 2

CREATING THE BASIC PATTERN

MEASUREMENTS

MEASUREMENTS ARE THE FOUNDATION of pattern drafting. They establish basic axes which are natural to the body (see Figures 3 through 6). These axes are then used to reconstruct the shape of the body onto the paper. They must, therefore, be taken with complete accuracy. One incorrect measurement can distort an entire pattern. The importance of accurate measurements cannot be overstressed.

There are many different ways to take measurements and also many different measurement charts. The pattern-drafting instructions in this book are based on the specific measurements and the method of taking them described as follows.

The measurement chart is divided into two basic groups of measurements, Girth and Length. The Girth measurements are taken horizontally and most of them go around the entire circumference of the body. These measurements, basically speaking, give the size of the body. The Length measurements are taken vertically and their primary purpose is to give the distances between the individual Girth measurements (and also between the Girth measurements and the floor).

The measurements should be taken snugly but not tightly (unless otherwise specified) with the subject standing in a relaxed, upright position in stockinged feet. The measurements should be taken over any foundation garments that are going to be used, such as bras, corsets, or padding. They should not be taken over bulky clothing, such as knitted sweaters, as this can distort the measurements. The approximate length of various measurements are given in parentheses. If the measurements, when they are taken, do not agree with those in parentheses, recheck carefully.

When the reader is taking his or her own measurements, then the aid of a friend should be enlisted as it is the only way to get truly accurate results.

The exact relationship between Girth and Length measurements is exceedingly important; it is the heart of this system of drafting. It is therefore advisable that the reader should, in some way, mark the critical intersections. A length of string or bias tape can be tied around the neck, chest, waist, and hips. A thin length of masking tape or chalk can be used to mark the shoulder seam. If a thin, tight-fitting sweater is worn the various axes can be marked directly on it with long basting stitches, masking tape, or tailor's chalk.

Once the drafter has had some experience in taking measurements these markings will no longer be necessary (except for a length of bias tape around the waist). An experienced drafter can take a complete set of measurements in two or three minutes. The beginner is advised to take up to a half-hour or longer. If accurate measurements are not taken initially, then hours can be wasted at the drafting table.

MEASUREMENT CHART

Name ______________________________

GIRTH

Body

Neck ________

Neck Width* ________

Chest ________

Front Chest ________

Back Chest ________

Rib Cage ________

Waist ________

Hips ________

Bust-to-Bust* ________

Across Shoulder* ________

Arm

Biceps ________

Above Elbow ________

Below Elbow ________

Wrist ________

Palm ________

Leg

Highest Point ________

Above Knee ________

Below Knee ________

Ankle ________

LENGTH

Body

Center Front to:

Chest ________

Rib Cage ________

Waist ________

Floor ________

Side Front-to-Bust ________

Side Front ________

Center Back ________

Side Back ________

Armpit-to-Waist ________

Arm

Shoulder-to-Elbow ________

Shoulder-to-Wrist ________

Underarm-to-Wrist ________

Leg

Waist to:

Hips ________

Above Knee ________

Below Knee ________

Floor ________

Inseam ________

* These measurements are not taken around the circumference.

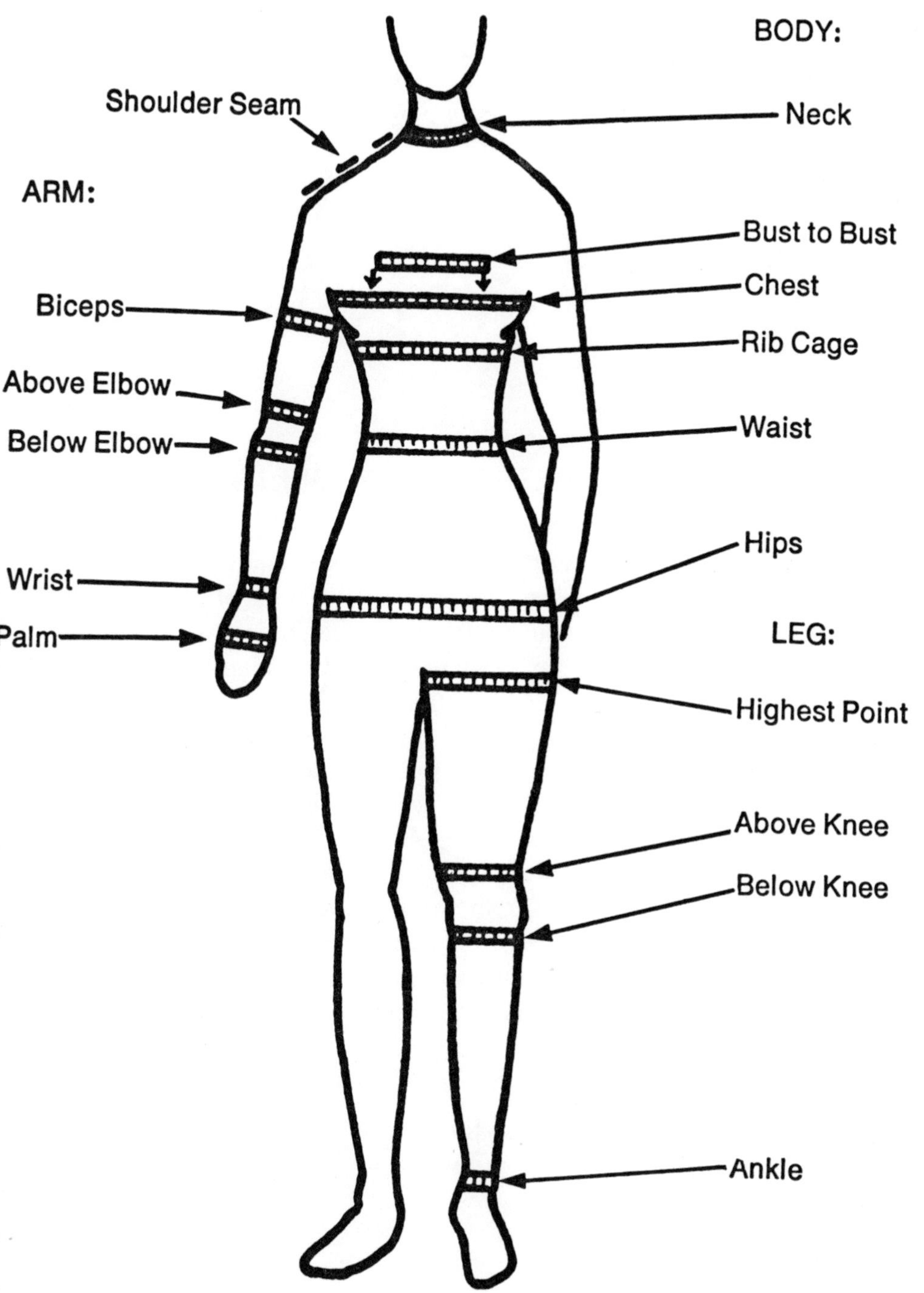
GIRTH MEASUREMENTS (Front View)
BODY:
Neck
Shoulder Seam
ARM:
Bust to Bust
Chest
Biceps
Rib Cage
Above Elbow
Below Elbow
Waist
Hips
Wrist
Palm
LEG:
Highest Point
Above Knee
Below Knee
Ankle

Figure 3

GIRTH MEASUREMENTS (Back View)

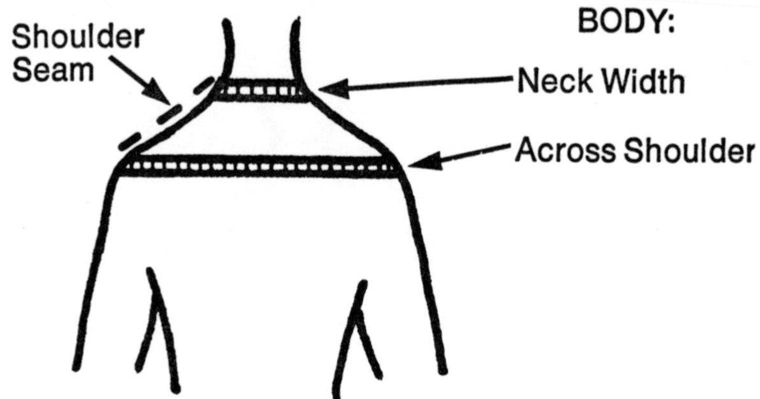

Figure 4

GIRTH MEASUREMENTS

BODY

NECK The first measurement is the neck circumference. It should be taken just over the large vertebra at the base of the neck in back and over the collarbone in front. It should follow the shape of a simple neckline. The measurement should be snug but not tight. This Neck measurement is one of the axes which can be marked to help take other measurements.

The shoulder seam can also be marked to clarify later measurements. If a tight sweater is being used the shoulder seam of the sweater will probably supply the correct line. Otherwise, mark the shoulder seam with masking tape or chalk. The shoulder seam should run down the top of the shoulder from the base of the neck, where the neck measurement was marked, to the end of the shoulder where the fitted sleeve is normally set in. This seam will *not* be used as a measurement, only as a reference for other measurements.

NECK WIDTH This measurement is taken straight across the base of the neck from one side to the other. It should run from the neck end of the left shoulder seam to the neck end of the right shoulder seam. (It should be between 4½″ and 6″.)

Across The Shoulder This is taken straight across the top of the back from one shoulder point to the other. This measurement runs from the outside of the left shoulder seam (the sleeve seam end) to the outside of the right shoulder seam.

Chest The standard Chest measurement is taken around the fullest part of the chest and over the shoulder blades. For women this measurement can be divided into a Front Chest measurement and a Back Chest measurement. To take these accurately, make a mark indicating the normal side seam of a well-fitted dress on both sides of the subject being measured. Measure from one side-seam line to the other across the back. This will be the Back Chest measurement; measuring across the front will give the Front Chest measurement. The Chest is another measurement which should be marked for future reference.

Bust To Bust This measurement is taken from the tip of one bust to the tip of the other.

Rib Cage The Rib Cage measurement is taken just below the bust on women and at an equivalent point on men. This measurement does not go over the shoulder blades. Mark the location of this line for future measurements.

Waist This is taken at the natural waistline just below the bottom of the rib cage. Be careful not to take men's measurements at the pants' waistline as this is rarely the natural waistline. The waist is one axis which should always be marked by a length of bias tape or string regardless of the experience of the drafter.

Hips The Hip measurement is taken over the fullest part of the hips. It should not be taken over wallets, checkbooks, or car keys. Mark the position of the Hip measurement for future reference.

ARM

Biceps The Biceps measurement is made around the fullest part of the upper arm.

ABOVE ELBOW This is the circumference of the arm directly above the elbow.

BELOW ELBOW This is the circumference of the arm directly below the elbow.

WRIST The circumference of the wrist.

PALM A circumference measurement taken around the largest part of the hand. This measurement is used to check finished patterns at the wrist to make sure the hand will be able to get through the final garment.

LEG *(These measurements are for pants only.)*

HIGHEST POINT The circumference of the leg at the crotch.

ABOVE KNEE The circumference of the leg just above the knee.

BELOW KNEE The circumference of the leg just below the knee.

ANKLE The circumference of the ankle.

LENGTH MEASUREMENTS

BODY

CENTER FRONT TO: CHEST, RIB CAGE, WAIST, FLOOR This measurement is taken down the center of the front of the body. It starts at the base of the neck, where the neck circumference measurement was made. Measure down to the Chest circumference measurement, then down from the neckline to the Rib Cage, then to the Waist, and finally, down to the floor. These measurements must coincide with the earlier Girth measurements.

SIDE FRONT Find the point where the shoulder seam line intersects with the neckline. Measure from this point down to the Waist. This

LENGTH MEASUREMENTS (Front View)

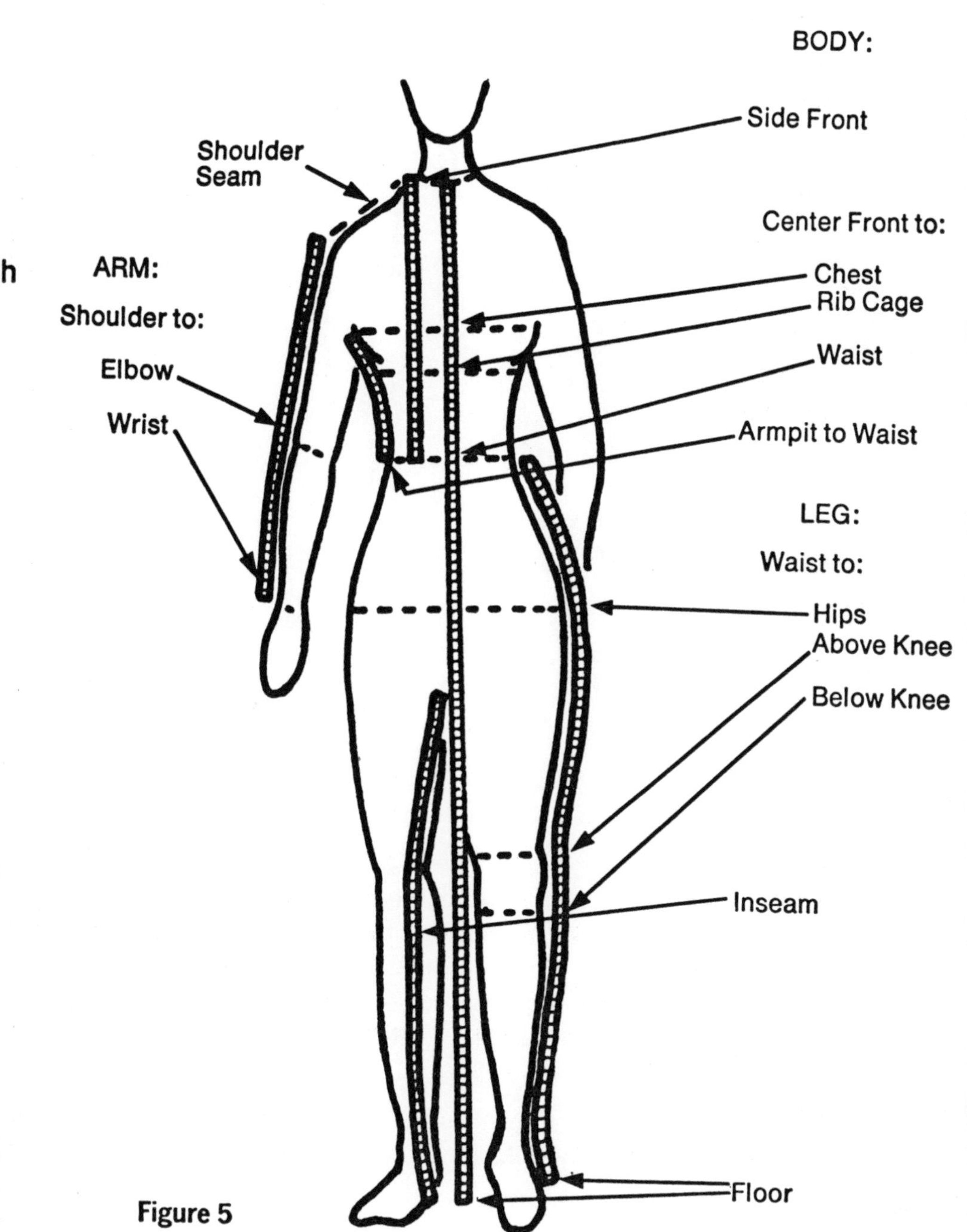

Figure 5

LENGTH MEASUREMENTS (Back View)

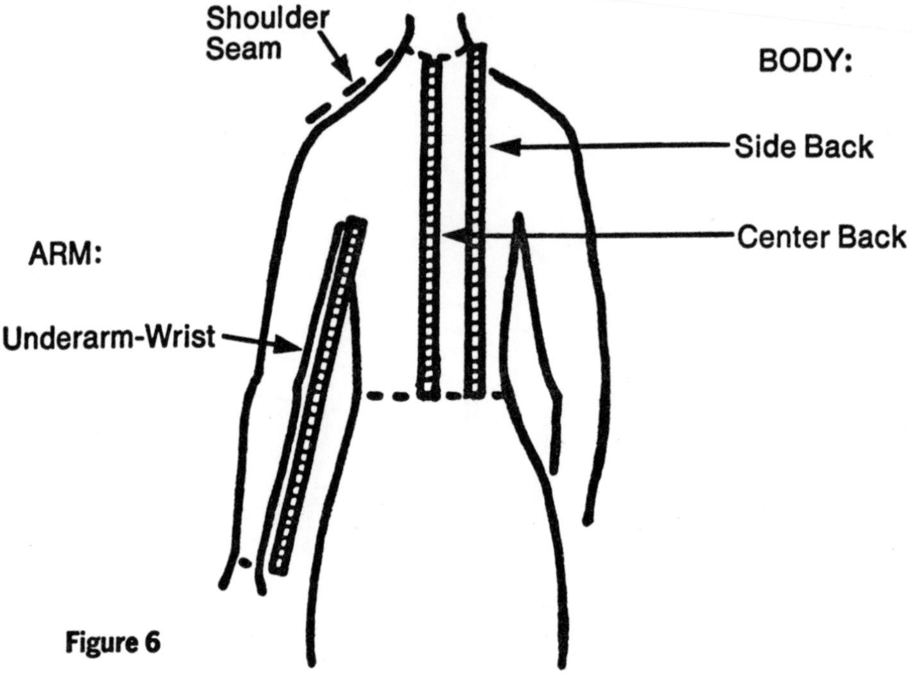

Figure 6

measurement is parallel to Center Front. (This measurement is usually 3″ longer than the Center Front to Waist measurement.)

Side Front To Bust (Women Only) This is the same as the Side Front measurement, but it stops at the Bust line instead of going down to the Waist.

Center Back The Center Back measurement is taken down the spinal column from the large vertebra at the base of the neck to the waist. Measure from the place where the neck was marked to the place where the waist was marked. (It is approximately 2″ longer than the Center Front to Waist measurement.)

Side Back Start at the point where the shoulder seam line touches the neckline and measure down to the waistline. This measurement is taken parallel to the Center Back.

Armpit To Waist This is taken down the side of the body from a comfortable point under the armpit to the waist. Do not push the tape too high in the armpit.

ARM

Shoulder To Elbow Measure from the tip of the shoulder to the elbow with the arm hanging naturally.

Shoulder To Wrist Measure from the tip of the shoulder to the wrist with the arm bent slightly. The tape should go over the elbow.

Underarm To Wrist This measurement is taken from a comfortable point in the armpit to the wrist. The arm should be hanging naturally to the side.

LEG

Waist To: Hips, Above Knee, Below Knee, Floor The basic Leg Length measurements are taken down the side of the body from the Waist to the Hips, Above Knee, Below Knee, and the floor. These measurements should coincide with the circumference measurements taken for the Leg Girth.

Inseam (Pants Only) The other Leg Length measurement is taken down the inside of the leg from the crotch to the floor. The person being measured should hold the top of the tape in a comfortable position in the crotch.

Not all of the measurements listed on this chart are required by the patterns in this book but they will be required at some time in the pattern drafter's work.

ADVICE ON DRAFTING

Materials needed to draft patterns:

Large sheets of paper. The tracing paper or sketch paper used by architectural drafters is best because it is semi-transparent and comes in rolls. Do not get the drafting vellum as this is very expensive. The less expensive tracing paper is about 10¢ a yard for a 24" wide roll. The 24" roll is a good size and can be obtained from stores which carry drafting supplies. Failing this, brown wrapping paper or newsprint may be used.

Cardboard cutting board marked off in inch squares (this is to be used only with the semi-transparent tracing paper). Drafting time can be cut almost in half by using semi-transparent paper and a cardboard cutting board. The 1" markings on the cutting board make it very easy to draw right angles and parallel lines, two functions which are frequently performed in drafting.

A yardstick. Or a long straight-edge used in conjunction with a measuring tape.

A tape measure.

A pencil and an eraser.

Something to mark right angles with. A T-square or a triangle is best, but the corner of a book, box, or sheet of paper will do.

Masking tape to secure the paper to the drafting surface.

Felt-tip marking pens, or crayons.

Good fabric scissors and paper scissors. Do not try to use fabric scissors to cut paper because the paper will dull the blades very quickly. Nothing is more tedious than trying to cut fabric with poor or dull scissors.

Pins

Hints for Successful Drafting

1. Fasten the paper to the drafting table with tape to keep it from slipping or rolling up.

2. Mark the names of the lines on the pattern as it is being drafted. This will help identify these lines during subsequent steps. Include the

measurements and the calculations used to achieve them. This will be useful for checking back if a mistake has been made.

3. When the pattern is transferred to the muslin, mark the seam lines with a felt-tip marker. The muslin is meant to be expendable. Its only function is to serve as a means of fitting the pattern. The corrected seam lines from the fitting should be marked with a different color for clarity.

4. The initial patterns and the trial muslin copies will be well marked up by the end of the drafting process. It is therefore a good idea to correct the initial patterns after the muslin has been fitted and corrected. Make a final version from the corrected pattern. If tracing paper is being used, the pattern may simply be traced. If the paper is opaque, the new copy may be transferred from the old pattern by using carbon paper and a marking wheel. Mark the seam lines as well as the seam allowance lines.

5. Write any pertinent information desired on the final pattern such as: the name of the person the pattern is for, the name of the pattern and the pattern part (i.e. Basic Bodice, Front; etc.), and the date the pattern was drafted.

6. Once the final copy has been made, throw away the initial pattern and the muslin copy. They may have great sentimental value at this point but saving them will only create confusion later on.

7. Do not try to keep final patterns on muslin as they will tend to distort during storage.

THE BASIC BODICE PATTERN

The first pattern to be drafted is the bodice. It is perhaps the most important pattern. It will be used as the basis for drafting dresses, coats, jackets, robes, shirts, and blouses. In fact, almost every garment which covers the top of the body utilizes the Basic Bodice pattern as a point of departure.

In later sections the methods of deriving other styles from the basic patterns will be explained. But the first step is to develop a good fitting basic pattern. If the measurements are accurate and the drafting is carefully executed, this is not difficult to do.

Two methods of creating a basic bodice are described here: drafting and draping. Drafting is the process of translating the body's measurements into a shape on a sheet of paper which will fit the body of the wearer when it is cut and sewn in fabric. Draping, on the other hand, is done by fitting the fabric directly on the body of the wearer, pinning in the darts, and marking the seam lines, the neckline, and the armholes. These markings are then transferred to paper to create the final pattern.

For some designs draping is easier and faster than drafting. For others, drafting is either the best or easiest method to use. The reader should learn both techniques in order to become a skilled drafter.

DRAFTING THE BASIC BODICE

The bodice pattern is drafted by dividing the upper body, from the base of the neck to the waist, into four sections: front right, front left, back right, back left. One pattern is drafted for the two front sections and another pattern is drafted for the two back sections. This can be done because the body is basically symmetrical. Any asymmetrical differences between the left and right sides will be corrected during the fitting process.

Front Section

The front section of the bodice is drafted to cover the shaded area in Figure 7. The other front section will be cut by reversing the pattern on the material.

FRONT SECTION OF BODICE

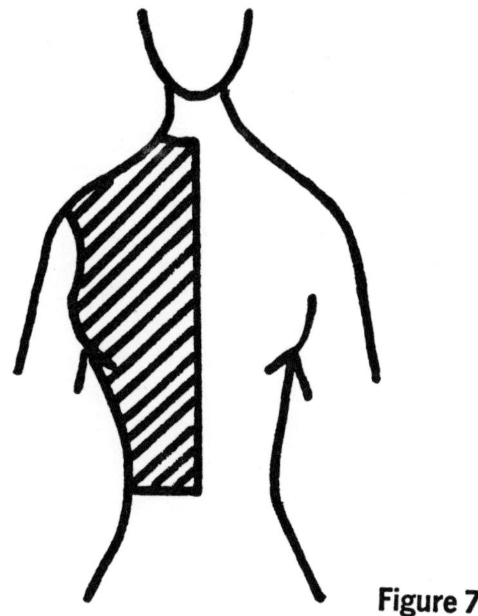

Figure 7

Front and back measurements needed for this pattern:

Center Front to Waist ________
Waist ________
Neck Width ________
Across the Shoulder ________
Chest (Men) ________
Front Chest (Women) ________
Side Front Length ________
Armpit to Waist ________
Bust to Bust (Women) ________
Side Front to Chest (Women) ________
Center Back to Waist ________
Back Chest (Women) ________
Side Back ________

The measurements are listed here in the order they will be needed. The reader may want to copy these measurements onto a separate sheet of paper which may be kept at the working area.

FRONT BODICE PATTERN (Steps 1 to 4)
The Basic Axes

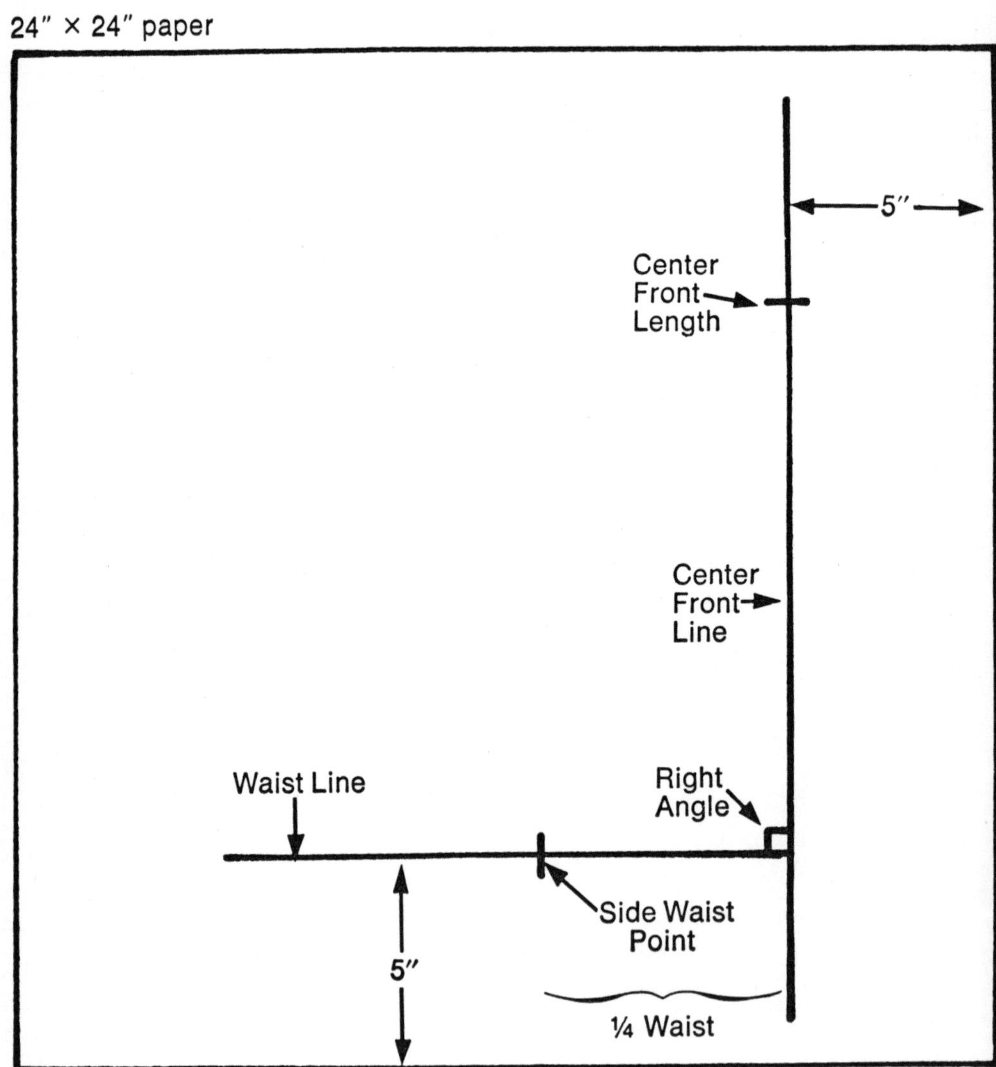

Figure 8

STEP 1. On a sheet of paper approximately 24″ by 24″, draw a vertical line approximately 5″ in from the right side of the paper (see Figure 8). This will be the Center Front line.

STEP 2. About 5″ from the bottom of the paper draw a line at right angles to the Center Front line. This will be the Waist line.

STEP 3. Now mark off the Center Front to Waist measurement on the Center Front line.

STEP 4. Mark off one-fourth of the Waist measurement on the Waist line. This is the Side Waist Point.

The Center Front line and the Waist line serve as the basic axes from which the front section of the bodice will be drafted. Only one-fourth of the Waist measurement is used because the body has been divided into four sections and this pattern is for half of the front. Other subsequent Girth measurements will also be divided by four. The wide margins at the right and bottom of the paper are for seam allowances.

FRONT BODICE PATTERN (Steps 5 to 7)
Basic Reference Lines

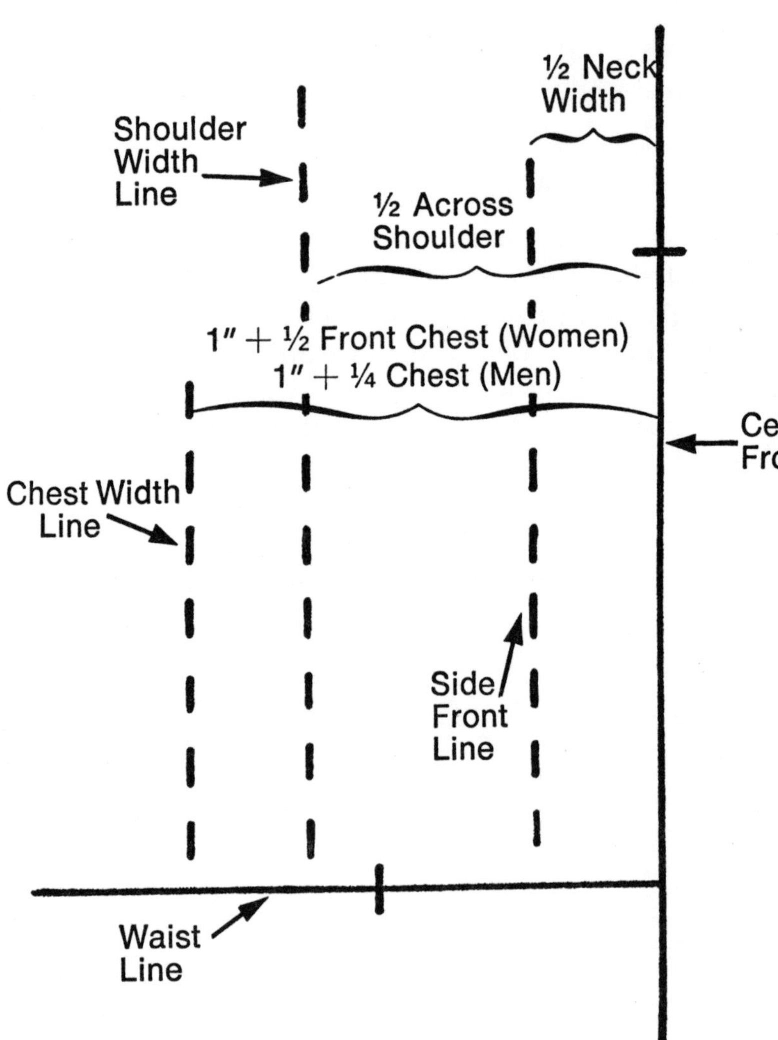

Figure 9

The next two steps use lengths that are one-half the measurement because the measurements were not taken around the circumference of the body.

STEP 5. Draw a line parallel to the Center Front line at a distance of one-half the Neck Width away (see Figure 9). This is the Side Front line.

STEP 6. Draw a second line parallel to the Center Front line at a distance of one-half the Across the Shoulder measurement away. This measurement will determine the Shoulder Point and is the Shoulder Width line.

STEP 7. Draw a third line parallel to the Center Front line at a distance of one inch plus one-half of the Front Chest measurement for women, or one inch plus one-fourth of the entire Chest measurement for men. This is the Chest Width line.

One inch is added to compensate for the movement of the arms in relation to the body and for the movement of the chest.

FRONT BODICE PATTERN (Steps 8 & 9)

The Shoulder Seam

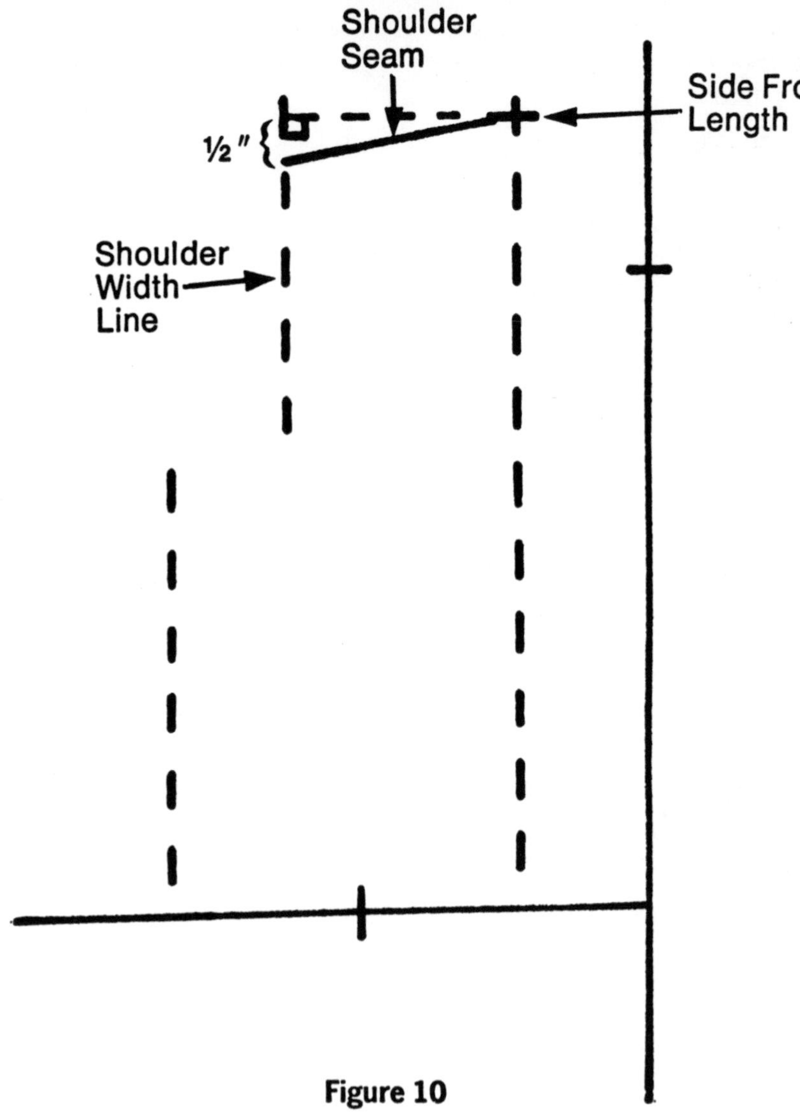

Figure 10

Step 8. On the Side Front line mark off the Side Front length measuring from the Waist line (Figure 10).

Step 9. Draw a slightly sloping line from the top of the Side Front line to the Shoulder Width line. The angle of this line must be estimated. This is the Shoulder Seam line.

The actual slope of the Shoulder Seam will be determined during the fitting process. It is suggested that beginning drafters keep this line almost parallel to the Waist line as it is always easy to increase the angle of the slope during the fitting but very difficult to decrease it. A slope of about one-half inch down from the parallel can be used as a beginning approximation.

FRONT BODICE PATTERN (Step 10)

The Side Seam

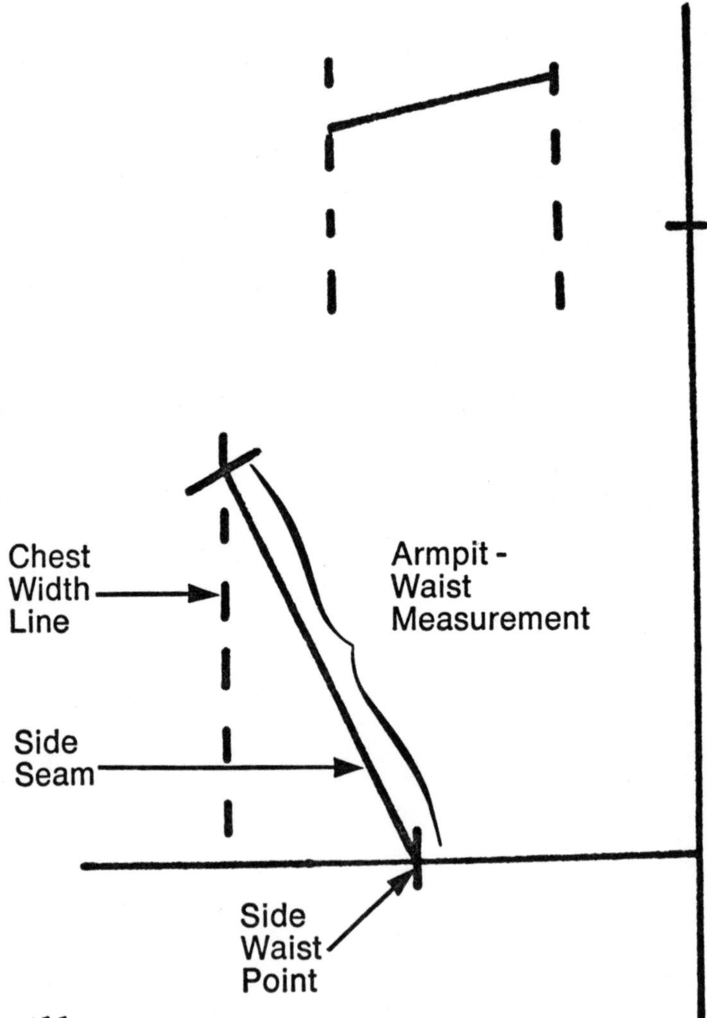

Figure 11

STEP 10. Strike a radius from the Side Waist point with the Armpit-to-Waist measurement so that it intersects the Chest Width line (Figure 11). To strike this radius, take a tape measure and find the length of the Armpit-to-Waist measurement. Put one end of this length on the Side Waist point and place the other end on the Chest Width line, holding the tape straight and taut. Mark this point and connect it to the Side Waist point. This line is the Side Seam line.

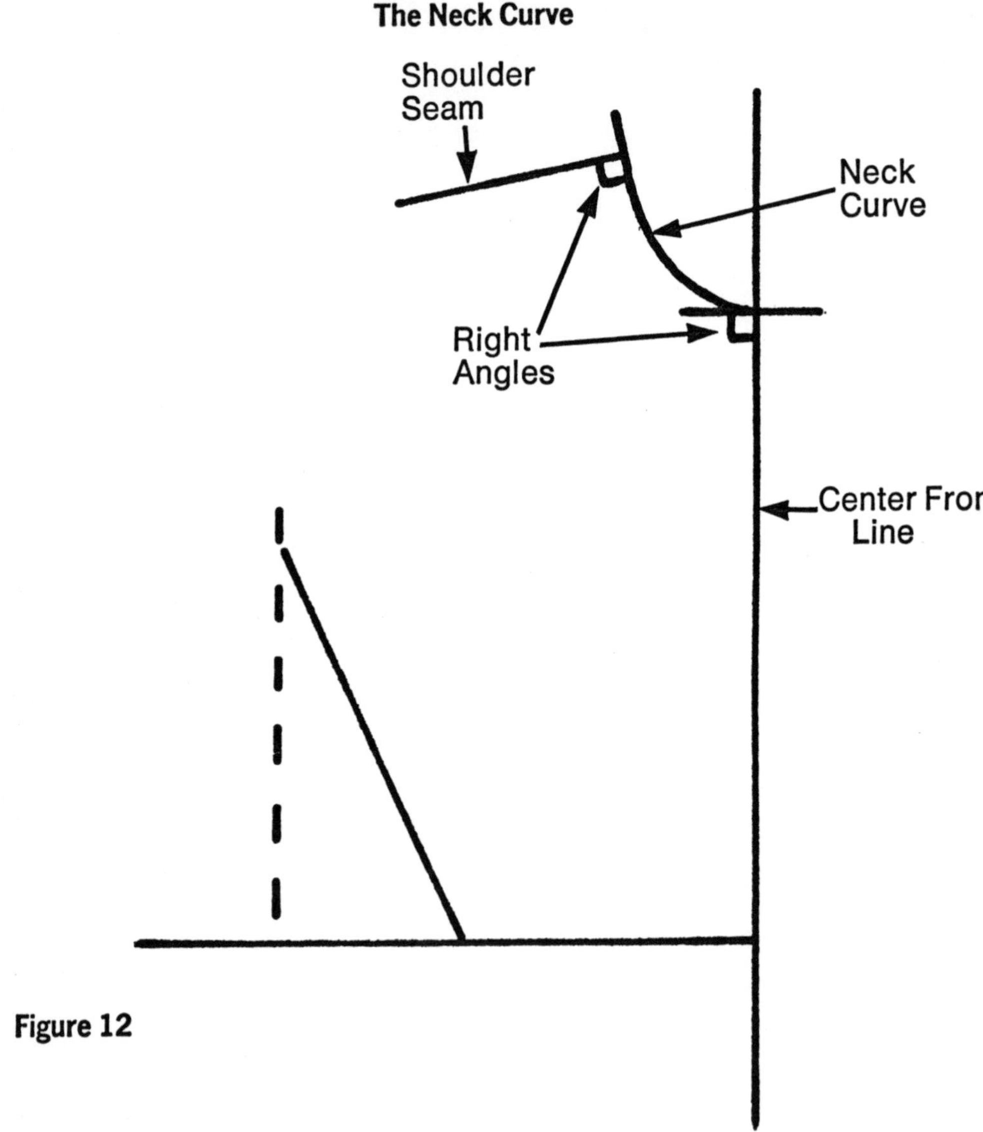
FRONT BODICE PATTERN (Step 11)
The Neck Curve
Shoulder Seam
Neck Curve
Right Angles
Center Front Line

Figure 12

STEP 11. The Neck curve is to be sketched in freehand (see Figure 12). It is almost semi-circular in shape. The intersections of the Neck curve with the Center Front line and the Shoulder Seam line should be perpendicular. If this is not done, there will be an uneven shape where the separate patterns are joined together (see Figure 13).

CURVING THE NECK LINE

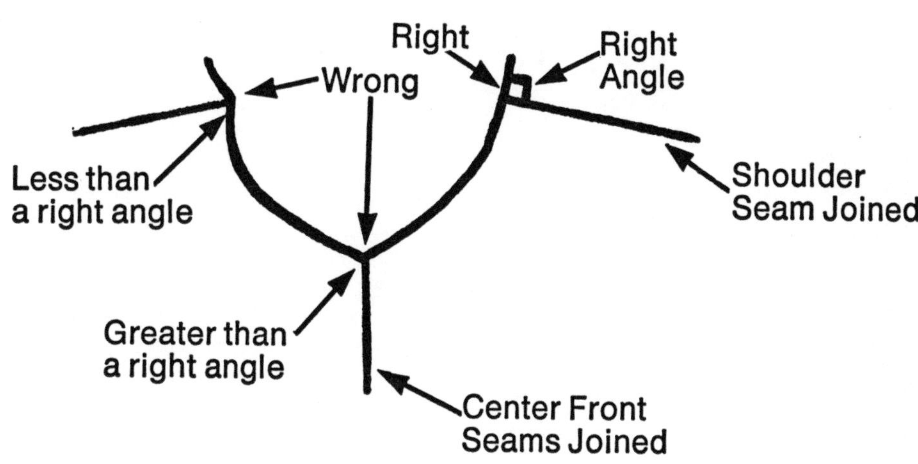

Figure 13

FRONT BODICE PATTERN (Step 12)

The Armhole Curve

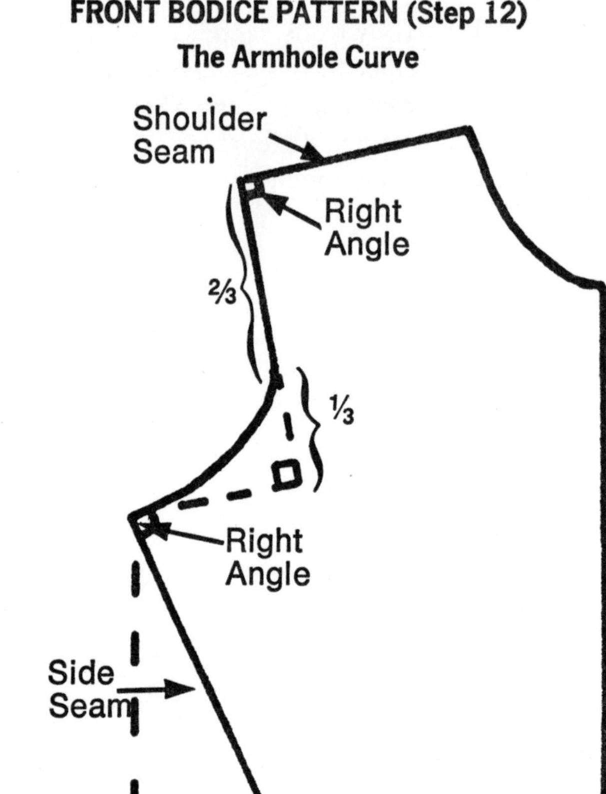

Figure 14

STEP 12. The Armhole curve is also sketched in freehand (Figure 14). This line runs at right angles to the Shoulder Seam line for about two-thirds the distance between the Shoulder Seam and the top of the Side Seam. It then curves in to meet the Side Seam line.

The basic pattern for the Front Section of the Fitted Bodice has now been drafted. For women's bodices it is necessary to add a dart to compensate for the bust. For men's bodices the pattern is complete except for seam allowances which will be discussed following the instructions for drafting darts. (page 52).

THE FRONT DART

The front dart on women's bodices is one of the few darts which may be drafted accurately because the exact location of the tip of the bust may be measured. Other patterns will have dart allowances added during the drafting, but the darts themselves will be fitted rather than drafted.

THE BUST DART (Steps 1 to 5)
Dart Centerline and Bust Point

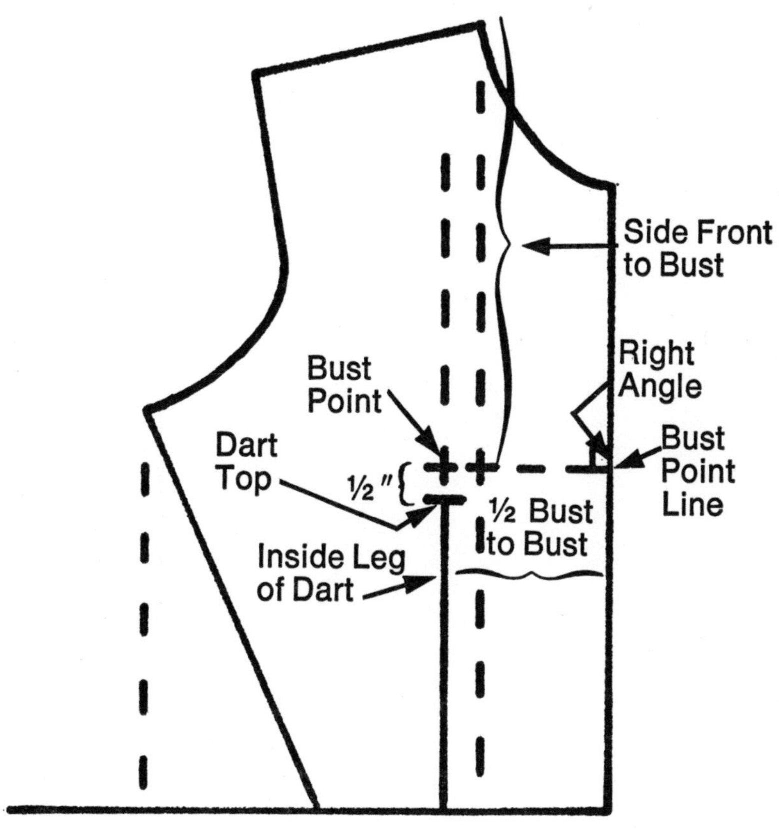

Figure 15

THE BUST DART (Steps 6 to 8)

Drawing in the Dart

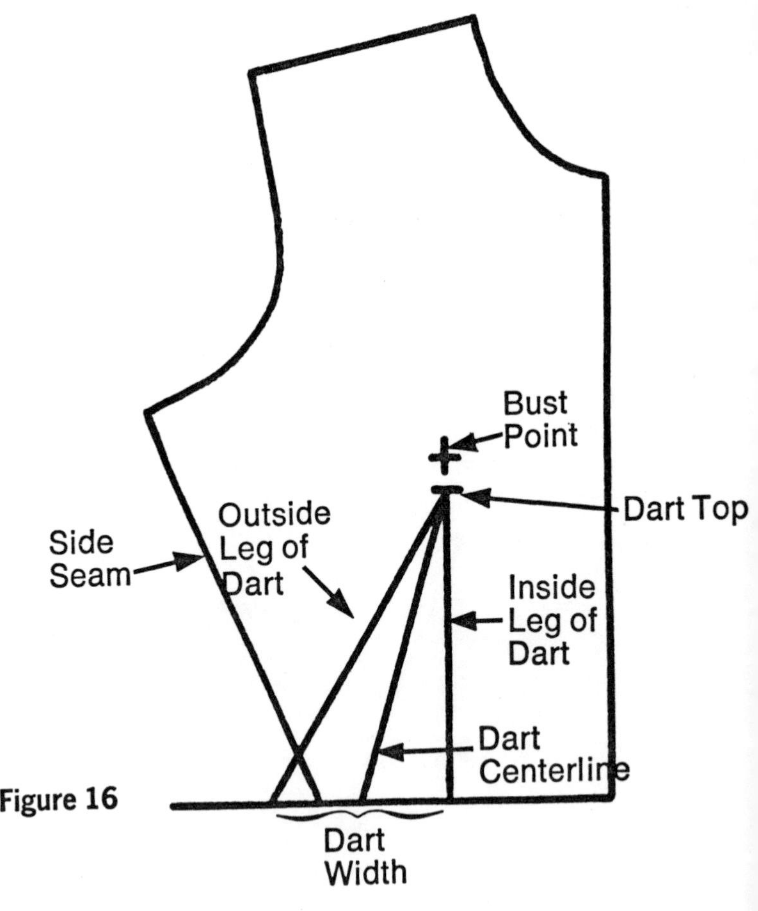

Figure 16

STEP 1. On the Side Front line, measure down from the Shoulder Seam and mark off the Side Front to Bust Length (Figure 15). Remember this measurement was taken from the shoulder down to the bust.

STEP 2. Draw a line perpendicular to the Center Front line so that it intersects the point established in Step 1. This is the Bust Point line.

STEP 3. Measure in on this line from the Center Front line one-half of the Bust to Bust measurement. Mark this point. This is the Bust Point.

STEP 4. At this point draw a perpendicular line down to the Waist line. This line will be the inside leg of the dart. It should be parallel to the Center Front line and slightly to the left of the Side Front line.

STEP 5. Measure down one-half inch from the Bust Point line along the Dart Centerline and mark this point clearly. This will be the Dart Top.

Steps 1, 2, and 3 establish the Bust Point on the pattern. The top of the dart is then placed ½″ below the Bust Point. The Front dart should not rest exactly on the tip of the bust because the maximum shaping of a dart occurs not at the point of the dart but just beyond it.

STEP 6. Find the correct Dart Width from the following chart and mark it on the Waist line starting from the inside leg of the dart (Figure 16).

DART WIDTHS

BUST (WAIST)	DART WIDTH
32″ (25″)	2″
34″ (26″)	3″
36″ (28″)	4″
38″ (30″)	5″
40″ (32″)	6″
42″ (34″)	7″

The Dart Width may be roughly adjusted to the waist size of the wearer by decreasing the dart size for waists larger than the listed size and increasing the darts for smaller waists.

a) If the actual Waist measurement is larger than the listed waist measurement, subtract the listed waist from the actual waist, divide the difference by four (the pattern is for a fourth of the body), and subtract this figure from the Dart Width listed. For example, if the actual measurements are: Chest 38″, Waist 34″; 1″ will be subtracted from the Dart Width. (Actual size 34″ minus listed size 30″ = 4″; divided by 4 this leaves 1″, and 1″ from the listed dart of 5″ = 4″. Thus 4″ is the Dart Width.)

b) If the actual Waist measurement is smaller than the listed size, subtract the actual size from the listed size, divide the difference by four, and *add* this to the Dart Width.

These Dart Widths are approximations. There are many factors which can affect the final dart size. For this reason the actual width will be determined during the fitting. Do not, therefore, spend too much time trying to calculate the correct width.

Step 7. Draw the outside leg of the dart by connecting the mark established in Step 6 to the Dart Top (Figure 16).

Step 8. Divide the Dart Width in half and draw a Dart Centerline.

The pattern will now be folded as if the dart were sewn so that the Waist line can be redrawn.

Step 9. Fold the pattern at the Dart Centerline and pin the dart closed as if it were sewn (Figure 17).

Step 10. Lay out the pattern so that the Waist line is flat.

The pattern will be a little difficult to handle for the preceding step because the dart will prevent the whole pattern from lying flat. Hold the top of the dart down on the drawing surface and pull up at the shoulder seam. This will put the pattern in the correct position, with the Waist line flat. Be sure the fold in the pattern follows the dart. Do this as accurately as possible but do not spend too

THE BUST DART (Steps 9 & 10)
Folding the Pattern

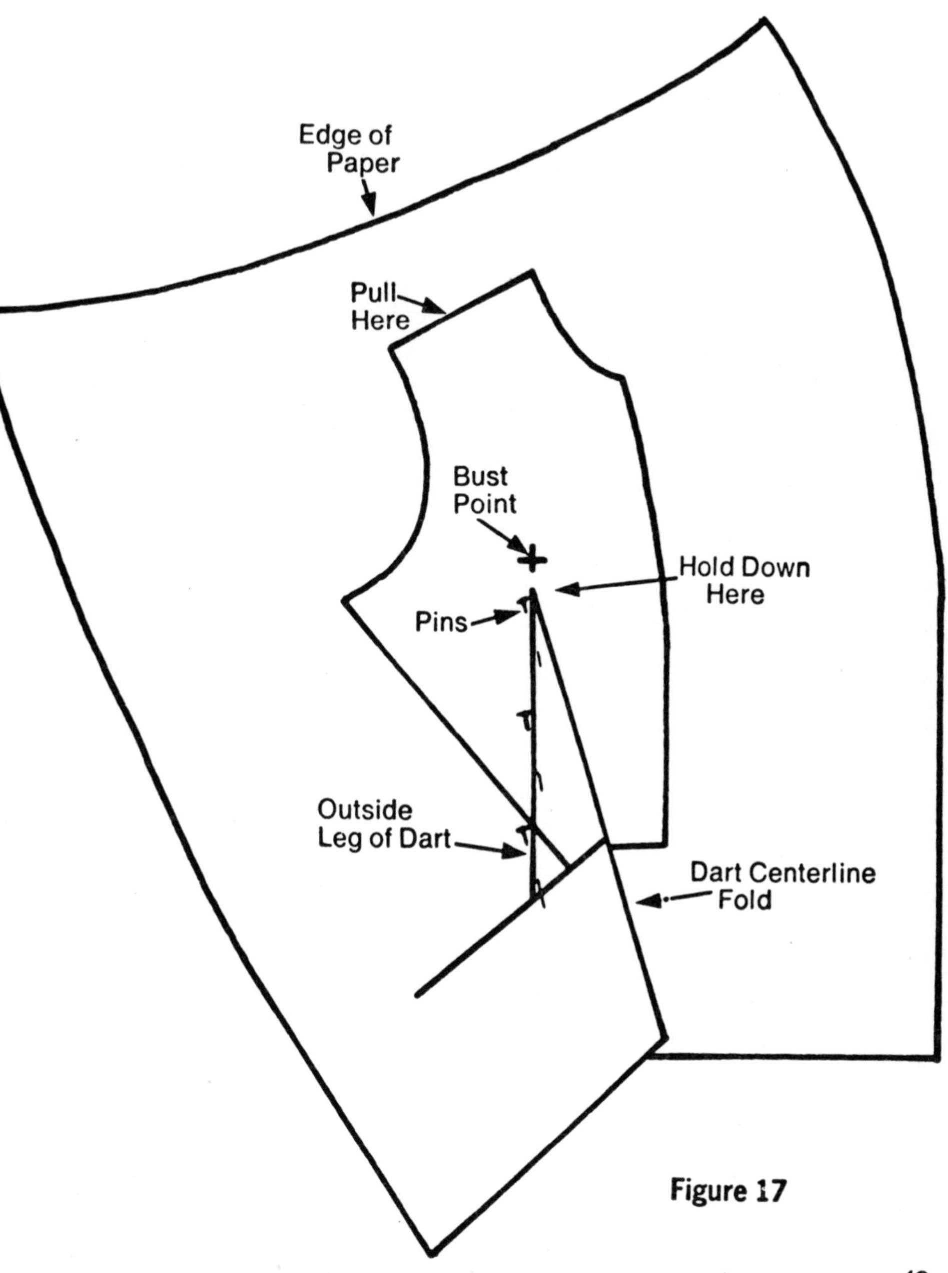

Figure 17

much time with it as the fitting will be used to correct any mistakes.

STEP 11. With the pattern in this position, extend the Waist line to the left, at right angles to the Center Front line (Figure 18).

STEP 12. Mark 1″ plus ¼ the Waist measurement on the new Waist line to establish the new Side Waist point.

STEP 13. Unpin and unfold the pattern.

STEP 14. Draw in a new Side Seam line by pivoting the Armpit to Waist measurement so that it intersects with the old Chest Width line. Use the new Side Waist mark as a starting point (Figure 19).

THE BUST DART (Steps 11 & 12)
Marking the Waistline

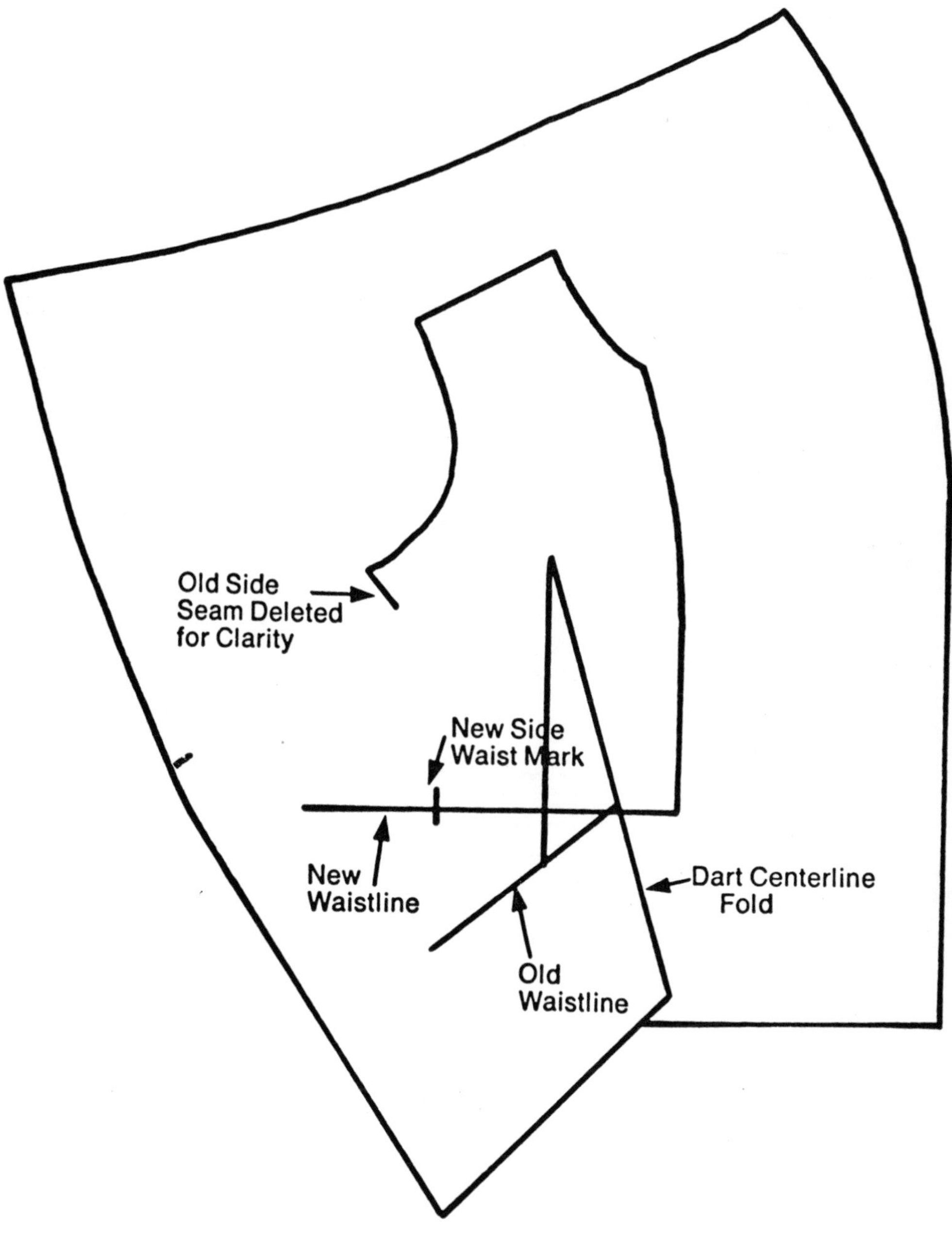

Figure 18

THE BUST DART (Steps 13 to 15)
Drawing in the New Side Seam

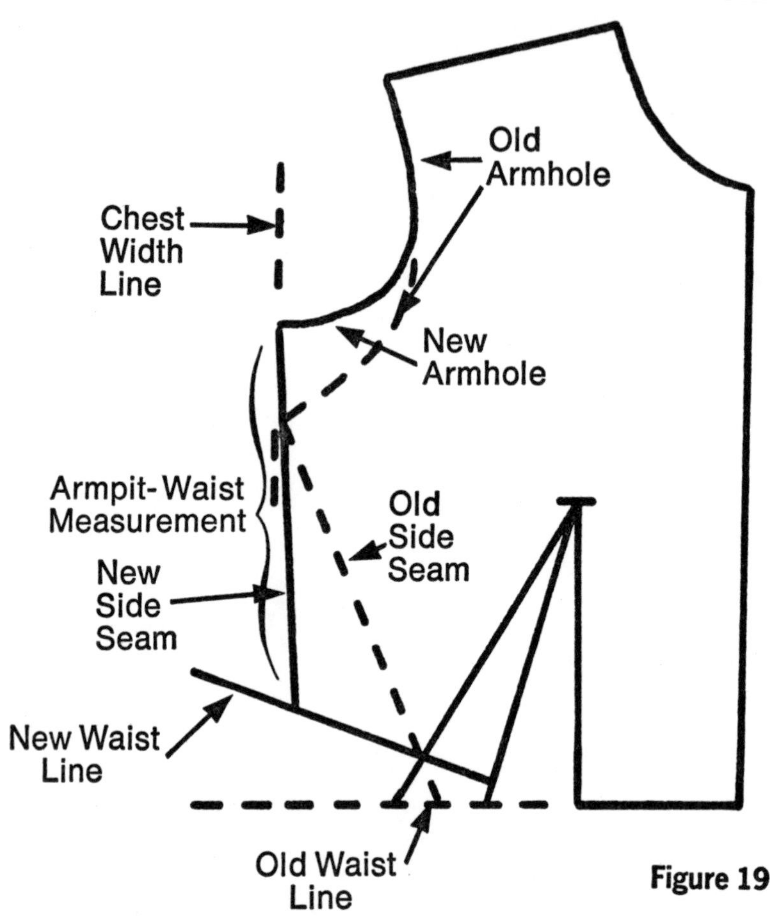

Figure 19

STEP 15. Reshape the new armhole into the old armhole.

STEP 16. Connect the new Waist to the old Waist line across the inside half of the dart. (Figure 20).

STEP 17. Add seam allowances as follows: Add a 2″ seam allowance to the Shoulder Seam, the Waist line, and the Side Seam. Add a 1″ seam allowance to the Neck and the Armhole. Do not exceed 1″ because a larger allowance will distort the bodice during the fitting.

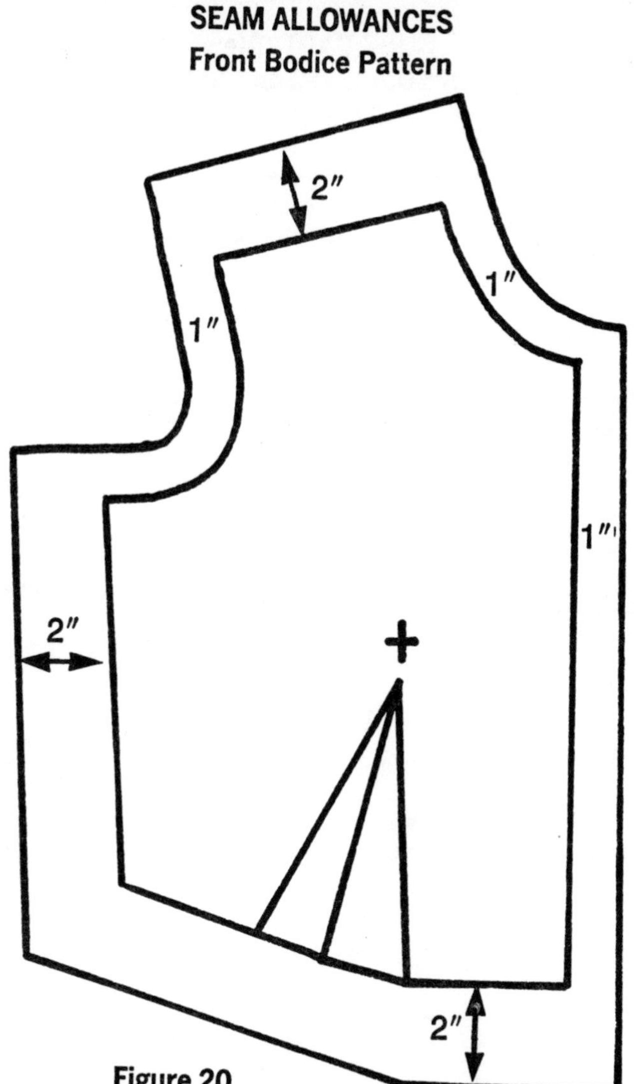

Figure 20

Leave a 1″ seam allowance down the Center Front line for a front opening in the bodice.

Back Bodice Pattern

The procedure for drafting the back section of the bodice pattern is essentially the same as the procedure for drafting the front section. The following steps should be followed. Note the differences in the two sections.

THE BACK BODICE (Steps 1 to 10)

The Initial Dimensions

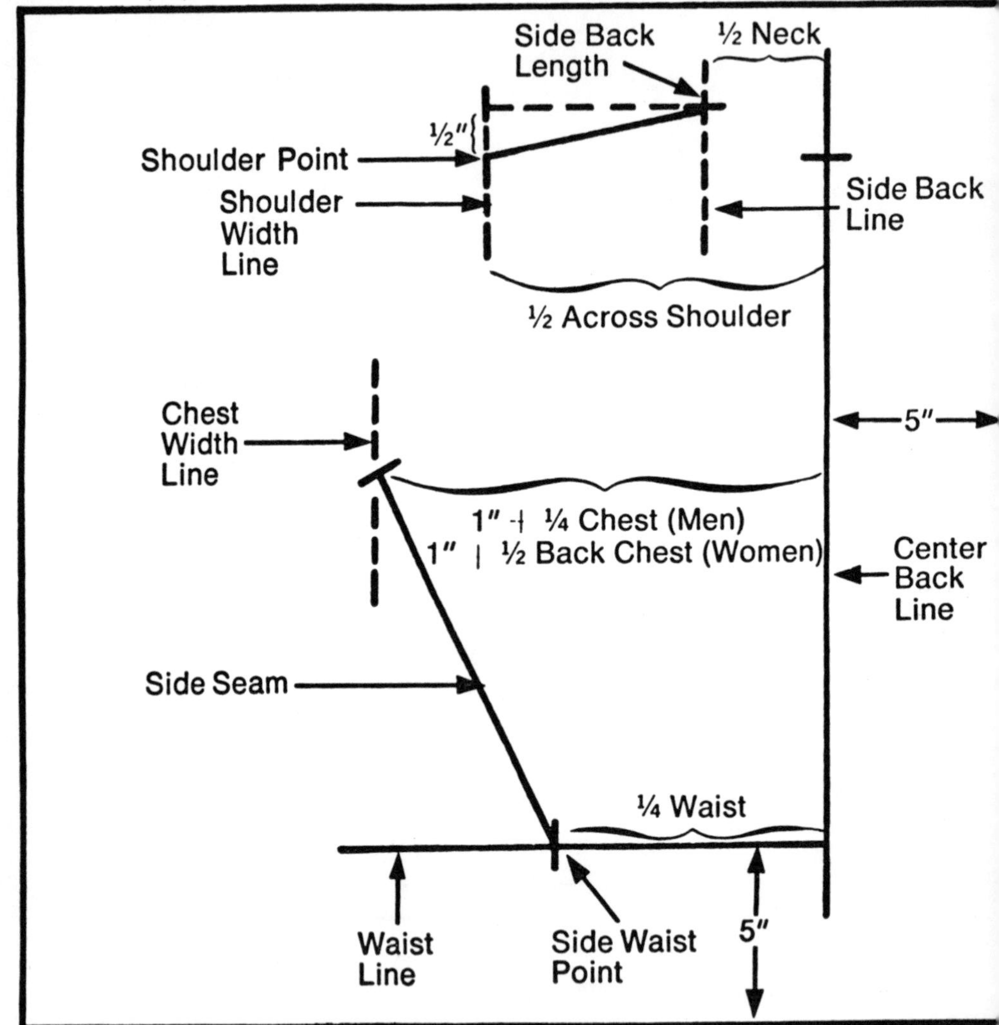

Figure 2

STEP 1. On a sheet of paper approximately 24" by 24", draw vertical line 5" in from the right side of the paper (see Figure 21 This will be the Center Back line.

STEP 2. About 5" from the bottom of the paper, draw a line

right angles to the Center Back line. This will be the Waist line.

Step 3. Now mark off the Center Back to Waist measurement on the Center Back line. (For most people this will be approximately 2″ longer than the Center Front to Waist measurement.)

Step 4. Mark off one-fourth of the Waist measurement on the Waist line. This is the Side Waist point.

Step 5. Draw a line parallel to the Center Back line at a distance of one-half the Neck Width away (see Figure 21). This is the Side Back line.

Step 6. Draw a second line parallel to the Center Back line at a distance of one-half the Across the Shoulder measurement away. This measurement will determine the Shoulder point and is the Shoulder Width line.

Step 7. Draw a third line parallel to the Center Back line at a distance of one inch plus one-half the Back Chest measurement for women, or one inch plus one-fourth of the entire Chest measurement for men. This is the Chest Width line. As with the Bodice Front pattern, one inch is added to compensate for the movement of the arms in relation to the body and for the movement of the chest.

Step 8. On the Side Back line mark off the Side Back length, measuring from the Waist line.

Step 9. Draw a slight sloping line from the top of the Side Back line to the Shoulder Width line. The angle of this line should be very slight, sloping about a half-inch down from the Side Back to the Shoulder Point. The correct slope will be determined during the fitting.

Step 10. Take a tape measure and, starting at the Side Waist point, measure off a length equal to the Armpit-to-Waist measurement. Mark the point where this measurement intersects with the Chest Width line. Draw a line connecting this point to the Side Waist point. This is the Side Seam line.

BACK BODICE PATTERN (Steps 11 to 13)

Neck and Armhole Curves

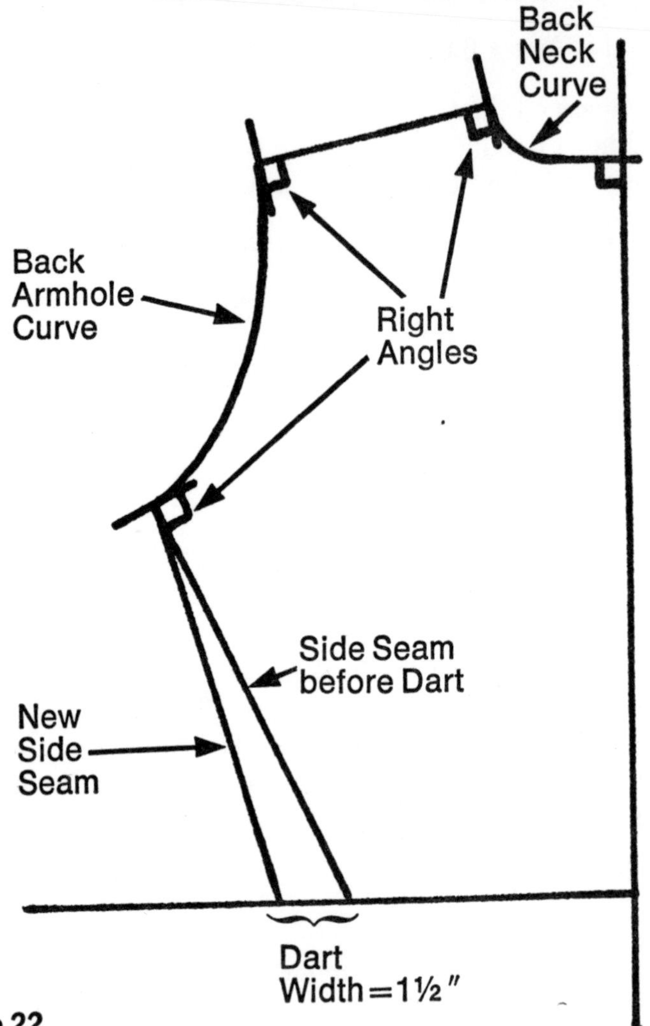

Figure 22

STEP 11. Draw in the Back Neck curve. This curve drops very quickly from the Shoulder Seam line to run at right angles to the Center Back line (see Figure 22). Remember to make the Neck curve at right angles to the Shoulder Seam.

STEP 12. The back Armhole curve is a very shallow curve. It starts out at right angles to the Shoulder Seam and curves slightly until it meets the Side Seam line, as indicated in Figure 22.

STEP 13. Add allowance for the Back Dart. Add about 1½″ to the Waist measurement and draw a new Side Seam line.

The actual placement of the dart will be established during the fitting session.

The allowance for the Back Dart is variable. As a rule it will not be as large as the front dart on women's bodices. On many patterns it is frequently left out, but it can add to the fitted appearance of a garment if it is included.

STEP 14. Add seam allowances as follows: Add 2″ at the Shoulder, Side Seam and Waist line. Add 1″ at the Neckline and Armhole curve.

The trial bodice will open in the front. Therefore, the Center Back line will be a fold line. No seam allowance is added to a fold line since it will be placed on the fold of the fabric.

After the seam allowances have been added, the pattern may be cut out.

The next step is to cut out a trial bodice in muslin so that the Basic Bodice may be fitted.

FITTING THE BODICE

It is important to master the fitting process because a garment is rarely, if ever, drafted perfectly. In addition to checking the fit, it is possible to improve the overall shape of the garment during the fitting. If a pattern has been well drafted, the fitting session can be short, sweet and fruitful. On the other hand, if a pattern has been poorly drafted, a good deal of time will be required to fit it. It may even have to be redrafted.

In making the trial muslin, be sure to mark darts and seam allowances carefully. Pin the darts closed. Pin the seams together at sides and shoulders.

Try on the muslin, with the pins and seam allowances showing. This makes it possible to repin seams and darts during the fitting

The Shoulder Seam

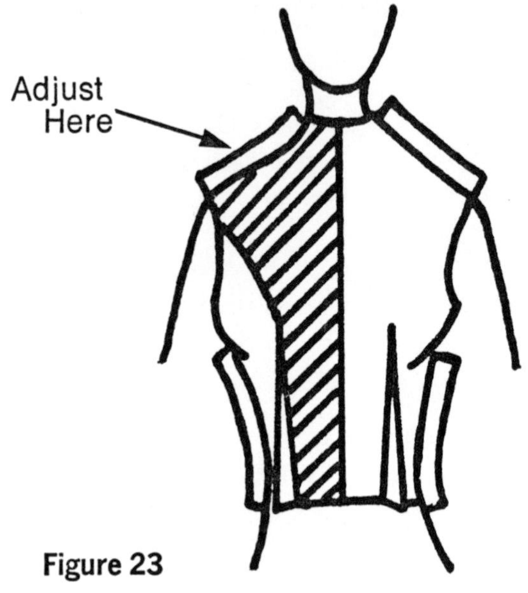

Figure 23

without removing the garment. Pin the garment closed on the center seam. Now check the muslin for fit.

STEP 1. Adjust the Shoulder Seam so that the muslin lies smoothly on the part of the body indicated by the shaded portion in Figure 23.

STEP 2. Keeping the shoulder and upper chest area flat, smooth out the fabric around the armhole and at the side-seam-to-dart area (Figure 24). Re-pin the side seam to make this part of the bodice lie absolutely smooth. Be sure that the Center Seam or Center Front line of the bodice stays properly aligned during the fitting. The Centerline may be pinned to an undergarment to facilitate this.

STEP 3. Now check the dart for proper placement and for proper fit. If the dart is not correctly placed, or is distorting the bodice in any way, remove it and repin it. The point of the dart should be placed just below the center of the bust. It should be adjusted so that the material in the shaded area of Diagram A, Figure 24, fits smoothly. Diagram B of Figure 24 shows where the excess material will be for a dart which is too small and a dart which is too large. As you adjust the

FITTING THE BODICE (Steps 2 & 3)
The Dart and Side Seam

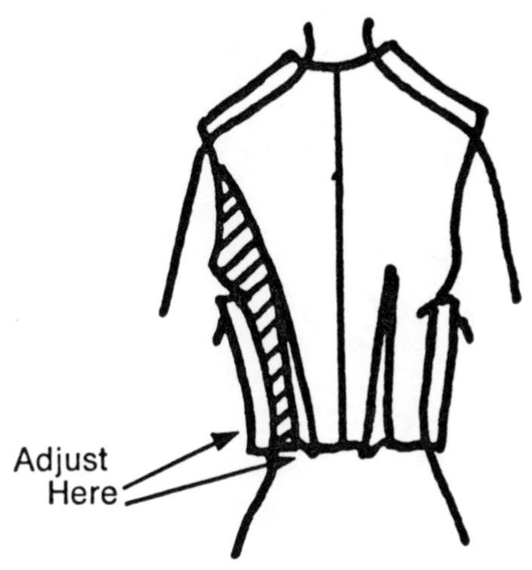

Diagram A

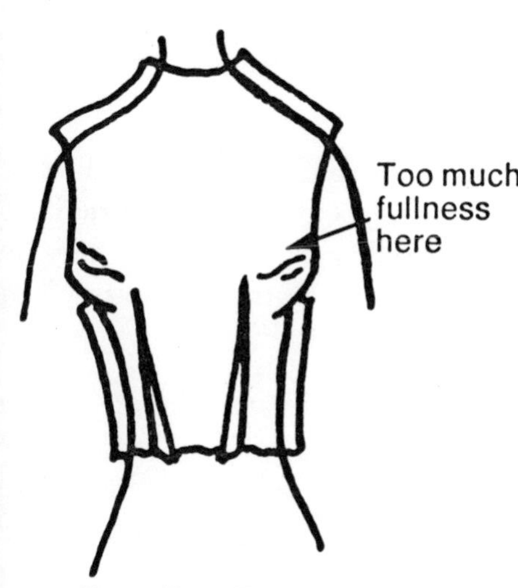

Front Dart Too Small

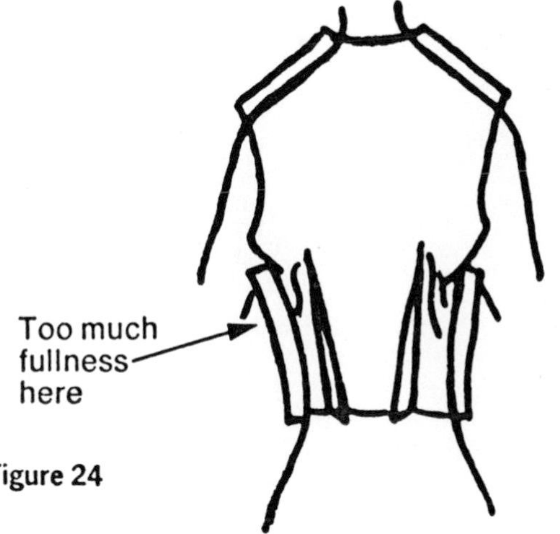

Front Dart Too Large

Figure 24

Diagram B

FITTING THE BODICE (Step 4)

The Shoulder Seam

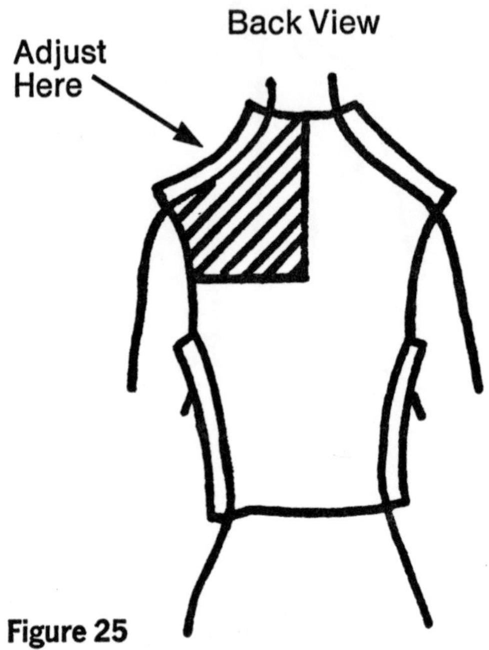

Figure 25

dart, make sure that the Center Front and the Side Seam remain in their proper locations.

Step 4. Adjust the Shoulder Seam so that the shaded area at the Bodice Back in Figure 25 fits smoothly. Be sure the Center Back line remains straight and in its proper place during the fitting. The muslin may be pinned to an undergarment along this line to keep the muslin in place during the fitting process.

Step 5. Now pin in the back dart, shaping the muslin up to the shoulder blade. To determine the exact placement of the dart, let the material hang freely. It should drape in slight folds as indicated in Figure 26. Change the fold into a dart and pin. Mark the top of the dart carefully.

Step 6. Adjust the Side Seam to remove any excess material from the lower portion of the back.

FITTING THE BODICE (Step 5)

The Back Dart

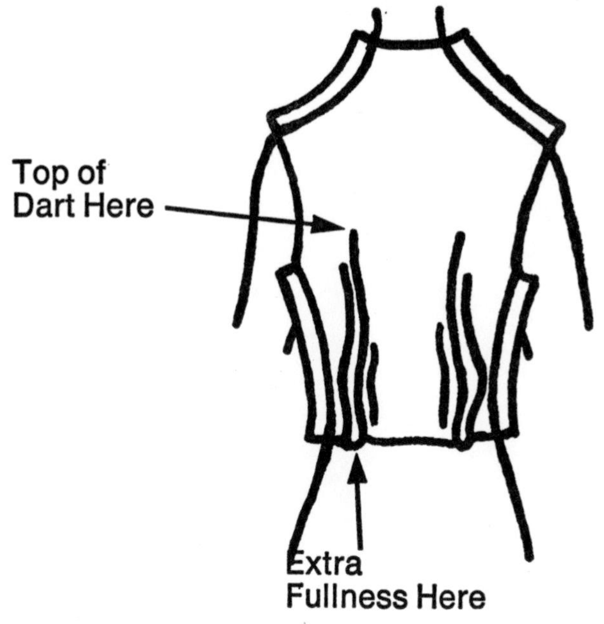

Figure 26

If the reader is fitting his or her own bodice, then assistance will be needed to help fit the back dart. A dress form is a good alternate. Or, if neither of these is available, the following may be done. Look in a mirror and mark the top of the back dart with a pencil by reaching over the shoulder. Gather the excess material at the waist and either mark this end of the dart or pin it.

STEP 7. Check now to make sure that the fitting of the Bodice Back has not altered or distorted the fitting of the Bodice Front. Make any necessary corrections until a satisfactory fit is achieved for both the front and the back of the Bodice.

The Armhole and Neck curves may now be checked. These lines occur quite simply where the arms and the neck meet the body. It does, however, take a little practice to determine these points accurately.

FITTING THE BODICE (Steps 8 & 9)

Neck and Armhole Curves

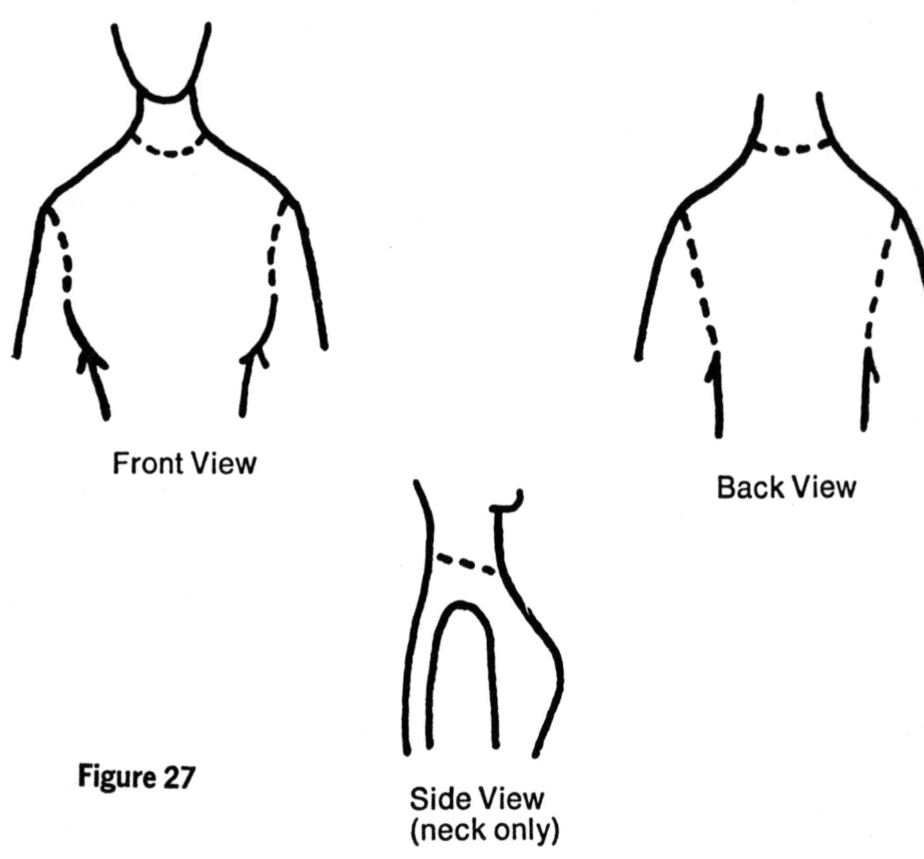

Figure 27

STEP 8. Figure 27 is a sketch of how the Neck curve should follow the contour of the body. Mark that line on the muslin bodice.

STEP 9. The Armhole curve can be determined by slowly lifting and lowering the arm directly away from the side of the body. The part of the body that is moving is the arm; the part that doesn't move is the shoulder. The Armhole curve should follow the separation.

If the drafter is having difficulty in seeing these lines, he should find some garment that fits properly to see how these points were drafted.

The corrected seam lines should now be marked with a felt-tip marker.

STEP 10. Mark the front and the back of the Shoulder seam lines.

STEP 11. Mark the front and the back of the Side Seams.

STEP 12. Tie a string around the Waist, and, using this as a guide, mark the Waist line all the way around.

STEP 13. Mark the top of the front and back darts. The sides and centerlines of the darts will be marked after the muslin is removed from the body.

STEP 14. Mark the Neckline and Armhole curves.

STEP 15. Remove the bodice and check the left side against the right side to make sure they match. Correct the seams as necessary. Go over all of the lines to make them perfectly clear, using a straightedge on seams that should be straight. Mark the centerlines and sides of the darts.

STEP 16. Machine baste the trial muslin together along the corrected seam and dart lines.

STEP 17. Try the bodice on again and make whatever adjustments are needed. Mark the corrections on the bodice using a different color from the earlier markings to avoid confusion.

The body of the bodice is now complete. This bodice should not be taken apart, however, until the sleeves and collars have had a trial fitting. Once this has been done, the muslin can be taken apart and the corrected markings indicated on the original pattern.

The final pattern should only be for one side of the body, either left or right, unless the wearer has an exceptionally asymmetrical figure that needs to be compensated for.

For women's patterns, it is a good idea to mark the Bust point in addition to the top of the dart. This will be needed later when the position of the dart is altered.

Seam lines as well as seam-allowance lines should be clearly indicated on the pattern. If the reader chooses, the seam allowances may be left off. This will make it easier for tracing later patterns. The pattern, however, should be clearly marked to indicate that seam allowances have been left off; this will avoid costly mistakes in both time and money.

The Basic Bodice pattern is now complete. This pattern will be the basis for many different styles of garments. It may also be used to adjust commercial patterns so that they will fit easily and perfectly, without all the trial and error fittings which working with commercial patterns normally requires.

DRAPING THE BODICE

Draping can be a useful supplement to drafting. The basic process of draping a pattern is to take a piece of material such as muslin, pin it on either a dress form or the person for whom the pattern is being made, draw the basic seam lines and darts onto the muslin, then remove it, add seam allowances, and cut. The specific procedure for draping the front pattern of the woman's Basic Bodice will be described here.

Use a piece of muslin approximately 36″ wide and 24″ long. If the muslin is to be draped directly onto someone, she should wear a tight-fitting top so that there will be something to pin the muslin to.

STEP 1. Place the muslin on the person for whom the pattern is being made so that the straight of the goods is on the Center Front axis. Pin down from the neck to the waist (Figure 28).

STEP 2. Slash the fabric at the neck so that it will fit smoothly over the shoulders. Smooth the material over the Front Plane of the body, pinning it at the shoulder seams.

STEP 3. Next, pin the material into a front dart so that it is smooth over the side plane of the body. Do not distort the material that has already been fitted.

DRAPING THE BODICE

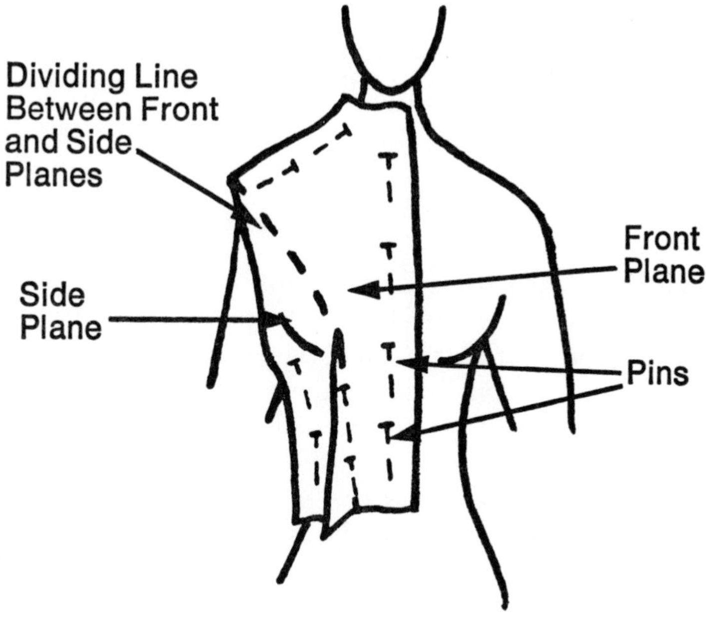

Figure 28

STEP 4. Remove any excess material from the side by pinning the Side Seam in place.

STEP 5. Mark the Center Front line, Neck curve, Shoulder Seam line, Armhole curve, Side Seam line, and Waist line directly onto the material.

STEP 6. Keeping the dart pinned, remove the fabric. Mark in the front dart. Then unpin it.

STEP 7. Spread the muslin out flat. Trace the dart and seam lines onto paper and add seam allowances. The pattern is complete.

The same principle of draping may be applied to other patterns —not only to the basic fitted patterns but also to completely original designs. The idea behind draping is that the material should be molded so that it assumes the shape of the final garment.

Draping is not difficult. Just be sure that the center seams and shoulders are well secured before folding and pinning other parts of the fabric.

THE BASIC SLEEVE PATTERN

The pattern for the Basic Fitted Sleeve is given here. It is the basis for many other sleeve styles, including the Shirt Sleeve, the Flared Sleeve and the Coat Sleeve, all of which are discussed in demonstration lessons in Section Four. Methods for drafting the Tunic Sleeve, the Raglan Sleeve and the Peasant Sleeve are given separately in Section Three.

The Fitted Sleeve pattern is one of the more straightforward patterns to draft. Its unique aspect is the Sleeve Cap. The function of the Sleeve Cap is, of course, to join the sleeve to the bodice.

Measurements needed for this pattern:

1. Shoulder-to-Wrist: ________
2. Wrist: ________
3. Undearm-to-Wrist: ________
4. Biceps: ________

Step 1. On a fresh sheet of paper draw a line that is the length of the Shoulder-to-Wrist measurement (Figure 29). This will be the Sleeve Centerline.

Step 2. At the bottom end of this line draw another line perpendicular to it. This will be the Wrist line. On the Wrist line mark off 1″ plus half of the Wrist measurement on either side of the Sleeve Centerline.

THE BASIC FITTED SLEEVE PATTERN (Steps 1 to 5)

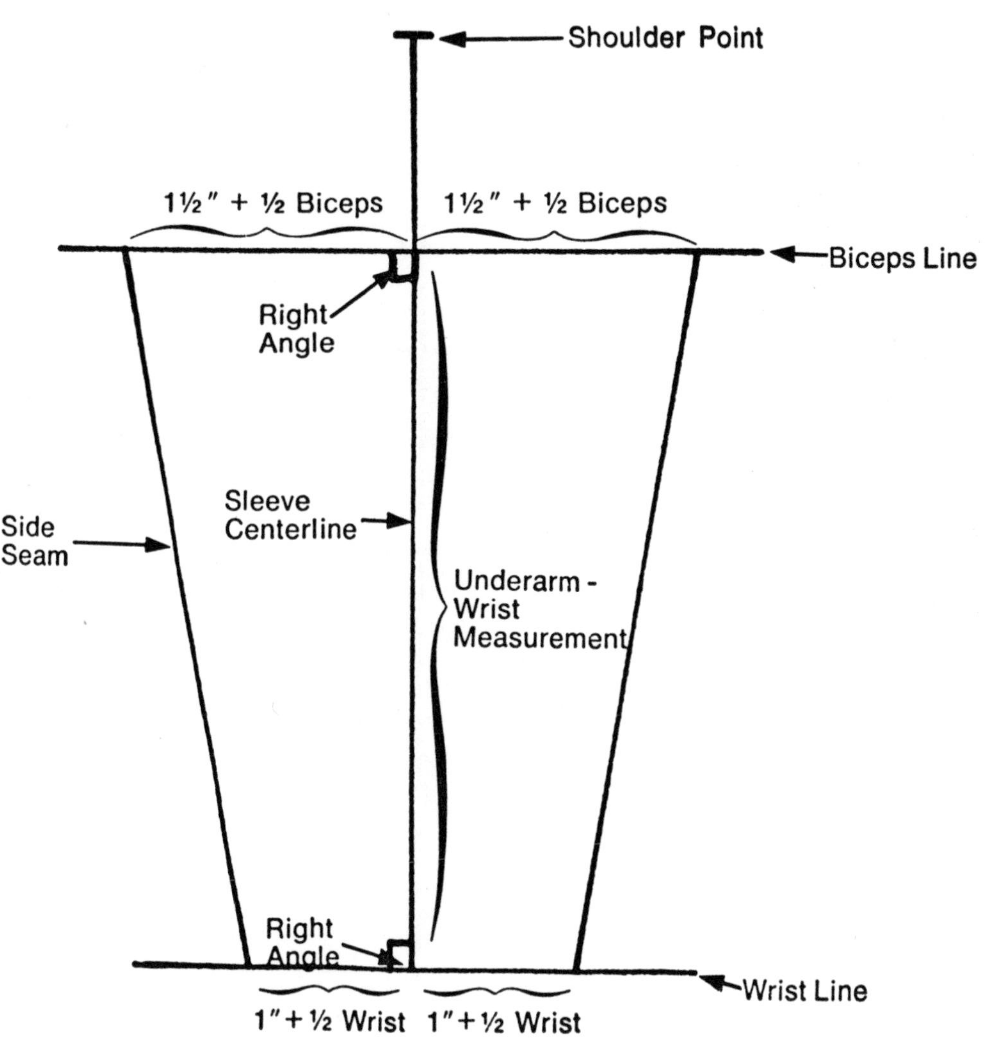

Figure 29

THE SLEEVE CAP (Steps 1 to 3)
The Basic Reference Points

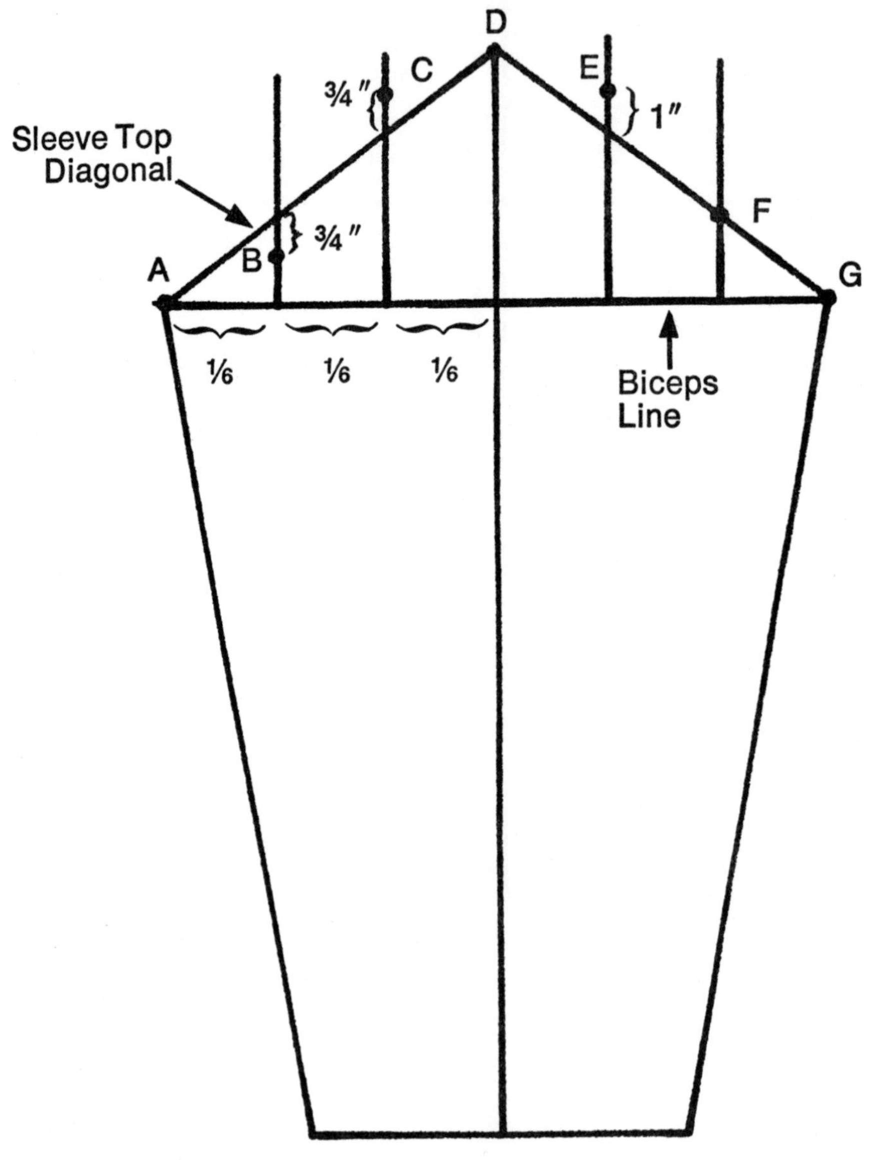

Figure 30

STEP 3. Measure up the Sleeve Centerline from the Wrist line, marking off a point that is the Underarm-to-Wrist length away. Draw a line at right angles to the Sleeve Centerline at this point. This will be the Biceps line. (The distance between the top of the sleeve and the Biceps line should be more than 5″ for a fitted sleeve.)

STEP 4. On the Biceps line mark off 1½″ plus half of the Biceps measurement on either side of the Sleeve Centerline.

STEP 5. The Side Seams of the sleeve may now be drawn by connecting the marks on the Biceps line with the marks on the Wrist line.

The sleeve pattern has now been drafted to cover the basic part of the arm. Notice that allowance has been added to the Wrist and Biceps measurement so that the arm will be free to move.

THE SLEEVE CAP

The Sleeve Cap is normally drafted so that the sleeve will hang neatly when the arm is at the side of the body. The optimum curve for this type of Sleeve Cap may be drafted in the following manner.

STEP 1. Divide the Biceps line into sixths. Construct lines perpendicular to the Biceps line from each of these points (Figure 30).

STEP 2. Draw lines connecting the top of the Sleeve Centerline to each end of the Biceps line. These are the Sleeve-Top Diagonals.

STEP 3. Mark points A, B, C, D, E, F, and G as indicated in Figure 30. Point B is ¾″ below the Sleeve-Top Diagonal and Point C is ¾″ above the Sleeve-Top Diagonal. Point E is 1″ above the Sleeve-Top Diagonal. All the other points are at the intersections of the Sleeve-Top Diagonal line and the dividing lines.

THE SLEEVE CAP (Step 4)
The Final Shape

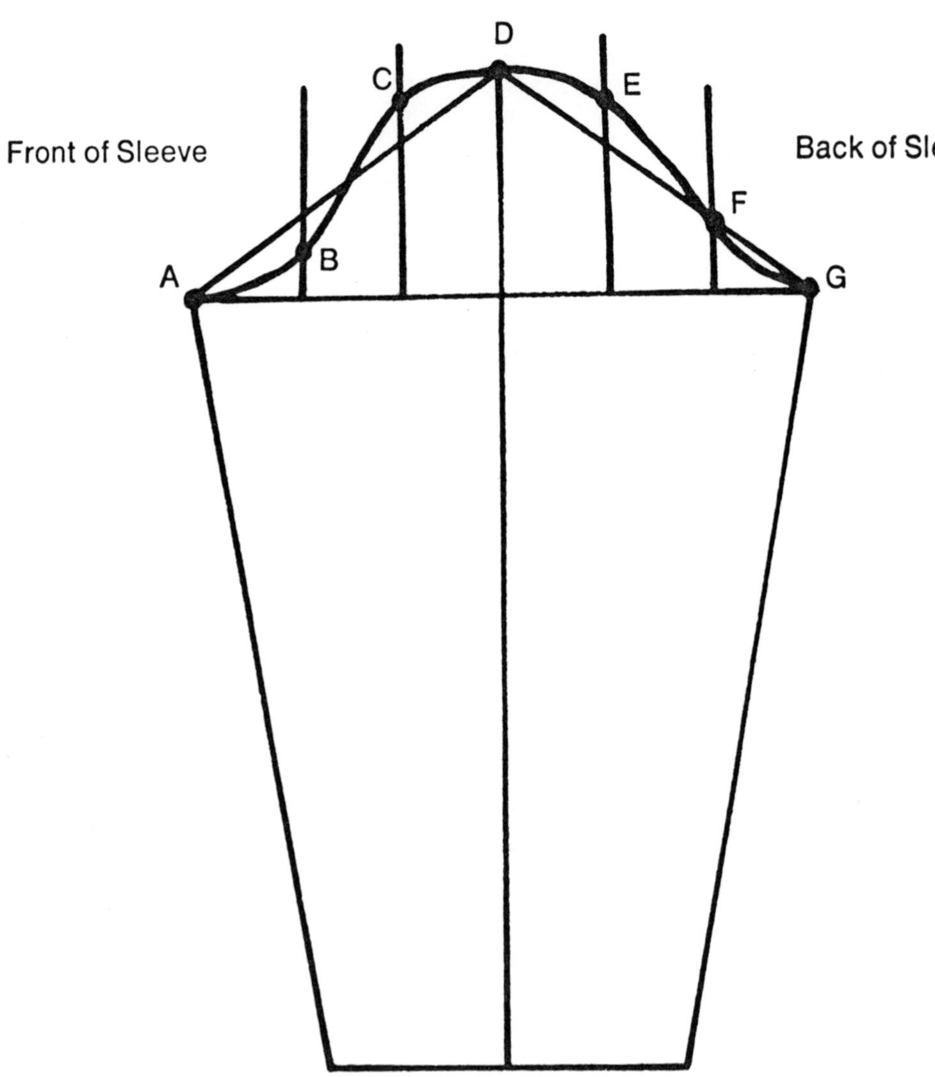

Figure 31

STEP 4. Draw the Sleeve Cap line by connecting these points. The finished Sleeve Cap should look like Figure 31. Take special note of how the Sleeve Cap is shaped differently in front and in back as it will be important to remember this when the sleeve is sewn in.

The circumference of the Sleeve Cap must now be checked against the circumference of the armhole opening to ensure a proper fit. The Sleeve Cap circumference should be 1″ longer than the armhole circumference. (The 1″ difference will be eased into the armhole.) Measure the armhole seam line and the Sleeve Cap line. Make the following alterations as necessary.

Step 5. If the necessary expansion is only an inch or two, the Sleeve Cap curve may be exaggerated as in Diagram A of Figure 32. This exaggeration will add a few inches to the circumference.

Step 6. If the necessary expansion cannot be achieved in this manner, it may be necessary to expand the entire sleeve at the Biceps line and redraw the Sleeve Cap curve. (See Diagram B, Figure 32.)

If the Sleeve Cap curve exceeds the armhole circumference by more than 1″, reduce the Sleeve Cap by doing just the opposite of what is suggested in Steps 5 and 6.

Adding a Dart

Fitted sleeves will sometimes have a dart at the elbow to facilitate movement of the arm at this point. This type of dart may be added by the following procedure.

Step 1. Lengthen the back seam line by the desired dart width (¾″ is recommended).

Step 2. Curve the Wrist line as indicated in Figure 33. Note that the intersection of the Wrist line and the Side Seam lines form right angles. This establishes the correct shape for the wrist when the sleeve is sewn in. (Refer back to the instructions for drafting the bodice Neckline, starting on page 42, including Figure 13 for clarification of the idea behind this rule.)

Step 3. Draw a line perpendicular to the Sleeve Centerline at the Shoulder-to-Elbow length. Extend this line to the Back Side seam. This is the Elbow line and it will form the top edge of the dart.

SLEEVE CAP ALTERATION (Steps 5 & 6)

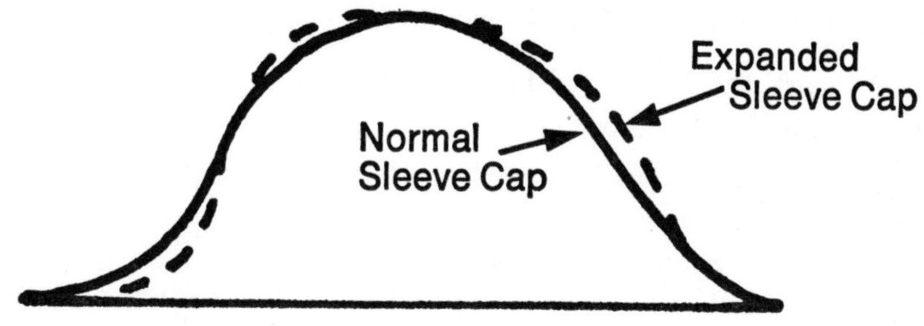

Sleeve Cap Curve Exaggerated

Diagram A

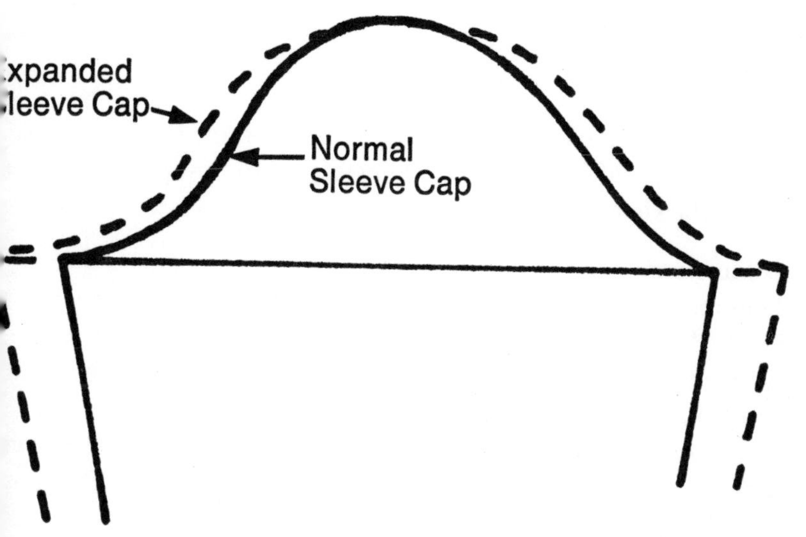

Sleeve Expanded

Diagram B

Figure 32

STEP 4. Mark a point half way between the Side Seam and the Sleeve Centerline of the Elbow line. This will be the end of the dart.

STEP 5. Mark the Dart Width on the Side Seam line. Connect this point to the end of the dart.

The basic pattern for the sleeve is now complete. Add 1″ seam allowances to the Side Seams and a 5/8″ seam allowance to the Sleeve Cap. Label the Front and Back halves of the Sleeve Cap for later identification. Cut out a sleeve in muslin for a trial fitting. Mark the Centerline on the muslin and label the Front and Back segments of the Sleeve Cap.

FITTING THE SLEEVE

The sleeve is fitted so that it will hang smoothly from the shoulder. If the sleeve is the wrong shape it will create folds either in the sleeve or in the shoulder of the bodice.

STEP 1. Pin the top of the Sleeve Cap seam to the point of the shoulder.

STEP 2. Match the Sleeve Cap seam line with the Armhole seam line as the arm hangs naturally.

STEP 3. Reshape the Sleeve Cap seam as necessary to eliminate any undesirable folds.

STEP 4. If alteration of the Sleeve Cap was necessary the Sleeve Cap Circumference should be rechecked to establish the proper allowance for setting in the sleeve.

VARYING THE SLEEVE SEAM

Different types of sleeves may require different seam locations. Alteration techniques will be discussed in Section Three but at this point the reader should understand how to locate the inside, front, outside, and back of the sleeve.

The seam locations are determined by the shape of the Sleeve Cap. Diagram A of Figure 34 illustrates the basic positions. Diagram B of Figure 34 illustrates the shape the Sleeve Cap would assume for different seam locations.

DRAFTING THE SLEEVE DART (Steps 1 to 5)

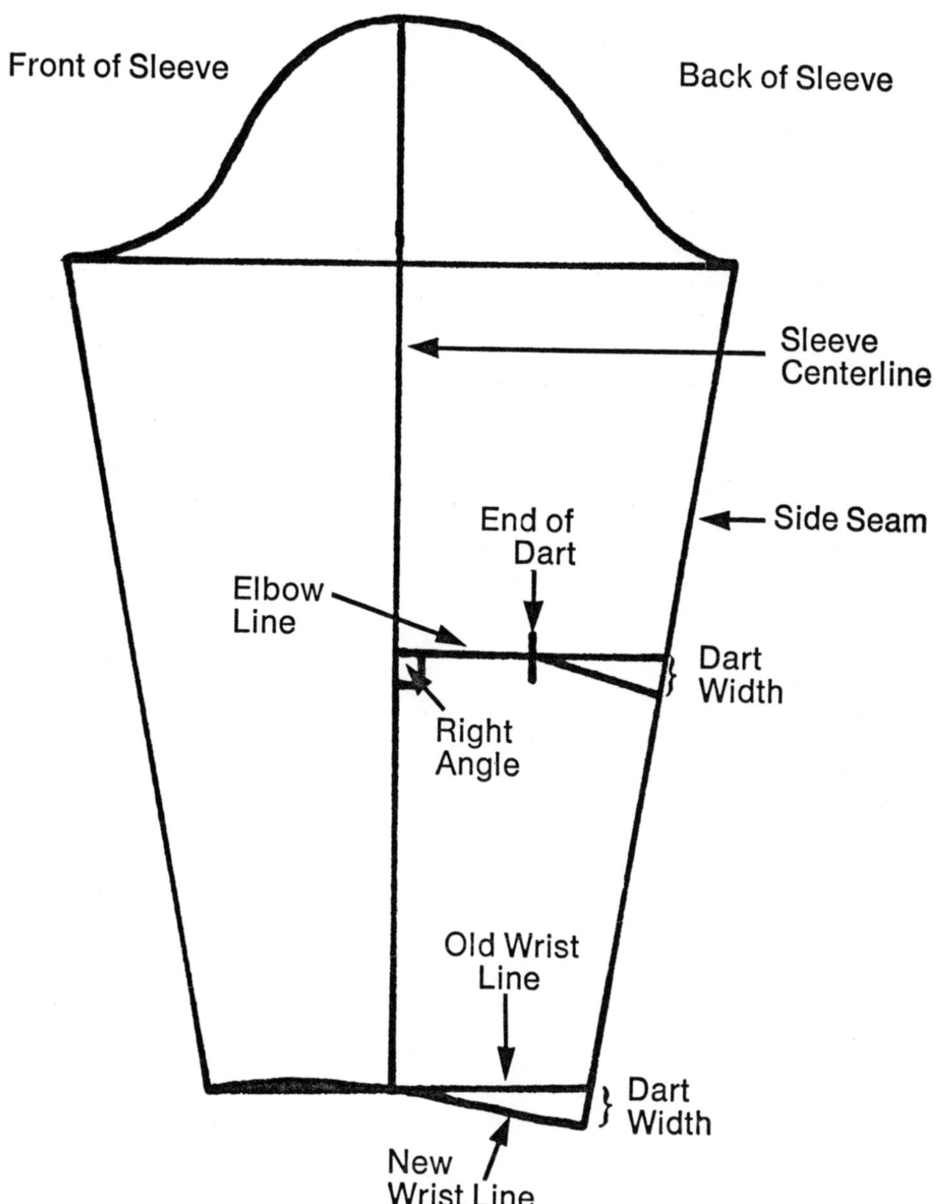

Figure 33

THE SLEEVE CAP AND SEAM LOCATIONS

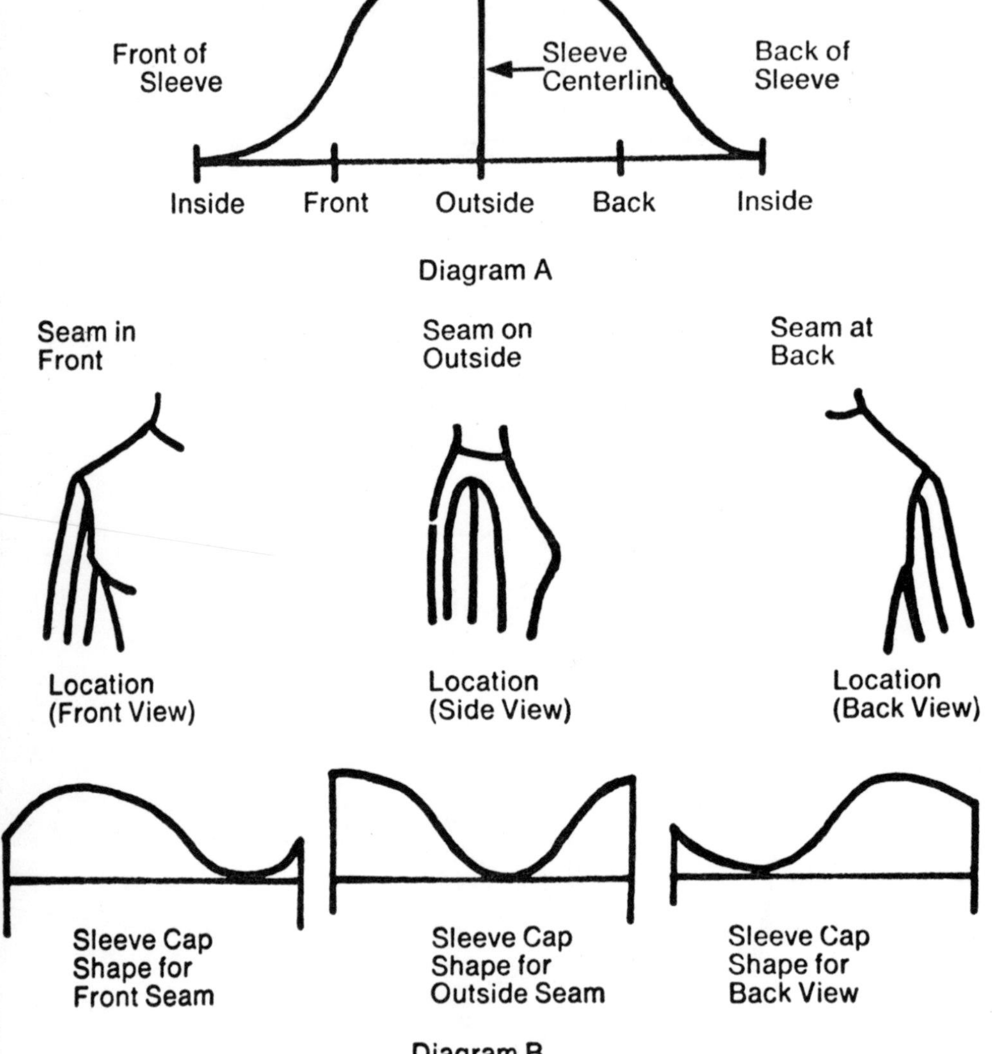

Figure 34

COLLAR PATTERNS

There are three basic types of collars: the Flat Collar, the Shirt Collar, and the Mandarin Collar. What distinguishes these three types from each other is the shape of the seam where it is sewn to the bodice. The Flat Collar has a concave seam line. The Shirt Collar has an almost straight seam line. And the Mandarin Collar has a convex seam line. Figure 35 illustrates the three basic types and their respective seam lines.

THE BASIC COLLARS

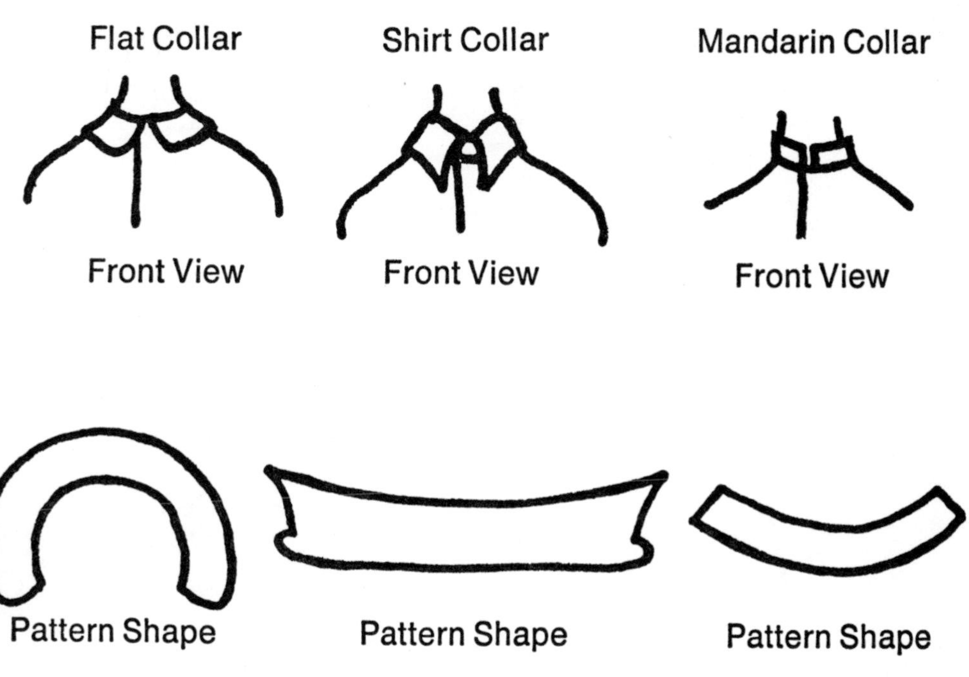

Figure 35

FLAT COLLAR PATTERN

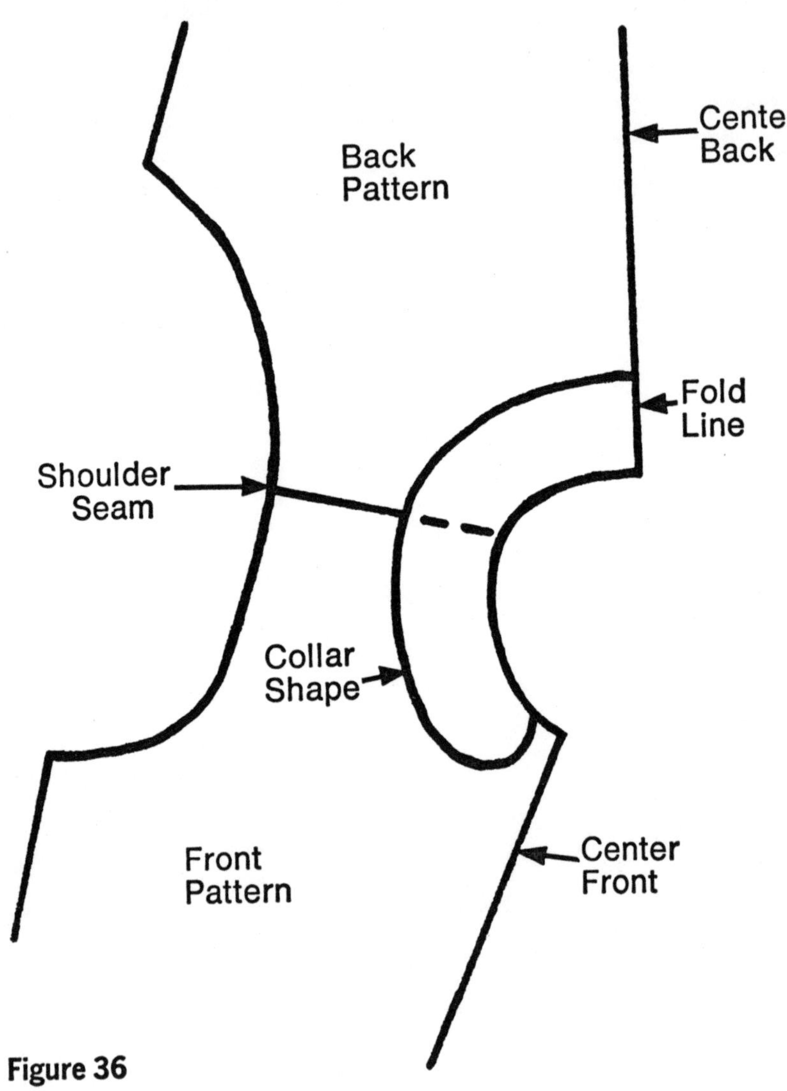

Figure 36

THE FLAT COLLAR

The Flat Collar, as the name implies, lies flat on the bodice. To achieve this, the shape of the collar seam that attaches to the bodice seam must be the same as the shape of the bodice Neck Seam. The Flat Collar may be drafted by the following technique.

STEP 1. Lay out the bodice pattern as if the Shoulder Seams were sewn (see Figure 36).

STEP 2. Trace this shape onto another sheet of paper.

STEP 3. Sketch in the desired shape of the Flat Collar.

STEP 4. Add seam allowances and cut.

With a Flat Collar of this nature it is not necessary to have any shoulder seams. The Center Back will be a fold line.

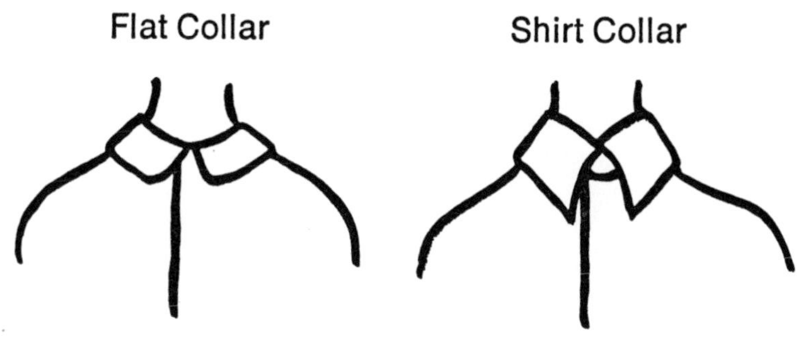

THE SHIRT COLLAR

A Shirt Collar is the type of collar most often seen on men's shirts. It stands up next to the neck briefly, then rolls over and falls away. This collar may be cut in a single piece or in two pieces. The procedure for drafting a single-piece collar will be described here. For a two-piece collar there is another seam at the Collar Fold line.

THE SHIRT COLLAR (Steps 1 to 4)
The Basic Dimensions

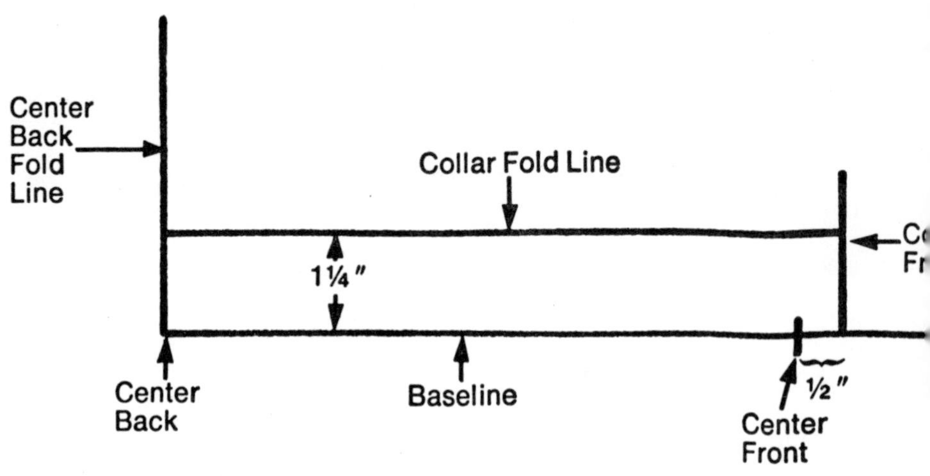

Figure 37

STEP 1. Draw a baseline for the collar. Mark off half of the Neck measurement. This will establish the Center Back and Center Front of the collar (see Figure 37).

STEP 2. Mark a point ½″ out from the Center Front mark on the Baseline and extend a perpendicular line. This will be the Collar Front.

The ½″ is added to the Baseline at the Center Front because this type of collar overlaps from one side to the other so that it may be buttoned.

STEP 3. Draw a line perpendicular to the Baseline at the Center Back. This will be the Center Back Fold line.

STEP 4. Draw a line parallel to the Baseline 1¼″ above it. This is the Collar Fold line.

The preceding steps establish the basic boundaries for the bottom part of the collar. This section may now be shaped.

THE SHIRT COLLAR (Steps 5 to 8)

Shaping the Bottom of the Collar

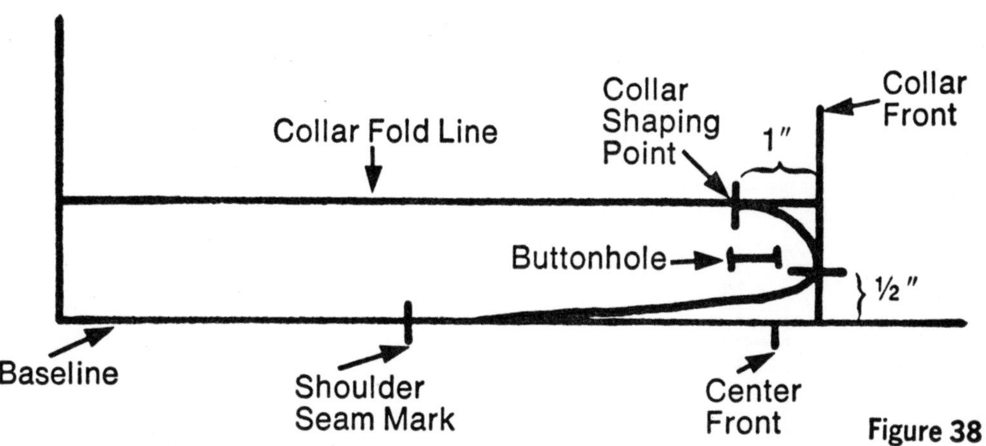

Figure 38

STEP 5. Measure the distance from the Shoulder Seam to Center Front on the bodice. Starting at the Center Front mark, mark this distance on the collar Baseline (Figure 38). This is the Shoulder Seam mark.

STEP 6. At the front of the collar make a mark ½″ above the Baseline. Draw a line from the Shoulder Seam mark, gradually curving it to this point.

The preceding steps shape the bottom of the collar so that it will follow the contour of the neck.

STEP 7. On the Collar Fold line mark a point 1″ from the Collar Front. This will be the Collar Shaping Point. Draw a curved line from this point to the Collar Front. This curve is strictly for appearance and does not affect the fit of the collar.

STEP 8. The buttonhole may be marked if a button is to be used. The line of the buttonhole is drafted halfway between the Baseline and the Collar Fold line. It starts at the Center Front mark. It should be of an appropriate length for the button being used.

This completes the bottom section of the collar. The shape of the top section can now be drawn in.

THE SHIRT COLLAR (Steps 9 to 12)
Shaping the Top

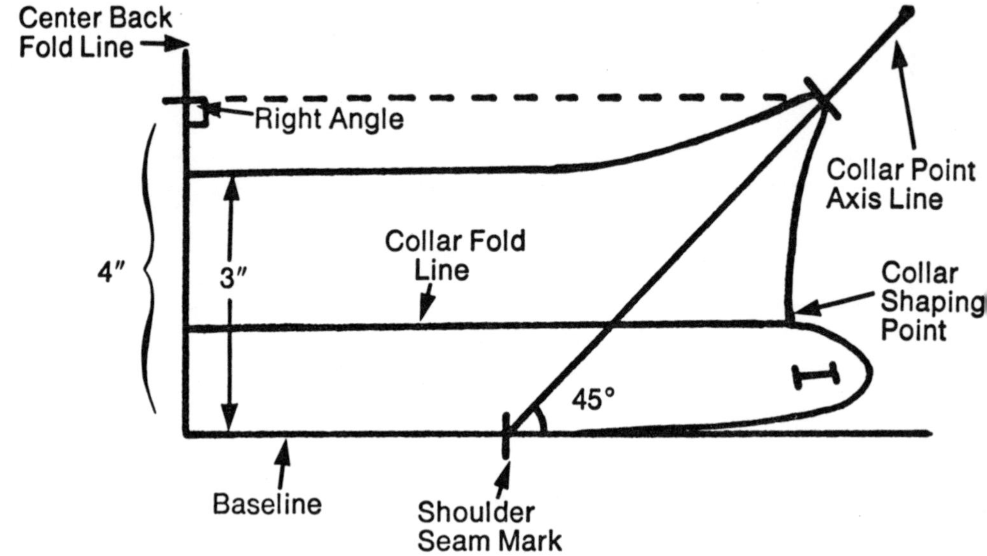

Figure 39

STEP 9. Draw a line from the Shoulder Seam mark at a 45 degree angle to the Baseline (see Figure 39). This is the Collar-Point Axis line.

The rest of the drafting process is a matter of sketching in the desired shape. The Collar-Point Axis line is equally applicable to conservative style collars or collars with extended points. The following discussion will describe a conservative dress shirt style.

STEP 10. Mark a point on the Center Back Fold line 3″ from the Baseline. This will be the top of the collar. Do not confuse the Center Back Fold line with the Collar Fold line. (For other styles of collars, it is recommended that this measurement be at least 3″ so that the fold-over part of the collar will cover the standing part of the collar.)

STEP 11. Mark another point on the Center Back Fold line 4″ from the Baseline. Extend this mark to the Collar-Point Axis line. This establishes the point of the collar.

STEP 12. Sketch in the top and side of the collar to the desired shape. The front edge of the top of the collar should start at the Collar Shaping point on the Collar Fold line.

STEP 13. Add seam allowances and cut.

Mandarin Collar

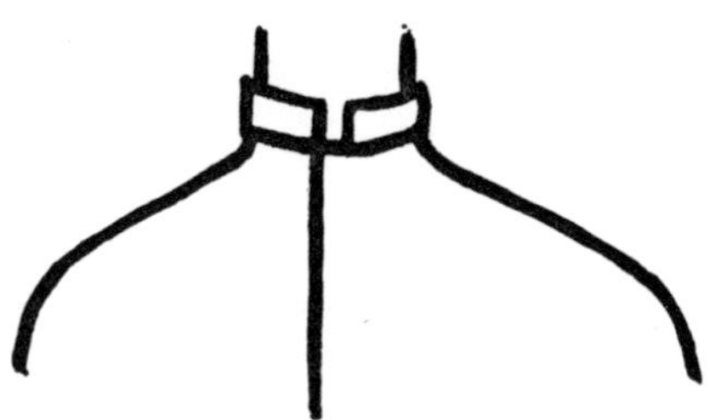

THE MANDARIN COLLAR

The Mandarin Collar is shaped so that it will stand up from the bodice neckline and fit smoothly around the neck. The basic dimensions of the Mandarin Collar will be drafted straight first. This strip will then be curved by a special technique so that the collar, when it is cut, will follow the shape of the neck. This shape is wide at the base and narrow at the top.

The technique of curving a seam line is an important one to master, as the drafter will have frequent opportunities to use it. It is used to curve such lines as the hem lines of skirts and the seam lines of wide cuffs. It can also be used to curve the seams of fitted waistbands.

THE MANDARIN COLLAR (Steps 1 to 9)
Establishing the Collar Dimensions

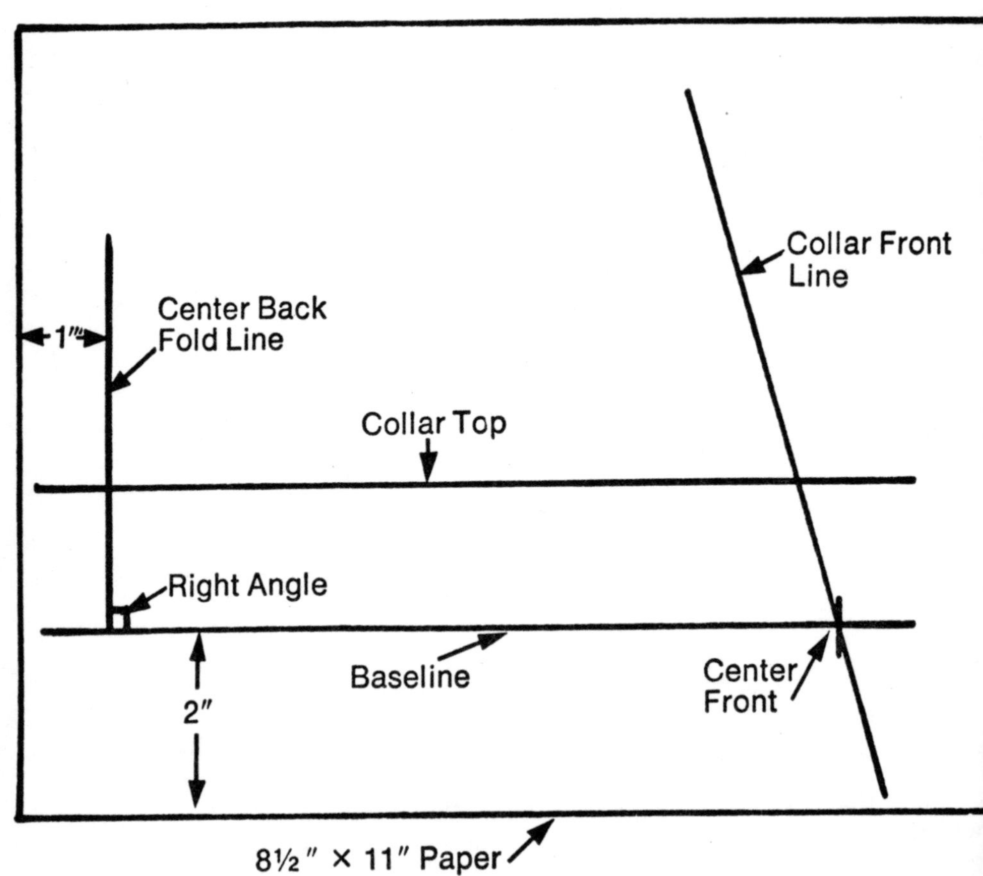

Figure 40

STEP 1. At a distance of 1″ from the left-hand edge of the paper, draw a vertical line. This is the Center Back Fold line.

STEP 2. At a distance of 2″ from the bottom edge of the paper, draw a line at right angles to the Center Back Fold line. This will be the Baseline. Extend the Baseline to the left-hand edge of the paper.

STEP 3. Measure the distance around the Neckline of the Basic Bodice. Divide this measurement in half. Mark the resulting length on the Baseline, starting from the Center Back Fold line and going to the right. This mark will be called the Center Front Point.

STEP 4. On the Center Back Fold line, measure up from the Baseline and mark the desired height of the finished collar.

STEP 5. From the point located in Step 4, draw a line parallel to the Baseline. This is the Collar Top line. Extend the Collar Top line to the left-hand edge of the paper.

STEP 6. On the person who is to wear the collar, measure up from the base of the neck the height of the finished collar.

STEP 7. At this height, measure the circumference of the wearer's neck. This measurement should be taken loosely. Mark off half this length on the Collar Top line, starting at the Center Fold line and going to the right.

STEP 8. Connect the point located by Step 7 with the Center Front Point on the Baseline. This will be a diagonal line called the Collar Front line.

STEP 9. Extend the line of the Collar Front up from the Collar Top.

The basic size of the collar has been determined by these steps. Now the collar seams must be curved so that the collar will stand up properly.

THE MANDARIN COLLAR (Steps 10 to 13)
Establishing the First Fold

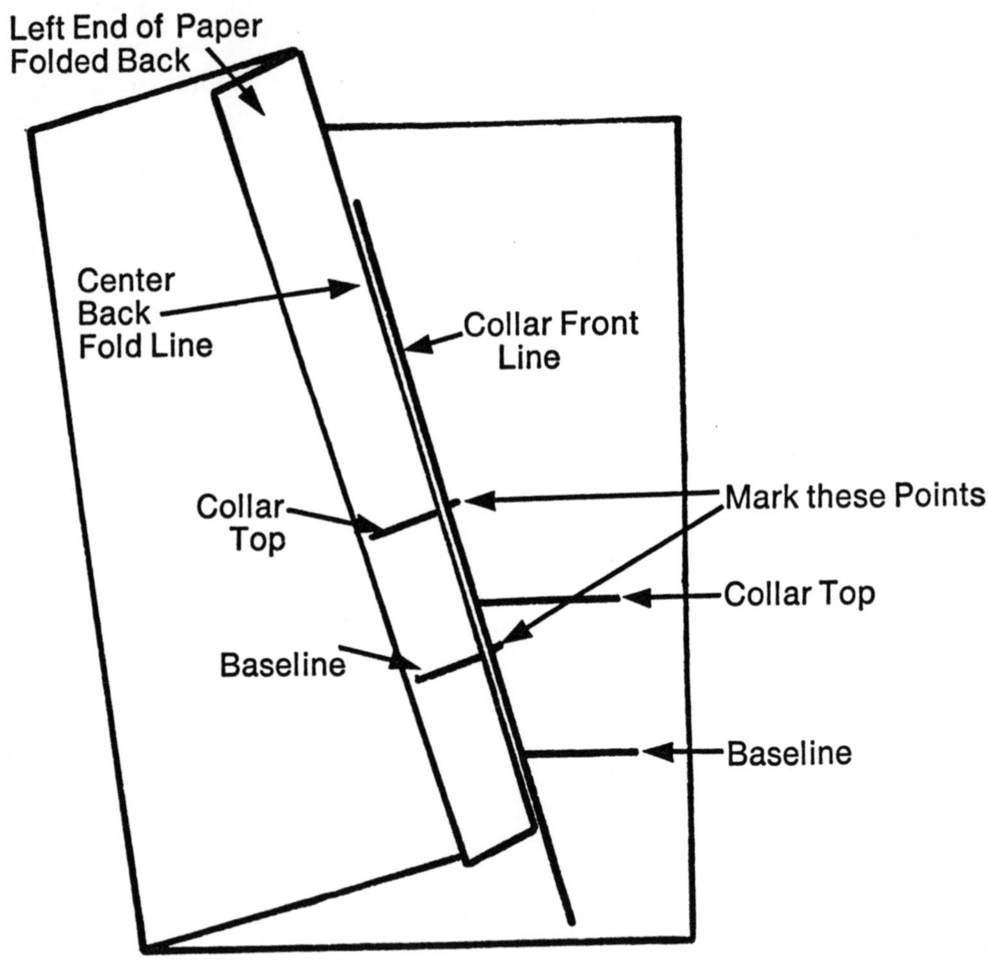

Figure 41

STEP 10. Fold the left-hand edge of the paper pattern backwards at the Center Back Fold line.

STEP 11. Now fold the pattern to the right, so that the Center Back Fold line coincides with the Collar Front line for its full length.

To do this, fold the paper on a diagonal. Most of the Center Back Fold line will land above the Collar Top line.

STEP 12. Crease the paper on the fold.

STEP 13. With the paper folded in this way, the Baseline and the Collar Top line at the Center Back Fold will appear on the folded back flap of the paper. Mark these points from the Center Back Fold line onto the Collar Front line.

THE MANDARIN COLLAR (Step 14)

The Second Fold

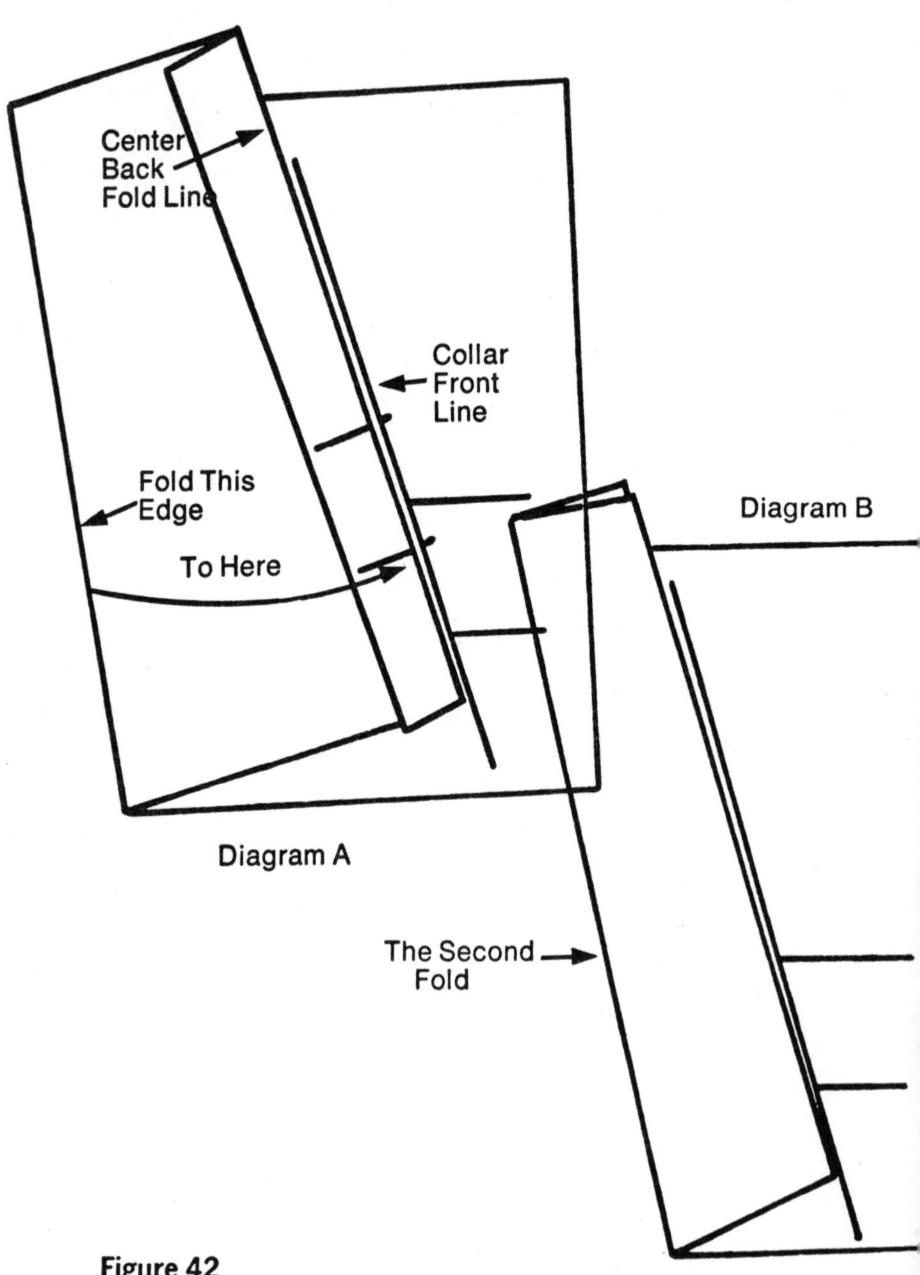

Figure 42

STEP 14. Without opening the folded pattern, fold it a second time, so that the left-hand edge of the folded pattern coincides with the Collar Front line (See Figure 42). Again this will be a diagonal fold. The pattern is now folded in fourths. Crease the new fold carefully.

STEP 15. Unfold the pattern. There should now be three creases in the pattern dividing the collar in fourths (See Figure 43).

STEP 16. Fold the pattern back from left to right again, this time so that the Center Back Fold line will coincide with the first crease to the left of the Collar Front line. Mark the points where the Collar Top line and the Baseline at the Center Back Fold land on this crease.

STEP 17. Move the pattern so that the Center Back Fold line lands on the middle crease. Again, mark the points where the Collar Top line and the Baseline extensions land on the middle crease.

THE MANDARIN COLLAR (Steps 15 to 24)
Curving the Collar

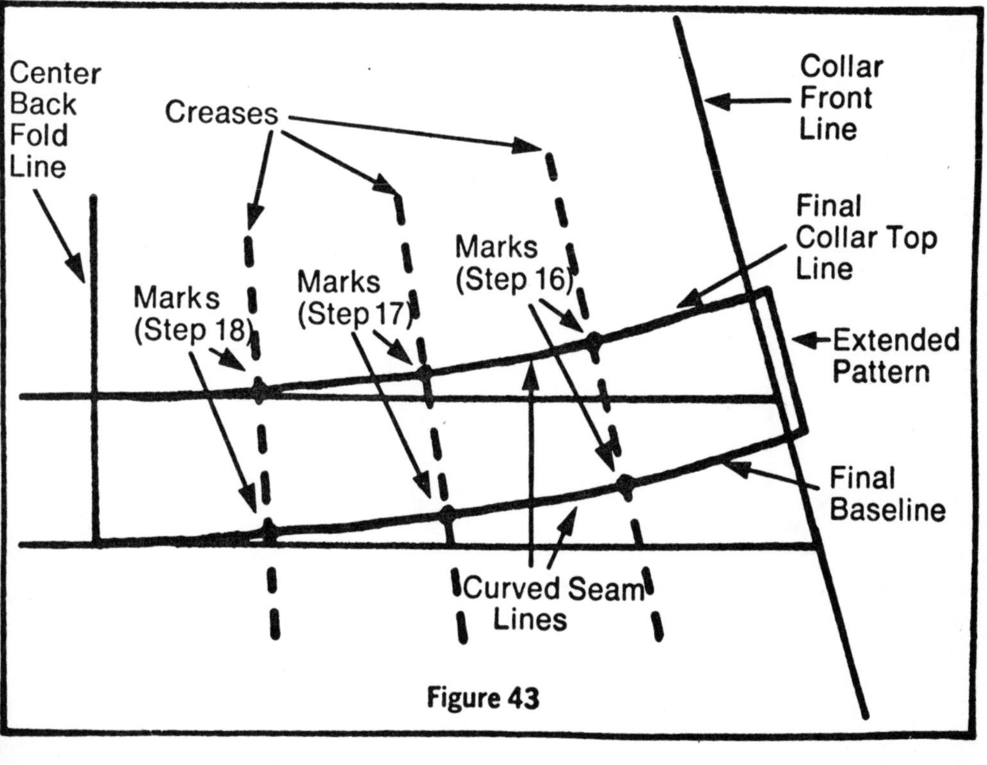

Figure 43

THE FITTED SKIRT PATTERN (Steps 1 to 7)

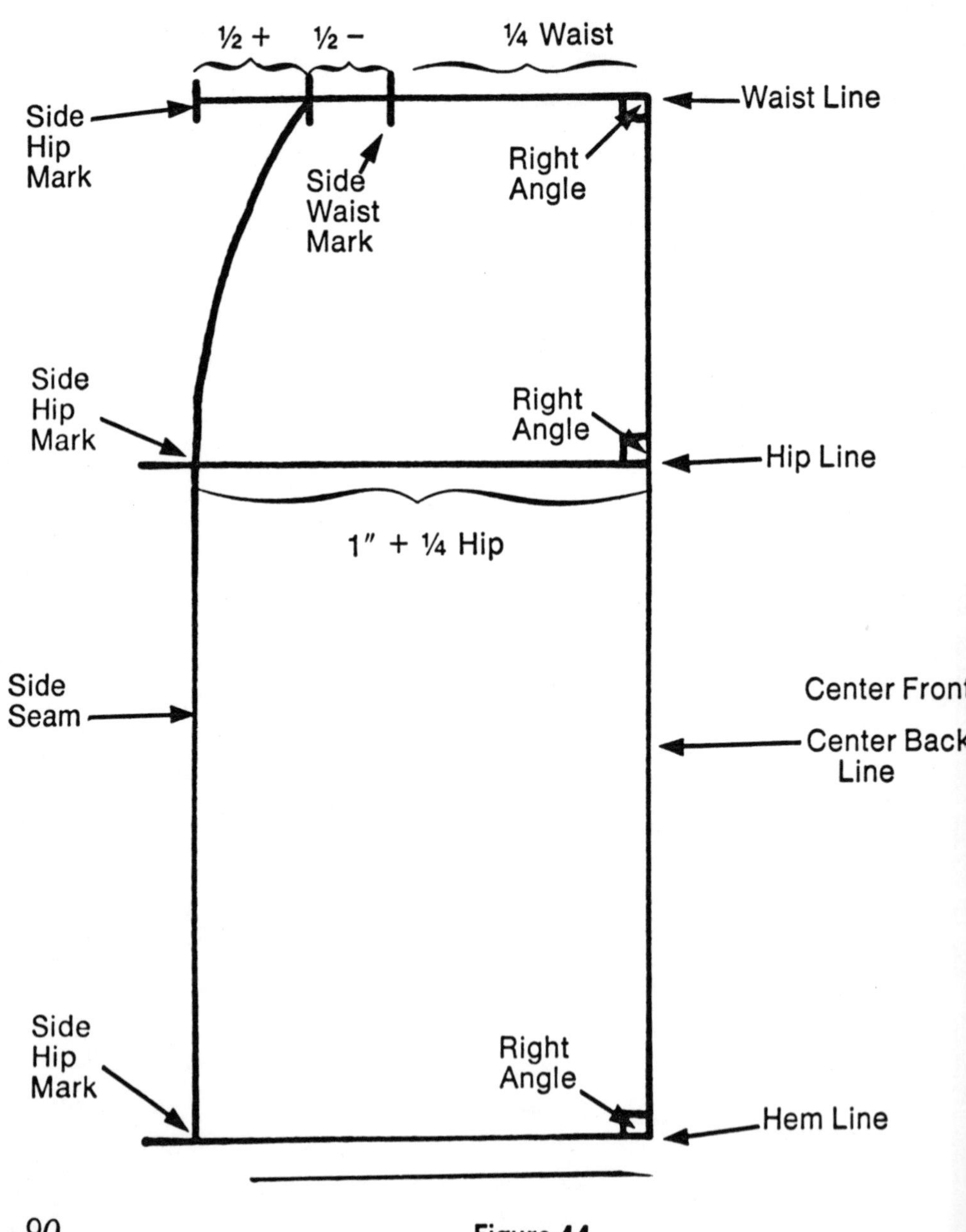

Figure 44

Step 18. Move the Center Back Fold line so that it coincides with the last crease. Mark the Collar Top and the Baseline on this crease.

Step 19. Open the pattern completely.

Step 20. Connect the points on the pattern, as shown in Figure 43. Connect the top marks to form the top curve of the collar and connect the bottom marks to form the bottom curve of the collar.

Step 21. Curving the collar will shorten the Baseline and the Collar Top line slightly. To correct this, measure the old straight Baseline and extend the new curved Baseline to the same length, continuing the curve freehand. Do the same with the Collar Top line.

Step 22. Connect the curved, extended Collar Top line and the curved and extended Baseline, to make a new Collar Front line.

Step 23. Add seam allowances and cut.

When cutting out this collar, be sure to place the Center Back Fold line on a fold of the fabric. This fold should be placed on the straight of the goods. Cut two collars. Sew them together on the Collar Top line and at the ends. Clip the corners, turn the collar inside out, and press. Attach the collar to the bodice neckline the same way a waistband is put on a skirt or a pair of pants.

THE BASIC FITTED SKIRT PATTERN

The Basic Fitted Skirt pattern is designed to cover the lower portion of the body in the same way that the bodice pattern is designed to cover the upper body. This is a basic pattern from which various other styles can be drafted. Both flared and pleated skirts, for example, can be drafted by adapting this pattern. Like the Basic Bodice pattern, the Basic Skirt pattern can serve as a guide for altering commercial patterns for a better fit.

The Fitted Skirt covers the region from the waist to the hips fairly snugly but with sufficient allowance for movement. From there it hangs straight down from the hips to the desired hem length. The skirt will be drafted using a single pattern for both the front and back sections. The difference in the shape of the body at the front and the back will be adjusted for during the fitting.

Measurements needed for this pattern:

1) Waist to Above the Knee ________
2) Waist to Hip ________
3) Hip ________
4) Waist ________

The Pattern

Step 1. Draw a vertical line that is the Waist to Above Knee measurement. This will be the Center Front/Center Back line of the skirt.

Step 2. At the top and bottom of this line draw lines perpendicular to it. These will be the Waist and Hem lines.

Step 3. On the Center Front/Center Back line mark off the Waist to Hip measurement. Draw a perpendicular line at this point. This is the Hip line.

Step 4. Mark off 1″ plus one-fourth of the Hip measurement on the Waist line, Hip line, and Hem line. These will be the Side Hip marks.

The one-inch allowance is added to enable the hips to move freely.

Step 5. On the Waist line mark off one-fourth the Waist measurement. This will be the Side Waist mark.

Step 6. Measuring from the Side Waist Mark, make a mark on the Waist line that is slightly less than half the distance between the Side Waist mark and the Side Hip mark. This will be the starting point for the Side Seam.

STEP 7. Draw in the Side Seam starting at the mark established by Step 6. Curve the line out to the Side Hip mark on the Hip line and continue it straight down to the Hem line Side Hip mark.

The principle behind the curved part of the Side Seam is that part of the shaping of the skirt will be done at the Side Seam and part of the shaping will be done by darts in the front and back. Thus the Side Seam starts at a point that is slightly less than half the difference between the Hip width and Waist measurement.

STEP 8. Seam and Hem allowances must now be added. Normally in a skirt of this type the Center Front will be a fold line and the Center Back will have a seam, therefore a 5/8-inch allowance will have to be added to the Center Back. If one pattern is used for both the front and back sections the Center Back seam allowance may be folded under when the front section is cut. 1½″ seam allowances are recommended for the Side Seams but 5/8″ is adequate for the Waist seam allowance. The amount of allowance that is added to the Hem line will depend on the desired Hem length.

The skirt should be cut in muslin and sewn down the entire length of the Side Seams and down the Center Back from the hips to the hem. The skirt is not sewn at the Center Back between the hips and the waist as this will be the closure for the skirt.

FITTING THE SKIRT

To fit the skirt, put it on the person who is to wear it and pin the Center Back seam closed.

STEP 1. Roughly pin out the dart allowances so that the skirt will hang from the proper location on the body.

STEP 2. Work one-fourth of the skirt at a time, pinning in the dart so that the skirt fits smoothly from the waist to the hips. Mark the ends of the darts carefully. It is not necessary to use the full dart allowance, as some of this allowance may be removed at the seams.

Only one half, either left or right, of the skirt should be fitted unless the wearer is asymmetrical. The other half will be corrected after the skirt has been removed. This assures a symmetrical shape for the darts and the seams.

STEP 3. After the front and back darts have been pinned in, reshape the side seams so that any excess dart allowance will be removed and also so that the skirt follows the contour of the hips at the side seam.

The Center Back seam and the Center Front seam (if there is one) should not be shaped. They should remain straight.

STEP 4. The fitted skirt may now be taken apart and the paper pattern corrected. It will be necessary to make a second paper pattern so that the front and back sections may be corrected separately.

SIMPLE WAISTBAND PATTERN

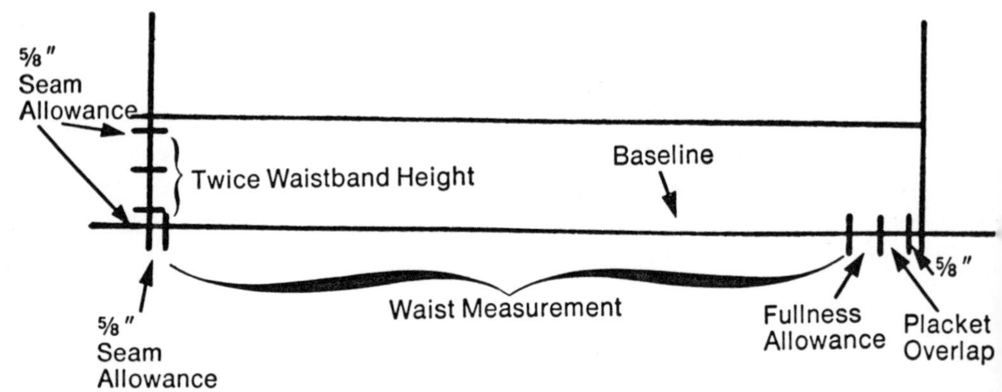

Figure 45

THE BASIC WAISTBAND

There are two kinds of waistbands: the simple, straight waistband, which is commonly used on skirts and trousers, and the shaped, or complex waistband, which fits over the hips and is shaped to follow the hips' contour. The simple waistband, described next, may be drafted for the Basic Skirt and the Basic Pants Pattern. The method for drafting the complex waistband is described in the demonstration lesson on drafting the flared hip-hugger pants.

STEP 1. Draw a horizontal line which will become the Baseline (Figure 45).

STEP 2. Mark off a distance on the Baseline which includes two ⅝″ seam allowances (or 1¼″), plus the Waist measurement, plus the desired placket overlap, plus, in the case of full skirts, an allowance for the fullness of the material. This distance will be the total length of the waistband.

The fullness allowance may be calculated by comparing the Waist measurement taken over undergarments with a measurement taken in the same place over the gathered skirt material. The difference between these measurements represents the necessary fullness allowance. For example, if the basic Waist circumference is 24″ and the same measurement taken over the skirt is 25″, the fullness allowence will be 1″ (25″ − 24″ = 1″).

STEP 3. Draw a line perpendicular to the Baseline at each end of the Waistband length measurement.

STEP 4. Measure up each of these lines the distance of two ⅝″ seam allowances (which is 1¼″), plus twice the desired height of the waistband.

STEP 5. Draw a line parallel to the Baseline connecting these points.

STEP 6. The pattern is now complete and may be cut out.

Note Carefully: This is one pattern in which the seam allowances are added as a part of the basic drafting procedure. Do not add any further seam allowances.

When the waistband is sewn, it is folded in half lengthwise. The two ends are sewn and clipped. The waistband is then turned and the skirt is set in.

THE BASIC PANTS PATTERN

The pants pattern is drafted in two sections, the front and the back. There is a dart in the back section to compensate for the shape of the hips, and there should be a dart in the front section of women's pants but not in the front section of men's pants. The pants should be fairly close fitting from the waist to just above the knee but should hang almost straight from the knee to the floor. The basic pants pattern should be drafted to fit at the natural waist. Subsequent patterns may be cut with a lower waist.

Measurements needed for this pattern:

A special measurement is needed for the pants pattern. This is the Front Waist to Crotch length. It is measured from the Waist line at the Center Front down to the point where the Inseam and the Center Front seam of the trousers meet.

1) Waist to Floor ________
2) Inseam ________
3) Leg, Highest Point ________
4) Waist ________
5) Waist to Hip ________
6) Hip ________
7) Waist to Crotch–Front ________

The Front Section

Step 1. Draw a vertical line of the Waist to Floor length. This is the Leg Centerline which divides most of the measurements for the pants pattern in half. (See Figure 46.)

Step 2. At the bottom of this line draw a line at right angles to it. Mark off 4″ on either side of the Leg Centerline. This is the Cuff line.

The circumference of the Cuff line is not taken from any particular measurement. It is set at 16″ so that there will be sufficient room for the foot to get through the pants leg.

FRONT PANTS PATTERN (Steps 1 to 5)

The Leg Section

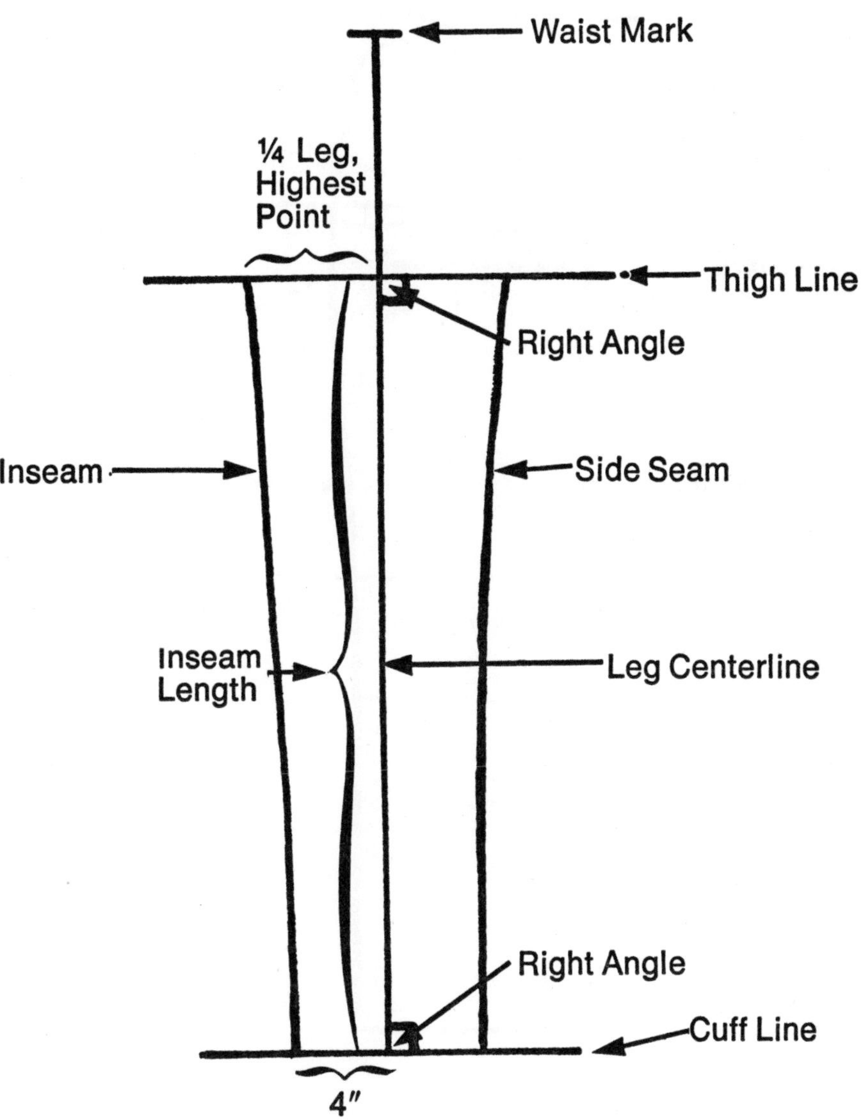

Figure 46

FRONT PANTS PATTERN (Steps 6 to 11)

The Top Section

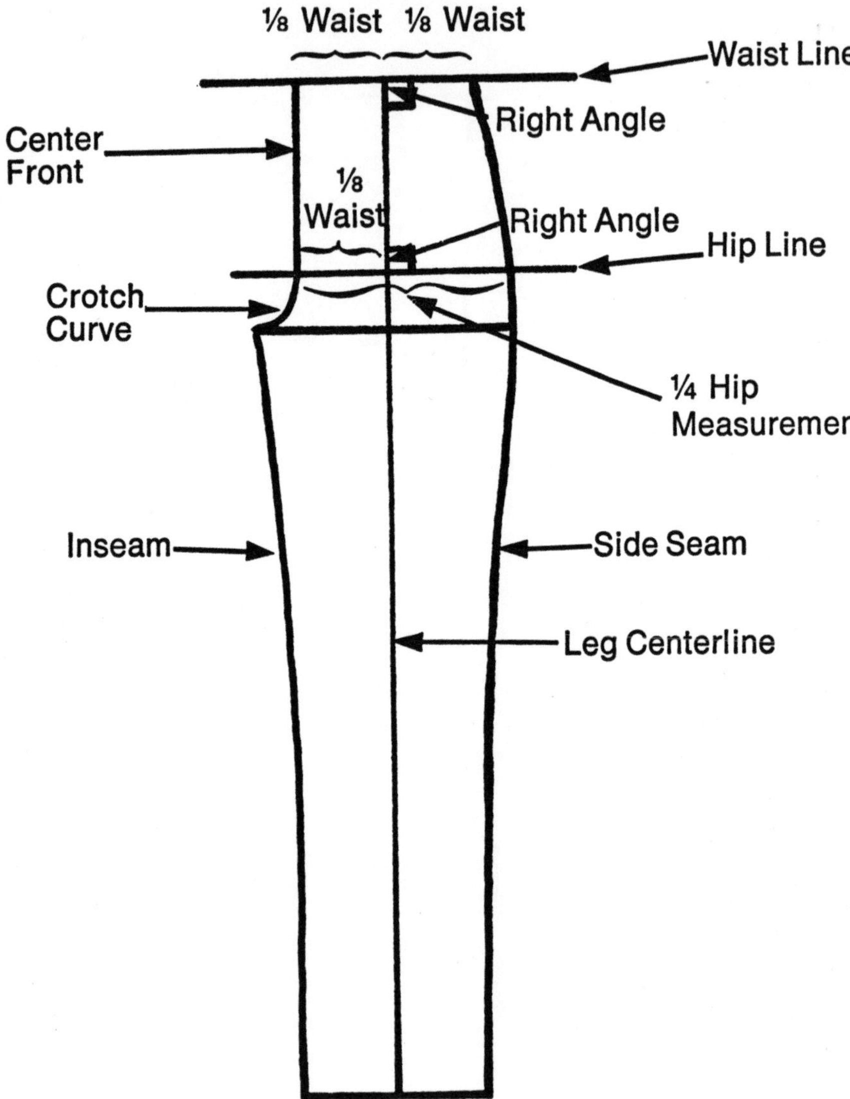

Figure 47

STEP 3. Mark the Inseam length on the Leg Centerline, measuring up from the Cuff line. Draw a line at right angles to the Leg Centerline at this point. This is the Thigh line.

STEP 4. Mark off one-fourth of the Leg, Highest Point measurement on the Thigh line to both sides of the Leg Centerline.

The Leg Girth measurements are divided in half for the front section of the leg pattern. These measurements are then bisected by the Leg Centerline, hence the one-fourth measurement.

STEP 5. The Inseam and the Side Seam lines may be drawn in for the leg portion of the pattern by connecting the points on the Cuff line to the points on the Thigh line with a slightly curving line.

Now that the leg section of the pants has been drafted, the upper portion must be drawn in.

STEP 6. Draw a perpendicular line at the top of the Leg Centerline (Figure 47). This is the Waist line.

STEP 7. Measure down the Leg Centerline the Waist to Hip measurement and draw another line perpendicular to the Leg Centerline. This is the Hip line.

STEP 8. Mark off one-eighth of the Waist measurement on both sides of the Waist line and on the Inseam side of the Hip line. Draw a line connecting the left Waist mark to this Hip mark. This line is the Center Front of the pants.

The Waist measurement is divided into eighths because this section of the pants is for one-fourth of the body. The Leg Centerline divides this measurement in half, therefore one-eighth of the total Waist measurement. The one-eighth Waist measurement is also used on the Hip line to establish a Center Front line that is parallel to the Leg Centerline.

STEP 9. Mark off one-fourth of the Hip measurement on the Hip line, starting at the Center Front as established in Step 8.

BACK PANTS PATTERN (Steps 1 to 5)
The Leg Section

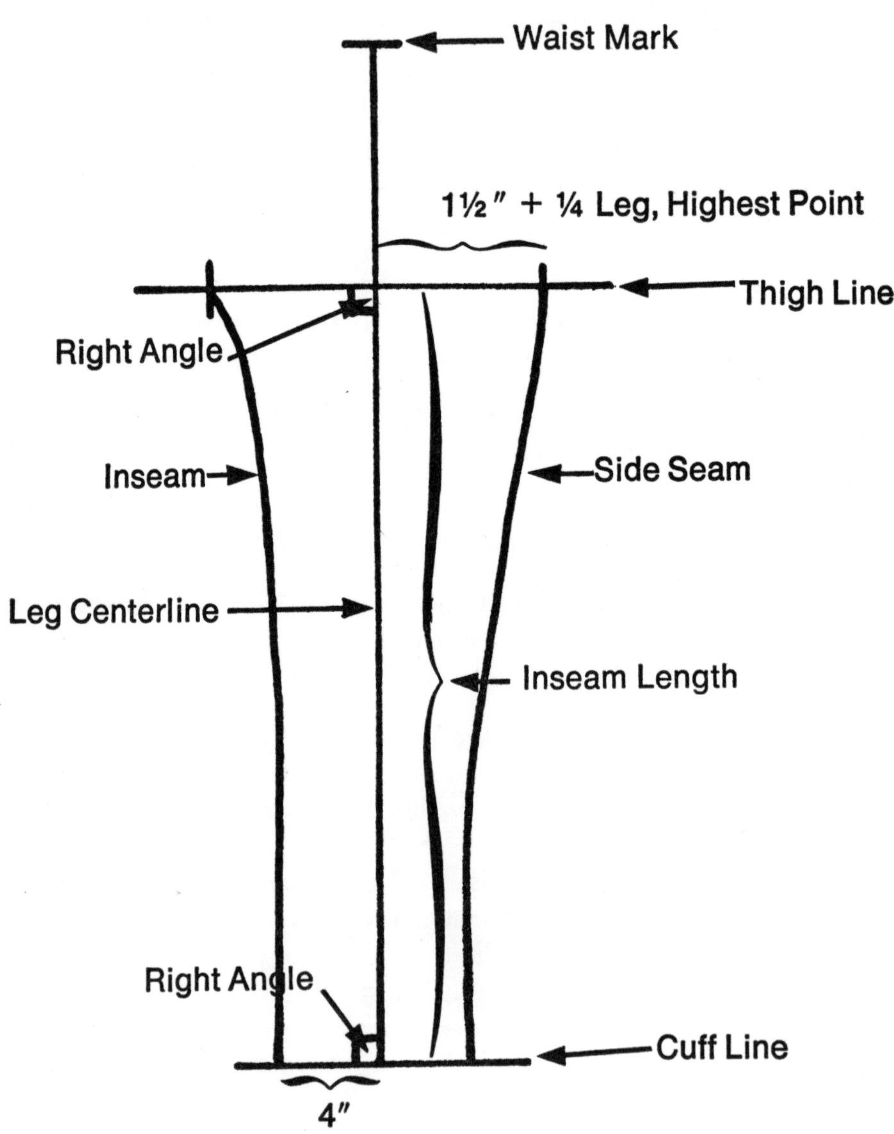

Figure 48

Notice that the Hip measurement is taken from the Center Front line rather than the Leg Centerline as the other measurements were.

Step 10. Draw in the Crotch curve by connecting the Inseam to the Center Front line (See Figure 47).

Measure the length of the Center Front line and the Crotch curve. Compare this to the Front Waist to Crotch measurement. Extend the pattern if it is necessary.

Step 11. Finish the Side seam by drawing a curved line through the Hip mark to the Side Waist point.

For women's pants a dart should be added in the front. In this case the Side seam will not curve completely to the Side Waist point. Use the technique described for drafting the Side seam of the fitted skirt.

Step 12. Add 2½″ seam allowances to the Inseam and the Side seam and ⅝″ allowance to the Center Front and Crotch lines. A 2½″ seam allowance should be added at the Waist line, to allow for the exact location of the Waist line during the fitting of the pants.

The Back Section

The back section is different from the front section in that allowance is added for the movement of the hips.

The first few steps for drafting the back section are the same as those for drafting the front section.

Step 1. Draw a vertical line of the Waist to Floor length. This is the Leg Centerline (See Figure 48).

Step 2. At the bottom of the Leg Centerline draw a perpendicular line and mark off 4″ on either side. This is the Cuff line.

Step 3. Mark off the Inseam length on the Leg Centerline and draw a perpendicular line at this point. This is the Thigh line.

BACK PANTS PATTERN (Steps 6 to 10)
The Hip and Waist Line

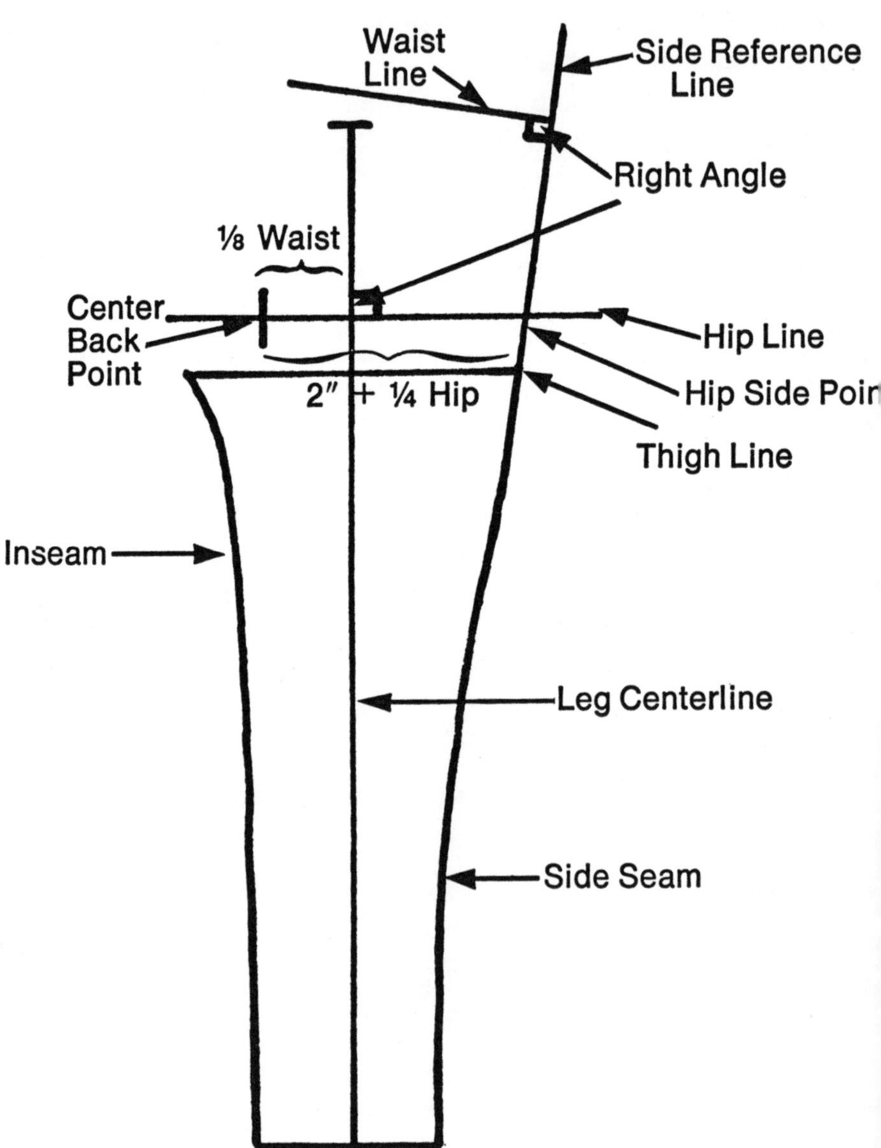

Figure 49

From this point the drafting procedure for the back section differs from the procedure for the front section.

STEP 4. On either side of the Thigh line mark off points 1½″ plus one-fourth the Leg, Highest Point measurement.

STEP 5. Draw in the Inseam and the Side seam lines by connecting the points on the Thigh line to the points on the Cuff line as is indicated in Figure 48. This completes the leg portion of the pattern.

The procedure for drafting the upper portion of the back section of the pants pattern is a little tricky. Effectively what has to happen is that extra material has to be added at Center Back so that the Waist line of the pants will not be pulled undesirably low when the wearer sits. The pattern is drafted in the following manner.

STEP 6. Measure down the Leg Centerline the Waist to Hip length and draw a perpendicular line for the Hip line (Figure 49).

STEP 7. Mark off one-eighth of the Waist measurement to the Inseam side of the Hip line, as was done for the front section. This establishes a Center Back point on the Hip line.

STEP 8. From this new point measure off 2″ plus one-fourth of the Hip measurement on the Hip line (measuring toward the Side Seam, not toward the Inseam). This establishes the Hip Side point.

STEP 9. Draw a straight line from the end of the Thigh line through this Hip Side point up beyond the Waist length. This will be the Side Reference line. It should angle away from the Leg Centerline.

STEP 10. Starting at the Hip Side point, on the Side Reference line mark off the Waist to Hip length and draw a line perpendicular from this point to establish the Waist line.

BACK PANTS PATTERN (Steps 11 to 14)
Establishing the Center Back and the Side Seams

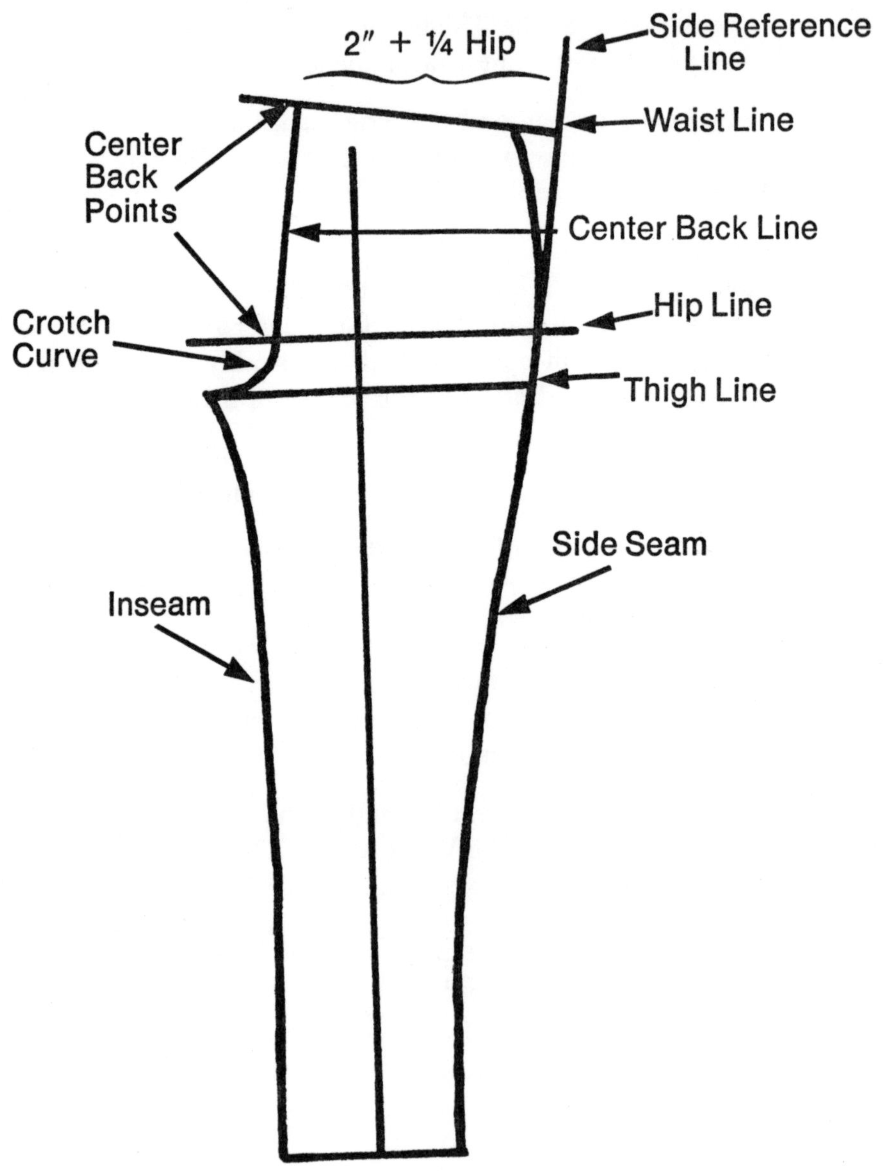

Figure 50

STEP 11. On the Waist line mark off the Hip line length (2″ plus one-fourth the Hip measurement) (See Figure 50). This establishes the Center Back point on the Waist line. Connect this to the Center Back point on the Hip line.

STEP 12. The Crotch seam may be completed by drawing a curved line from the Inseam to the Center Back line as indicated in Figure 50.

STEP 13. If the Waist line was raised on the pants front because of the Waist to Crotch measurement, raise the back Waist line now by the same amount.

STEP 14. The Side Seam should be extended from the Thigh line to the Waist line in a curve.

The Waist line as it is now drafted is longer than one-fourth the Waist measurement. The extra allowance will be used to create a dart for the Hips.

STEP 15. Add the same seam allowances used for the front section (2½″ at Side Seam and Inseam, ⅝″ at Center Back and Crotch, and 2½″ at the Waist line). Cut out the pattern.

There are no fold lines on pants patterns.

It is not necessary to draft a placket for the trial fitting, but a completed pair of men's pants will need both a placket and a waistband. Women's pants often use a simple zipper closing at the side or the center back. Instructions for drafting the placket used on all men's pants and some women's pants are provided on pages 110-111.

FITTING THE PANTS

A trial fitting may be made by cutting the pattern out in muslin and sewing it together. The front section should be sewn to the back section at the Inseam and the Side Seam on both legs. Be careful to reverse the pattern so that there are not two left legs or two right legs. One leg is then turned inside out and put inside the other with the good sides together. Pin the Center Back lines together and the Center Front lines together. Sew down the Center Back from the waist around the crotch to a point about 7″ from the waist on the Center Front seam. The muslin pants are now ready for fitting.

Step 1. Have the person for whom the pants are being made put them on. Pin the Center Front seam closed.

Step 2. Adjust and pin the back darts so that the pants fit smoothly over the hips. Mark the position of the darts.

Step 3. If women's pants are being made, pin in the front darts.

Step 4. Adjust the Inseam and the Side Seam for a smooth fit down the leg and to obtain the degree of tightness or flare desired. Do not, however, make the pants leg so tight that they cannot be pulled off over the foot.

Step 5. Tie a string around the Waist at the natural waist line. Mark this Waist line on the muslin using the string as a guide. Have the person trying on the pants sit and recheck the Waist line.

THE PLACKET

The placket is a means of making an opening at one end of a seam. The most common placket is the zipper closure on men's pants. Another variation of the placket is found on long-sleeved shirts at the cuff opening. Plackets may be closed either with buttons and buttonholes or with zippers. The placket is also used, sometimes, as a decorative or functional opening at the neckline of a dress.

The placket is normally drafted as a part of the pattern of the garment it is to be used on. This discussion describes it separately for the sake of clarity. If any difficulty is experienced in visualizing the placket, it is a good idea to follow the instructions and make a sample placket out of a few pieces of scrap muslin.

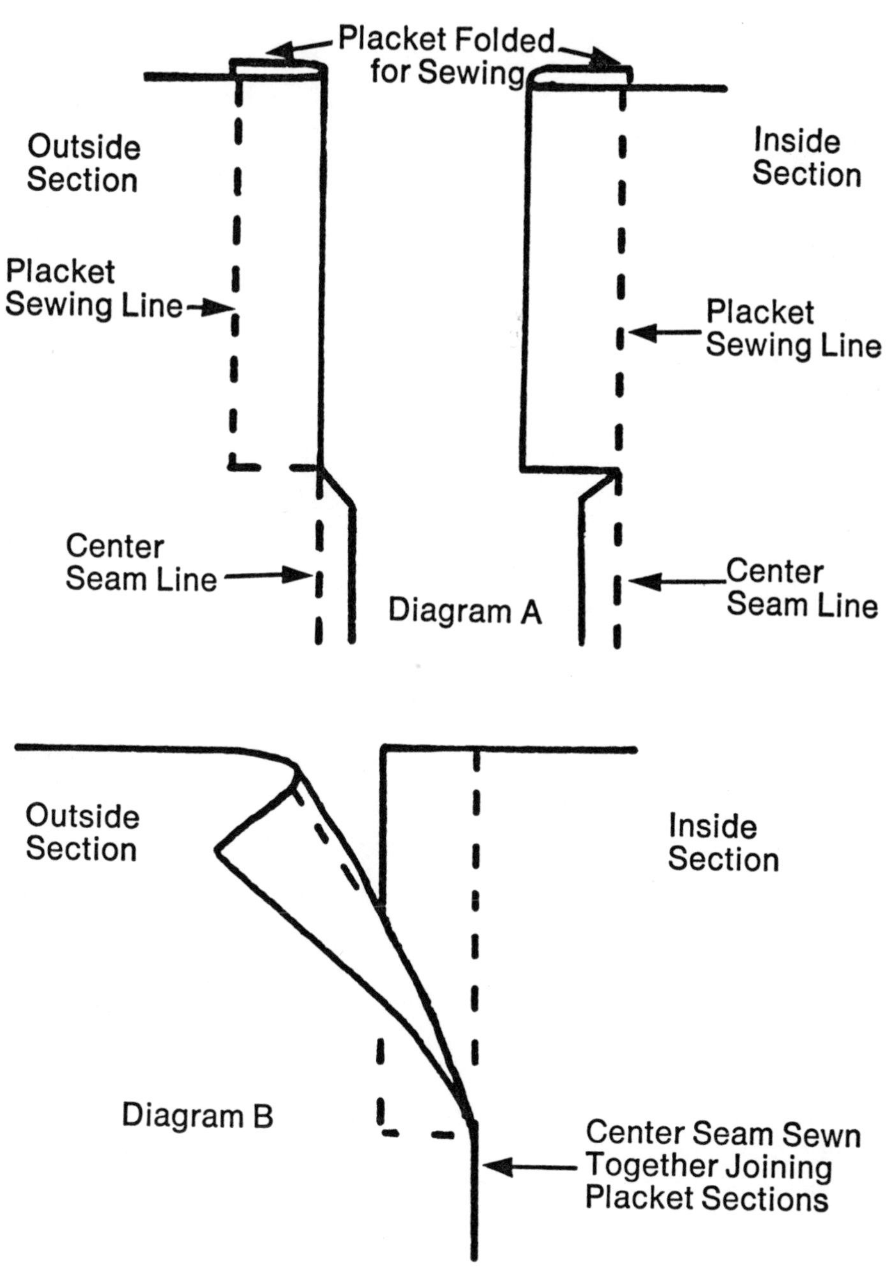
Placket Folded
for Sewing
Outside
Section
Inside
Section
Placket
Sewing Line
Placket
Sewing Line
Center
Seam Line
Diagram A
Center
Seam Line
Outside
Section
Inside
Section
Diagram B
Center Seam Sewn
Together Joining
Placket Sections

Figure 51

THE SKIRT PLACKET

A basic version of the placket is used on skirts that are made for the stage. This placket and the way it works is illustrated in Diagrams A & B of Figure 51. The stage skirt placket is described here because it illustrates the placket in one of its simplest forms. This placket is usually 12″ long and 1½″ to 2″ wide. It is drafted as a part of the skirt. The pattern for one half of the placket is wider than the pattern for the other half. The two halves will be illustrated separately but it is possible to draft one pattern using the dimensions of the wider section. This pattern may then be folded to the narrower dimensions when cutting the other section of the skirt.

STEP 1. Mark lines perpendicular to the skirt Center Back seam line at the waist and at a point 12″ below the waist (See Figure 52). (The placket can be put in at the Side Seam instead, if it is so desired. In this case, follow the directions given here, substituting the Side Seam for the Center Back line.)

STEP 2. On the outside section of the placket, draw a line parallel to the Center Back line 2″ away from it.

STEP 3. On the inside section draw a line parallel to the Center Back line 4″ away from it.

STEP 4. On the inside section 2″ from the Center Back line draw a fold line.

STEP 5. Add seam allowances around all edges.

When the placket is sewn, the seam allowances of both sections are pressed in, except at the waist, to give it a finished edge. The placket should then be slashed on the diagonal lines at the inside corners, and the outside corners should be clipped. The outside section of the placket is then folded to the inside of the garment at the Center Back line and top-stitched around the edge of the placket. (This is approximately 2″ in from the Center Back line.) The inside section is folded at the indicated fold line and top-stitched down the Center

PLACKET FOR STAGE SKIRTS

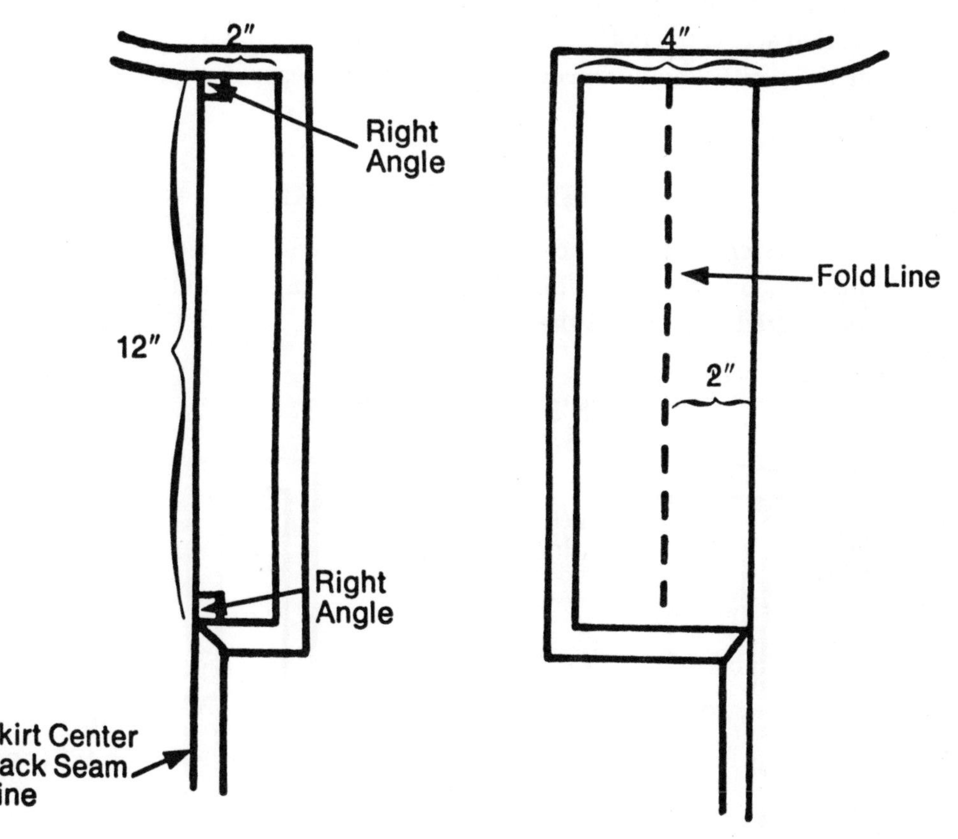

Outside Section

Inside Section

Figure 52

Back line and along the top and bottom of the placket. The two skirt panels are then sewn together down the Center Back seam, starting at the bottom of the placket. The outside section is sewn over the inside section across the bottom of the placket. This creates a lap-over opening at the waist which converts to an ordinary seam line (See Figure 51).

MEN'S PANTS PLACKETS

Men's pants plackets follow the same principle as the skirt placket, but they are drafted differently. They should still, however, be drafted as a part of the pants pattern.

MEN'S PANTS PLACKETS

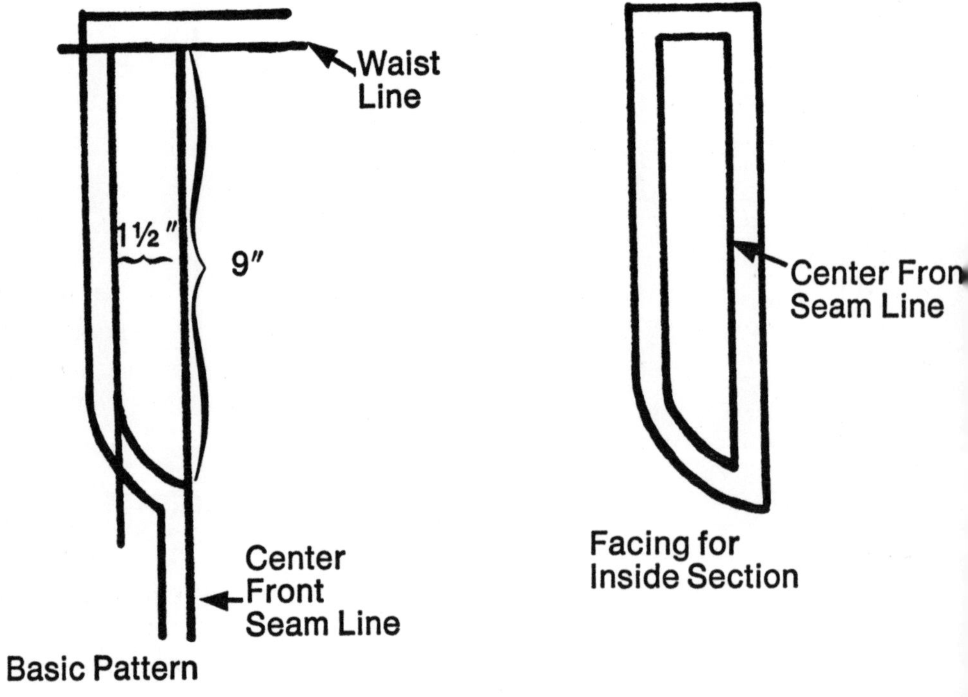

Figure 53

STEP 1. On the Front Pants pattern, extend the Waistline out 1½″ at the Center Front seamline. (see Figure 53)

STEP 2. Draw a line parallel to Center Front downwards from this point.

STEP 3. Curve the bottom of the placket from a point on the Center Front line that is 9″ down from the Waist line. This line curves out to the edge of the placket.

STEP 4. Add ⅝″ seam allowance to the pattern.

For men's pants this placket is added to both the outside and inside section at the Center Front line. The inside section then has a second piece added to it. (See Figure 53)

STEP 5. Trace the placket on a clean sheet of paper and include the Center Front line.

STEP 6. Add ⅝″ seam allowances to all the edges.

To sew this placket, the seam allowances for the outside section are clipped at the curves and turned under. The placket is then folded to the inside at the Center Front line. It is top-stitched to the body of the pants following the turned-under edge of the placket. If a zipper is to be used it may be first sewn to the placket extension before it is turned under for a cleaner finish. The inside placket is sewn by using the extra piece as a facing. This is sewn on the remaining section of the placket with the right sides together. This is clipped and turned to the inside. On the inside of the pants, the Center Front seam allowance of the facing is turned under, and the placket is top stitched down the Center Front line.

When the pants are assembled, the legs are sewn separately. One leg is then turned inside out and placed in the other leg so that the good sides are together. The crotch seam is sewn, starting at the Waist in the back, and continuing around to the base of the placket. Then the seam going across the base of the placket is sewn. Going back and forth two or three times will reinforce the opening.

FACINGS

Facings are perhaps one of the easiest patterns to draft. It is simply a duplicating, by tracing, of the particular seam that is to be faced.

FACING PATTERNS

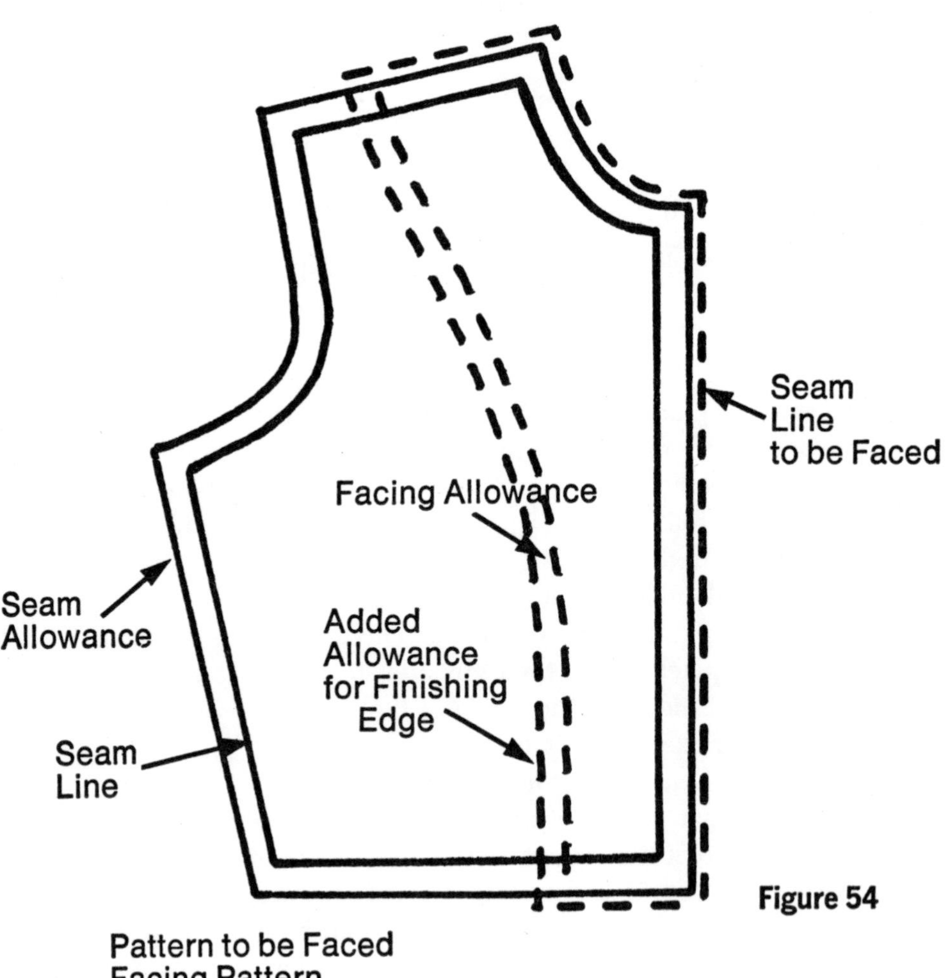

Figure 54

Figure 54 shows how a facing for a bodice front is drafted, but the principle of drafting any other facing pattern is the same.

Step 1. Lay out the pattern to be faced on a fresh sheet of paper.

Step 2. Trace around the pattern where the facing is to go.

Step 3. Remove the pattern.

Step 4. Draw in the shape of the facing. Add a sufficient allowance for finishing the facing's edges.

When the pattern that is being traced includes a seam allowance it is not necessary to add one. If this is not the case, a ⅝″ seam allowance should be added.

BASIC TECHNIQUES OF PATTERN ALTERATION

THE DRAFTING OF THE PATTERNS for the basic fitted garments is now complete. These patterns should be visualized as illustrating the basic form of the body. Clothes, however, do not follow the body exactly. They flare; they are gathered or pleated; their necklines are changed; and the waistlines are varied. To achieve these effects, the basic fitted patterns must be altered or new patterns must be drafted from scratch. This section describes the basic techniques of altering patterns to achieve new designs.

There are a large variety of different designs that can be achieved by altering patterns. Effectively, however, there are only two qualities that are being changed—the shape or the line of the garment.

For the purposes of this book, shape refers to how the garment fits the body. The shape is altered, for example, when an indented waist is changed to a straight waist as in Figure 55.

INDENTED AND STRAIGHT WAISTS

Figure 55

The line of a garment falls into one of two categories. It may be either external as in a neckline, or internal as in the case of seams. Figure 56 illustrates how a design may be altered both by changing the neckline and by adding seams. Neither of these techniques, in this instance, changes the shape of the garment.

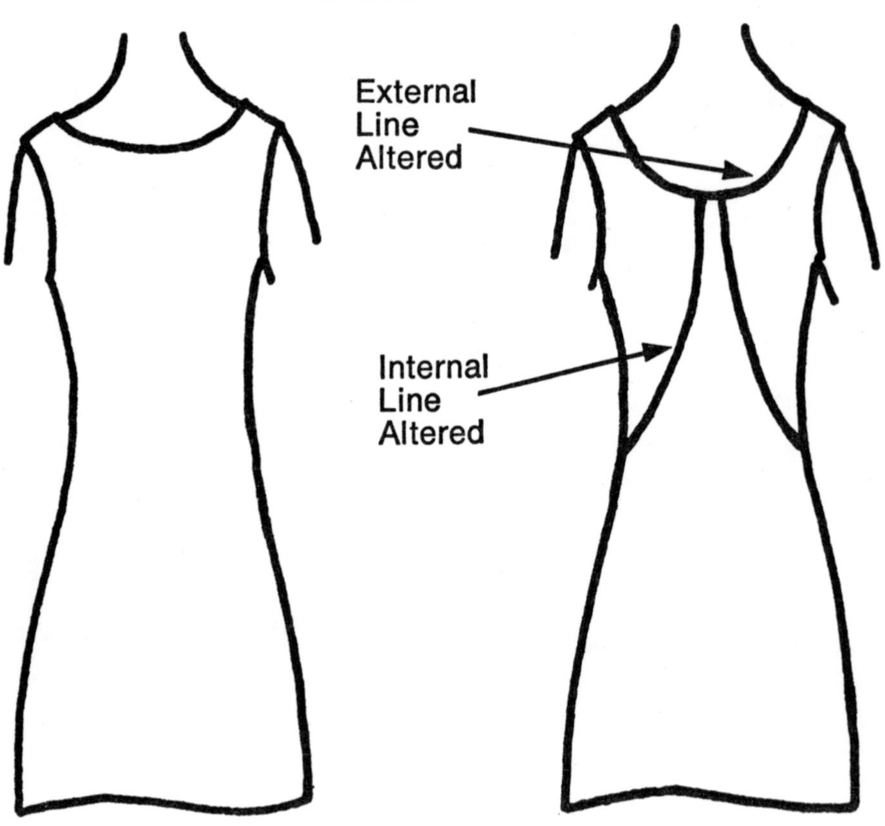

Figure 56

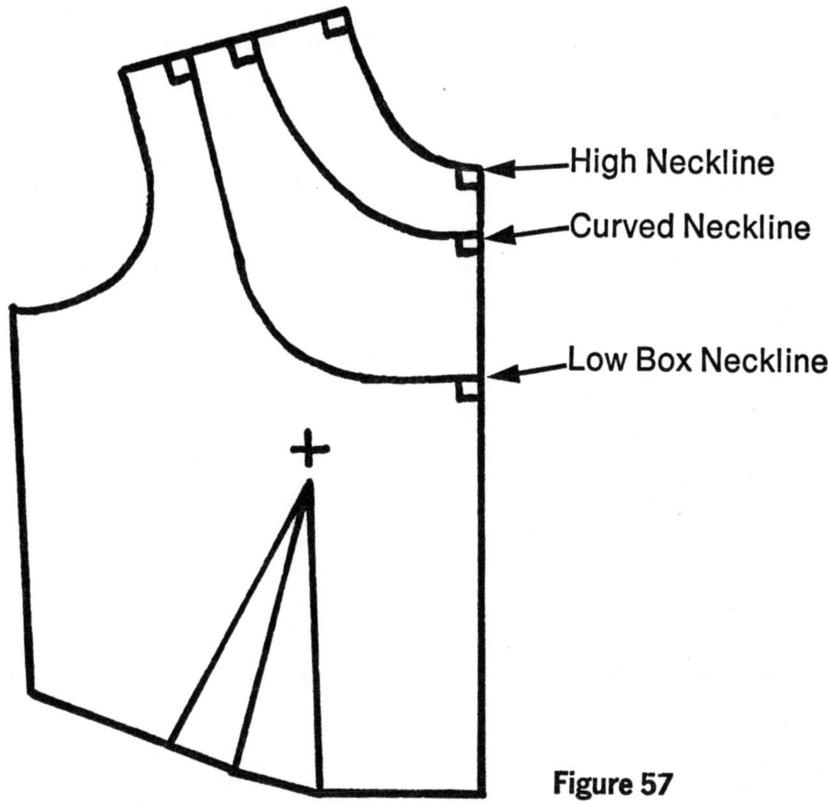

Figure 57

Six ways of changing the shape and line of a garment through pattern alteration will be discussed here: changing the external line of a garment; changing the location of darts; altering and changing seam placements; changing darts to seams; changing the shape of the pattern by cutting; and making pleats. Mastering these skills of pattern alteration is basic to creating original patterns.

CHANGING THE EXTERNAL LINE

Changing the external line of a garment, such as the neckline of a woman's dress, is exceedingly simple. All that is necessary is to sketch the desired shape directly onto the pattern.

There is no other alteration necessary because, as has been said earlier, the shape of the garment is not being changed. When the new neckline is tried on, however, some alteration of the fit may be required. For instance, when a high neckline is changed to a low neckline it may be necessary to add a dart at the corners of the neckline because of the shape of the body at this point.

The shape of an armhole for a sleeveless dress may be changed in the same way. The new lines, however, should always intersect the shoulder seams and the side seams at right angles to insure a continuous, smooth curve.

Hems and necklines may also be scalloped by drawing the desired scallop directly onto the pattern.

All of these variations will change the external line of the garment but will not affect the way it fits.

CHANGING DART LOCATIONS

There are two basic methods of altering dart locations. One is the pivot method and the other is the cutting method. This discussion will describe how to change the Front Dart on women's bodices by both methods. The principle involved is applicable to any dart.

It is preferable to alter the Front Dart on women's bodices by the pivot method rather than the cutting method because the pivot method rotates at the *Bust Point* while the cutting method is based on the *Top of the Dart,* which is lower. The dart created by the cutting method will have to be adjusted in a fitting session so that it points to the Bust Point.

The Pivot Method

Pivoting is based on transferring the wedge of the dart from one Seam line to another. There are several locations for the Front Dart. Figure 58 illustrates some of these.

POSSIBLE DART LOCATIONS

Figure 58

To illustrate the pivot method, the dart will be changed from the waist to the Side Seam position (Figure 59).

STEP 1. Place the original pattern on a piece of paper which will become the new pattern.

STEP 2. Draw a line on the original pattern to indicate the location of the new dart. In this example, this would be under the arm, about 2″ down from the armhole, on the Side Seam line. The dart will run from here toward the Bust Point.

PIVOTING THE DART (Steps 1 to 3)
Tracing the Original Pattern

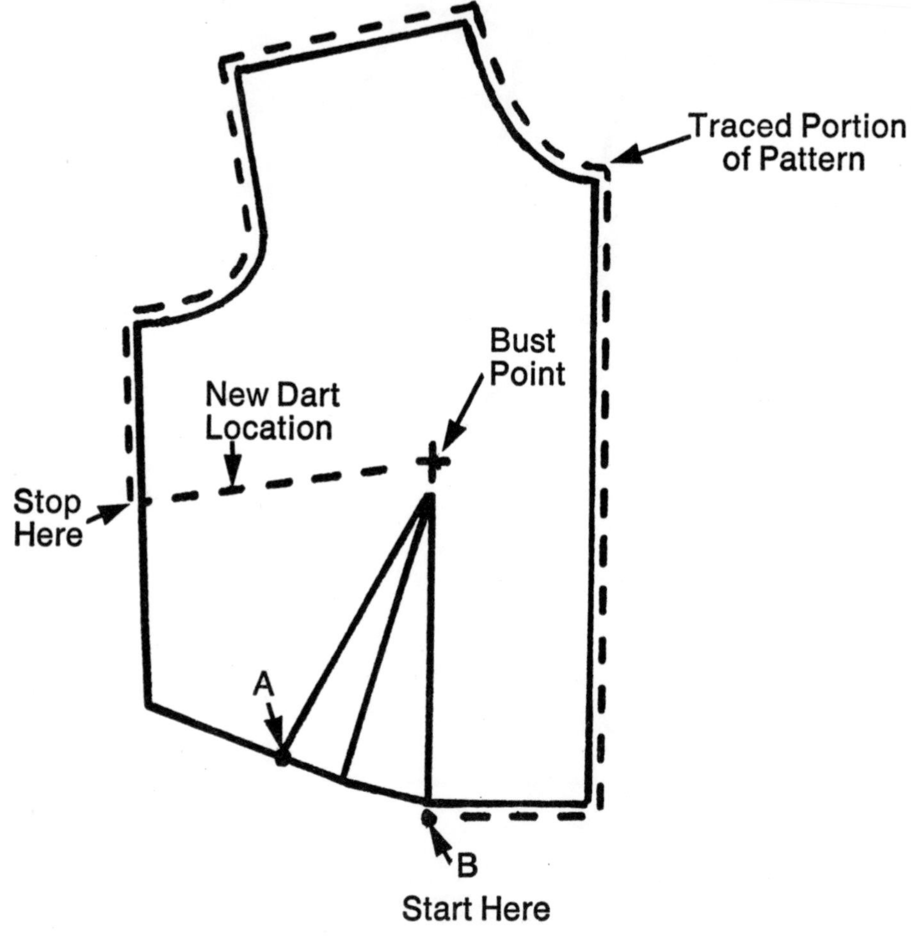

Figure 59

Step 3. Trace around the original pattern only where indicated by the dotted line in Figure 59.

Step 4. Now stick a pin in at the Bust Point, and using the pin as a pivot, close out the waist line dart by swivelling point A to point B (see Figure 60).

PIVOTING THE DART (Steps 4 & 5)
Swinging Out the Original Dart

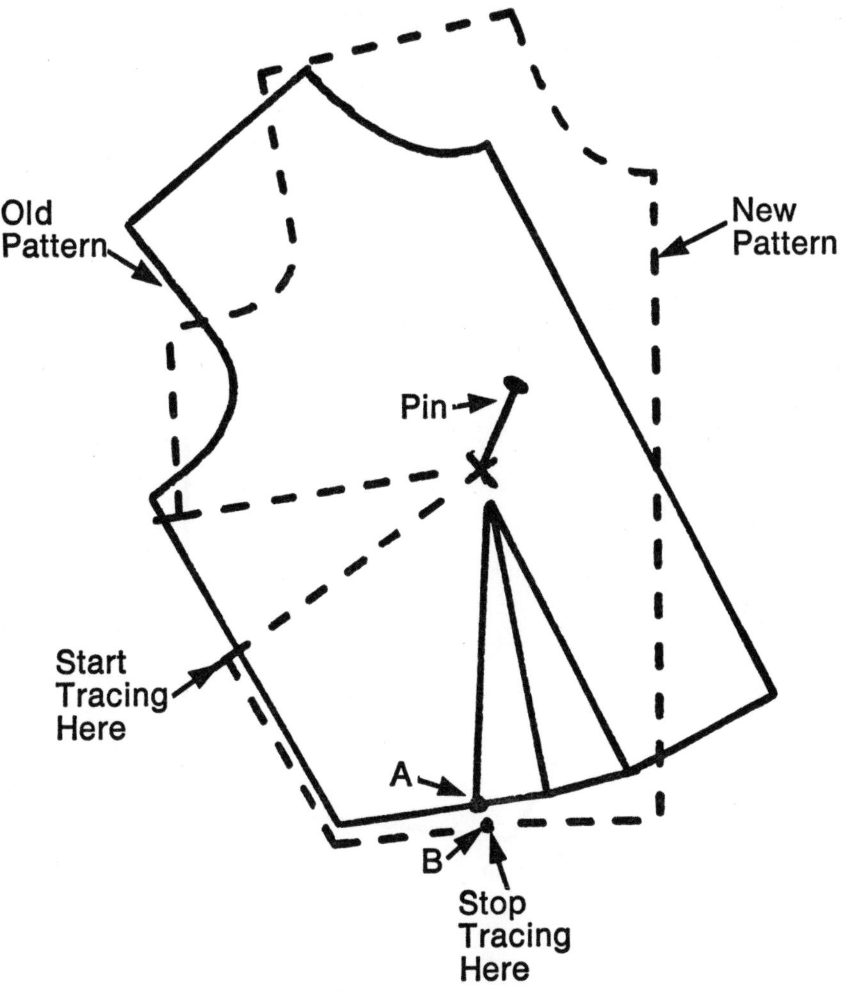

Figure 60

Note that the Bust Point is not the top of the dart, but is located about ½" higher up, at the true point of the bust. The true Bust Point is used for pivoting the dart because it will keep the finished dart line pointing at the bust.

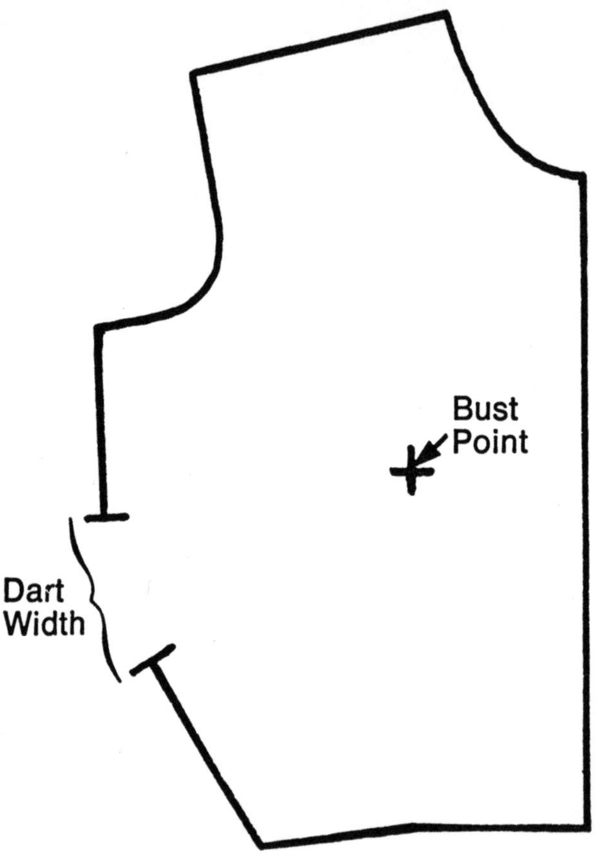

Figure 61

STEP 5. Now trace around the rest of the pattern, starting from the New Dart line marked on the original pattern and continuing to the closed-out dart.

STEP 6. The newly traced pattern should look like Figure 61. The pin hole used to pivot the pattern should be marked as indicated. This is the Bust Point.

PIVOTING THE DART (Steps 8 to 10)
Drawing the New Dart

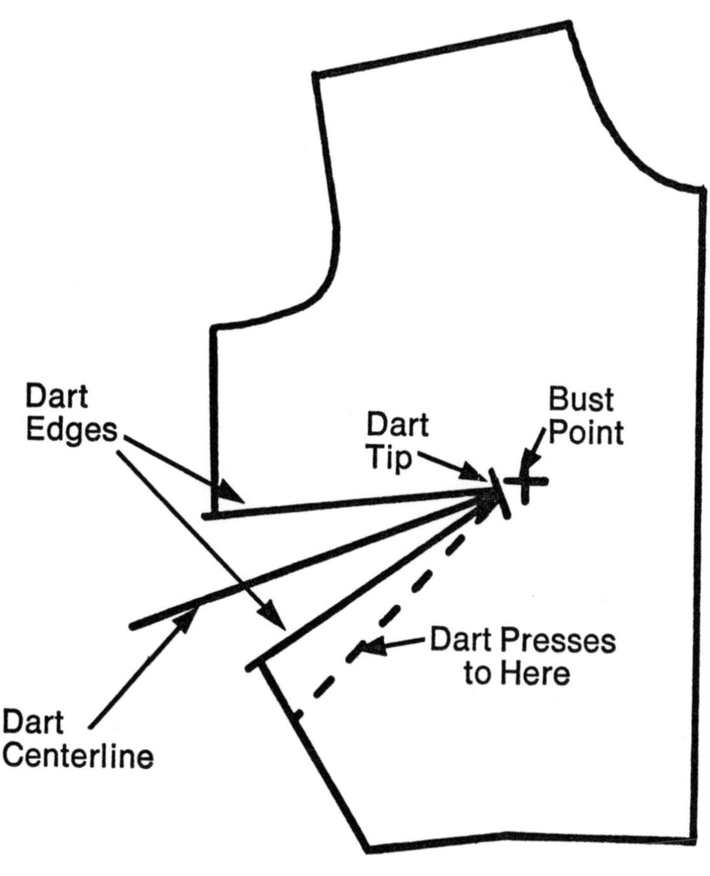

Figure 62

STEP 7. Round out the new waist line in a gradual curve.

STEP 8. Draw a new Dart Centerline by dividing the Dart Width in half and connecting this point to the Bust Point. (See Figure 62)

STEP 9. Mark a new top of the Dart ½″ from the Bust Point.

STEP 10. Now draw in the sides of the dart.

PIVOTING THE DART (Step 11)
The Finished Dart

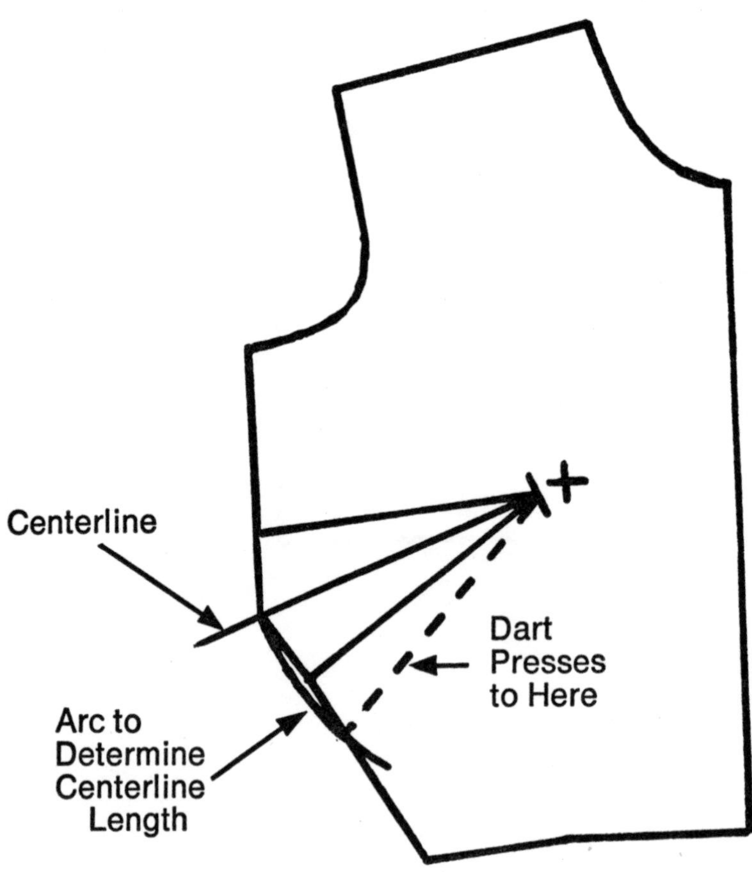

Figure 63

When the Dart is pressed down, after it has been sewn, the Centerline will be located as is shown by the dotted line in Figure 62. (This is half the Dart Width below the bottom side of the dart.) It is necessary to draft the end of the dart so that when the dart is pressed down the seam allowance of the end of the dart will match the seam allowance of the side seam.

STEP 11. Strike an arc on the Dart Centerline, using the tip of the dart as the pivot point and the length of the dotted line as the radius. The finished Dart will look like Figure 63.

PIVOTING TWO DARTS

For some designs the Front Dart will be divided into two darts. Women's shirtwaist dresses, for example, normally have one dart going to the waist and a second dart going to the side seam.

To split the dart by pivoting, the following procedure may be used.

PIVOTING TWO DARTS (Steps 1 & 2)

The First Step in Tracing

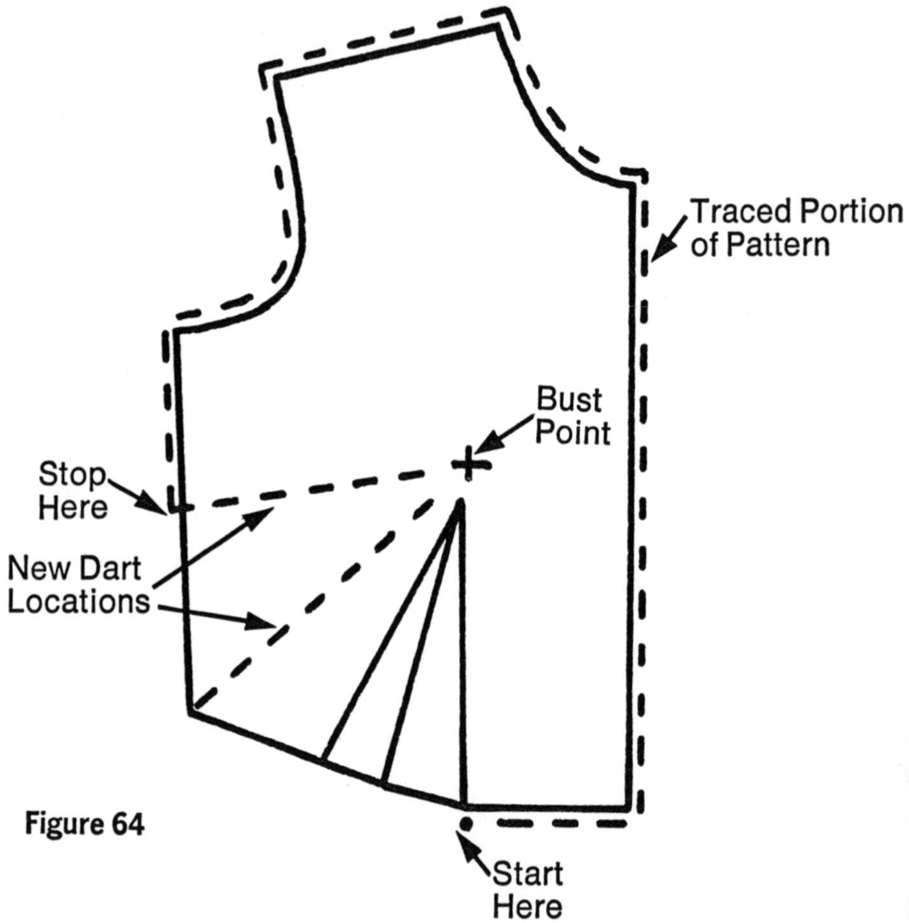

Figure 64

STEP 1. Draw in the two desired locations.

STEP 2. Trace around the pattern going around the Center Front line, neckline, etc. as was done for the single dart (Figure 64).

STEP 3. Pivot out *half* of the dart and trace to the second dart location (Figure 65).

PIVOTING TWO DARTS (Step 3)
The Second Tracing

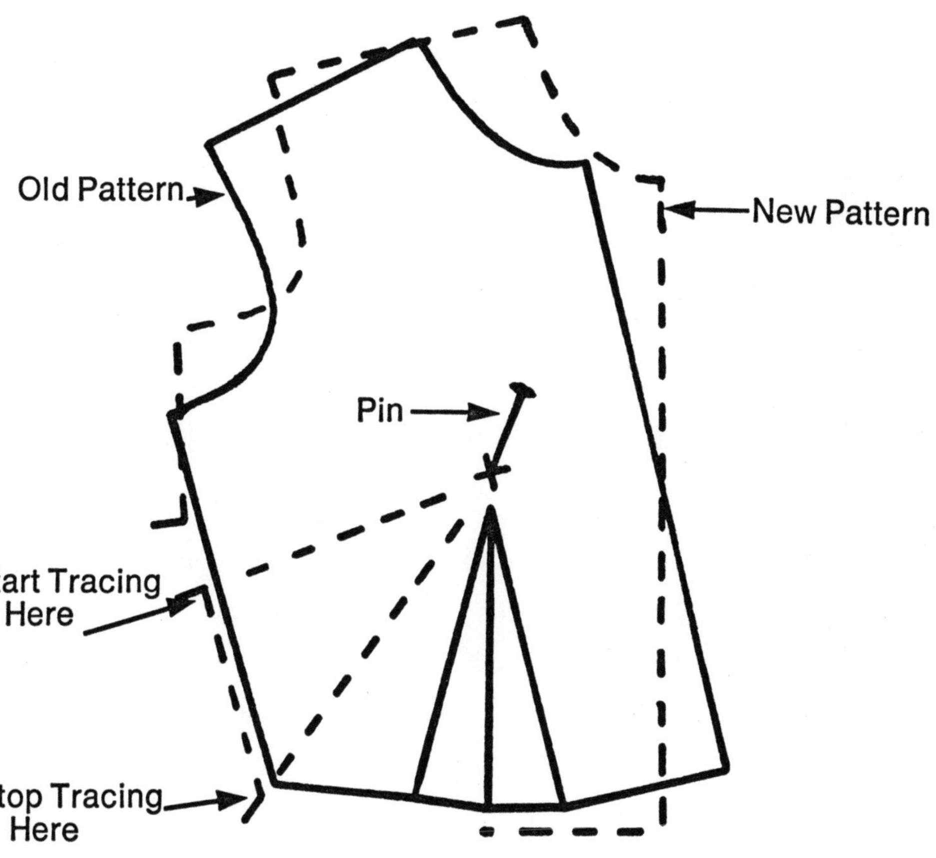

Figure 65

STEP 4. Pivot out the second half of the dart and complete the tracing.

The rest of the procedure is the same as that described for pivoting a single dart.

The Cutting Method

The principle behind the cutting method is the same as the pivot method. The wedge of the dart is transferred from one seam to another. Only the technique is different.

Step 1. From a tracing of the original pattern, cut out the triangular piece of material that makes the dart (See Figure 66).

Step 2. Make a cut where the new dart line is to go. This cut should be extended to the top of the dart. Close out the old dart by taping its sides together. This will automatically transfer the dart to the new location (See Figure 67).

Step 3. Place the cut pattern on a fresh sheet of paper.

Step 4. Trace around the pattern.

Step 5. Gradually curve the Waist line.

Step 6. Draw in a new dart tip ½" in from the Bust Point.

Step 7. Draw in the dart sides and draw the new Dart Centerline by dividing the Dart Width in half at the base.

Step 8. Draft the side point of the new dart by the same method used for the pivoted dart.

Cutting Two Darts

To divide a pattern into two darts by cutting, simply cut wherever the darts are desired. The dart widths may then be distributed by moving the cut pieces.

ALTERING DARTS BY CUTTING (Steps 1 & 2)
The Cutting

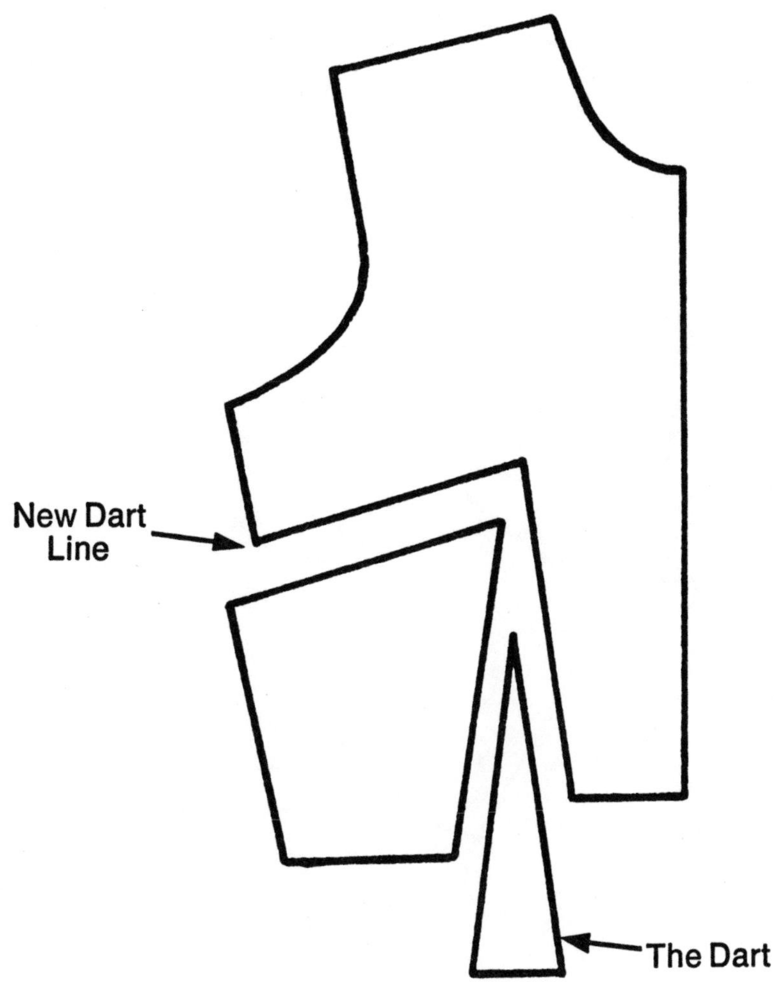

Figure 66

ALTERING DARTS BY CUTTING (Step 3 to 5)

The New Pattern

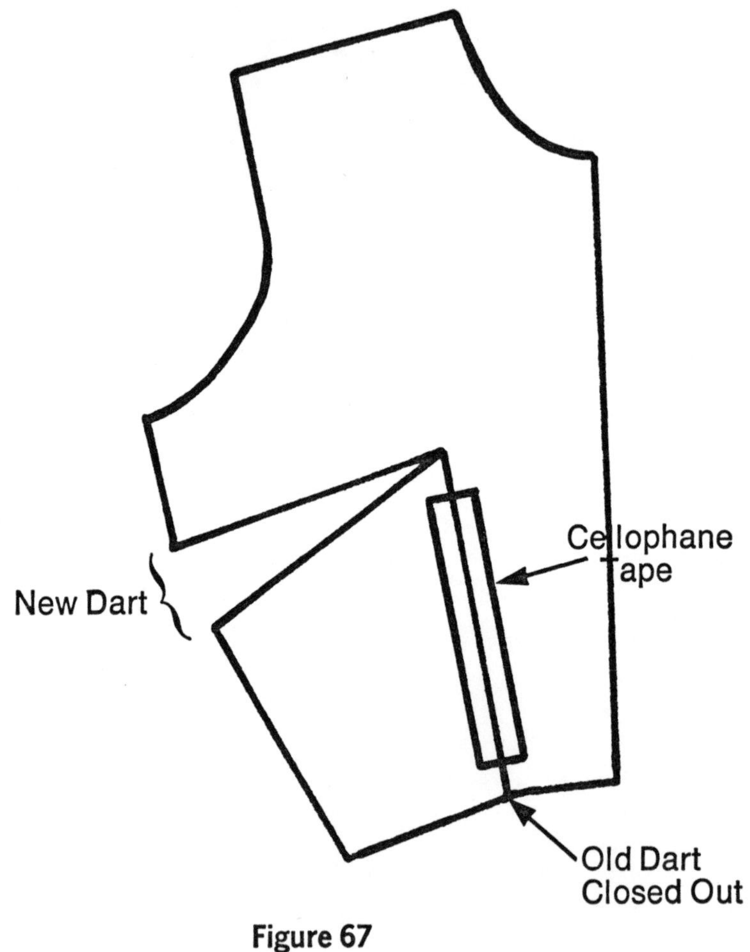

Figure 67

Diagrams A and B of Figure 68 illustrate how to make a bodice pattern for a shirtwaist dress. Notice how the waist dart is angled toward the Center Front line by a half of a dart width.

Altering the front dart for women's bodices has been described here because the dart was drafted. Most of the other darts were fitted. For fitted darts, the above principles can be used to change the

CUTTING TWO DARTS

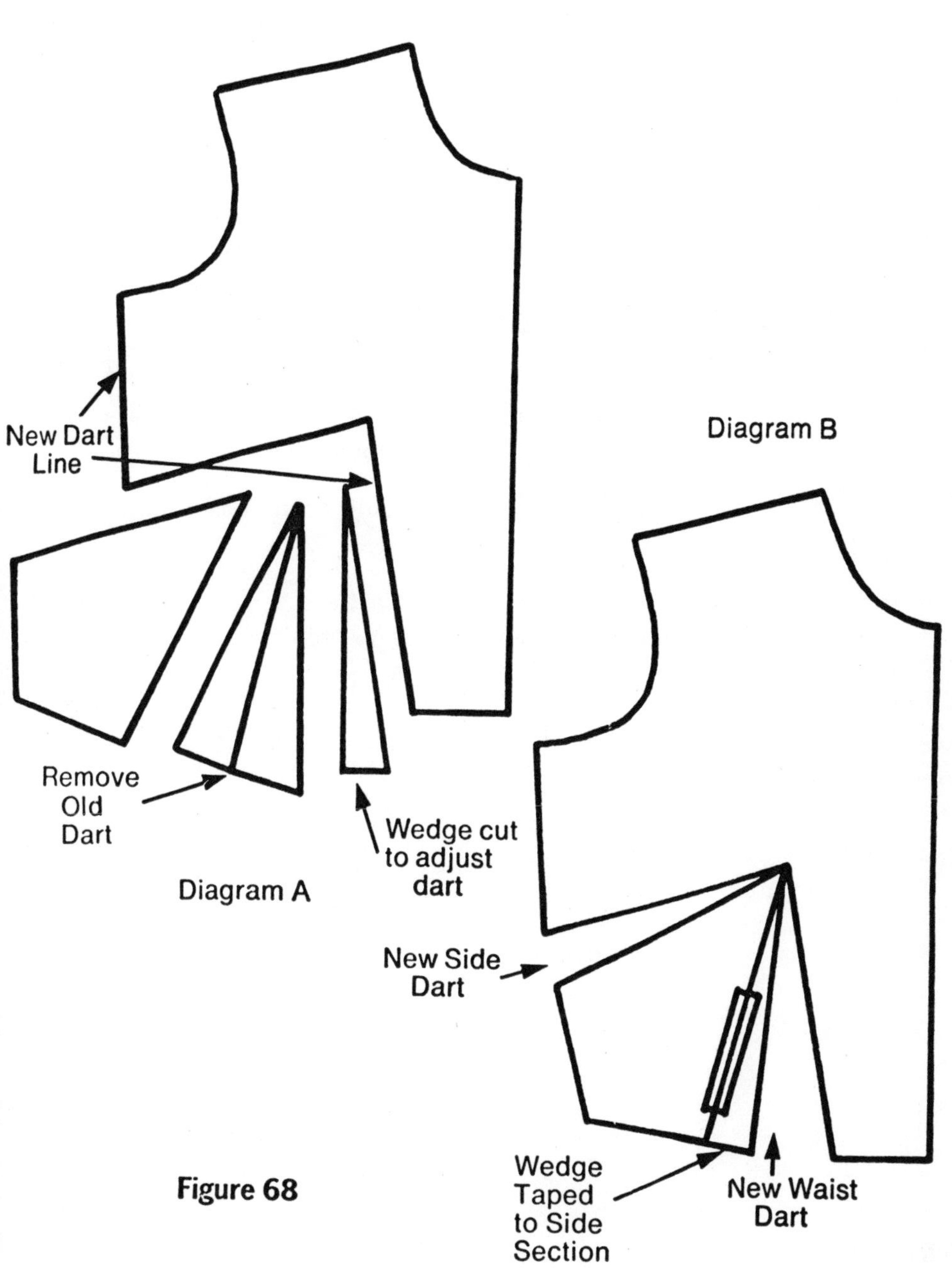

Figure 68

overall shape of the pattern, but the final dart placement should be determined in a fitting session.

CHANGING SEAM PLACEMENTS

The procedure for changing seams is another technique of pattern alteration which is essentially simple. The process for making a shirt yoke from the basic pattern will be described here because it requires both the addition and subtraction of seams.

Figure 69 shows how the basic bodice is sewn at the shoulder seams. No seam allowances are illustrated.

The shirt yoke being drafted has a front seam that is 1½″ forward of the normal shoulder seam and a seam across the back that is 2″ below the Center Back neck point.

STEP 1. Trace the front and back sections of the Basic Bodice pattern onto a fresh sheet of paper.

STEP 2. Cut straight across the back pattern 2″ down from the neck, measuring on the Center Back line (Figure 69).

STEP 3. On the front pattern, mark a line parallel to the shoulder seam 1½″ away. Cut on this line.

ALTERING SEAM LOCATIONS (Steps 1 to 3)
The Original Pattern

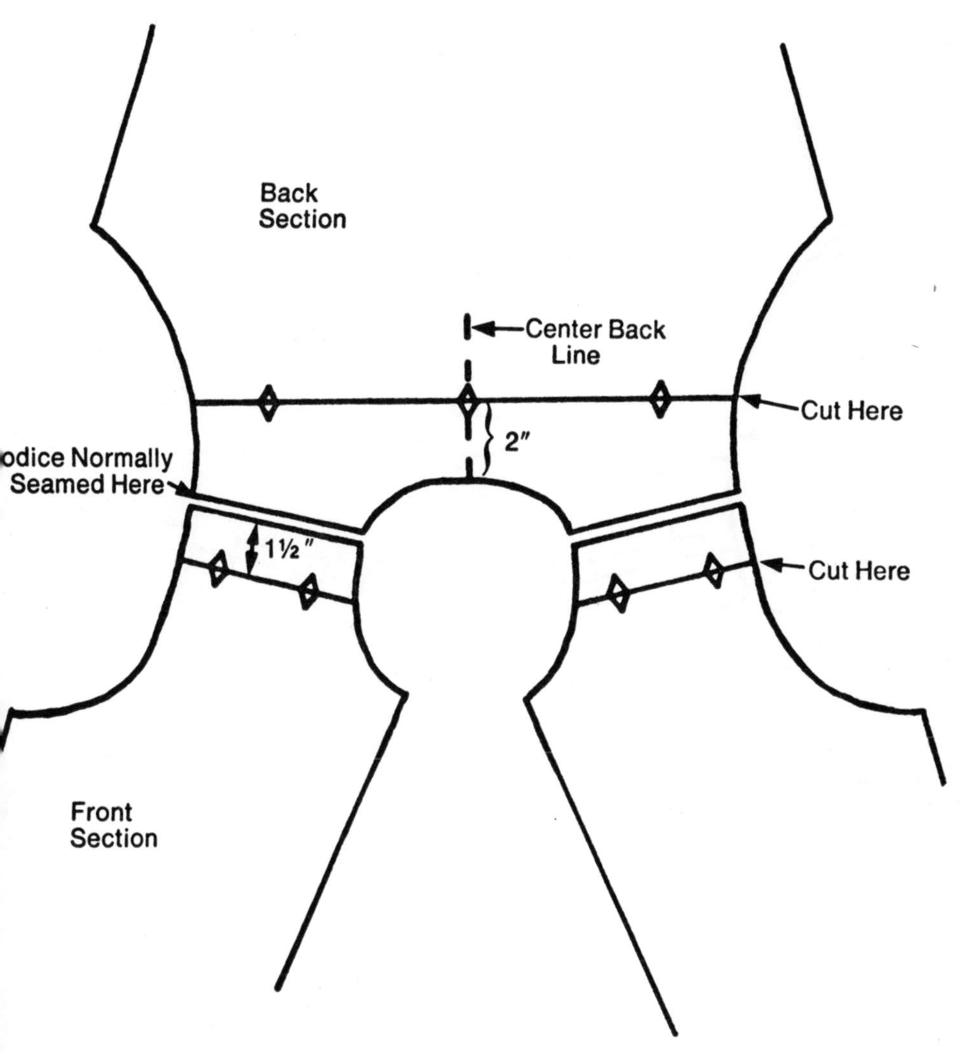

Figure 69

ALTERING SEAM LOCATIONS (Step 4)
The New Pattern

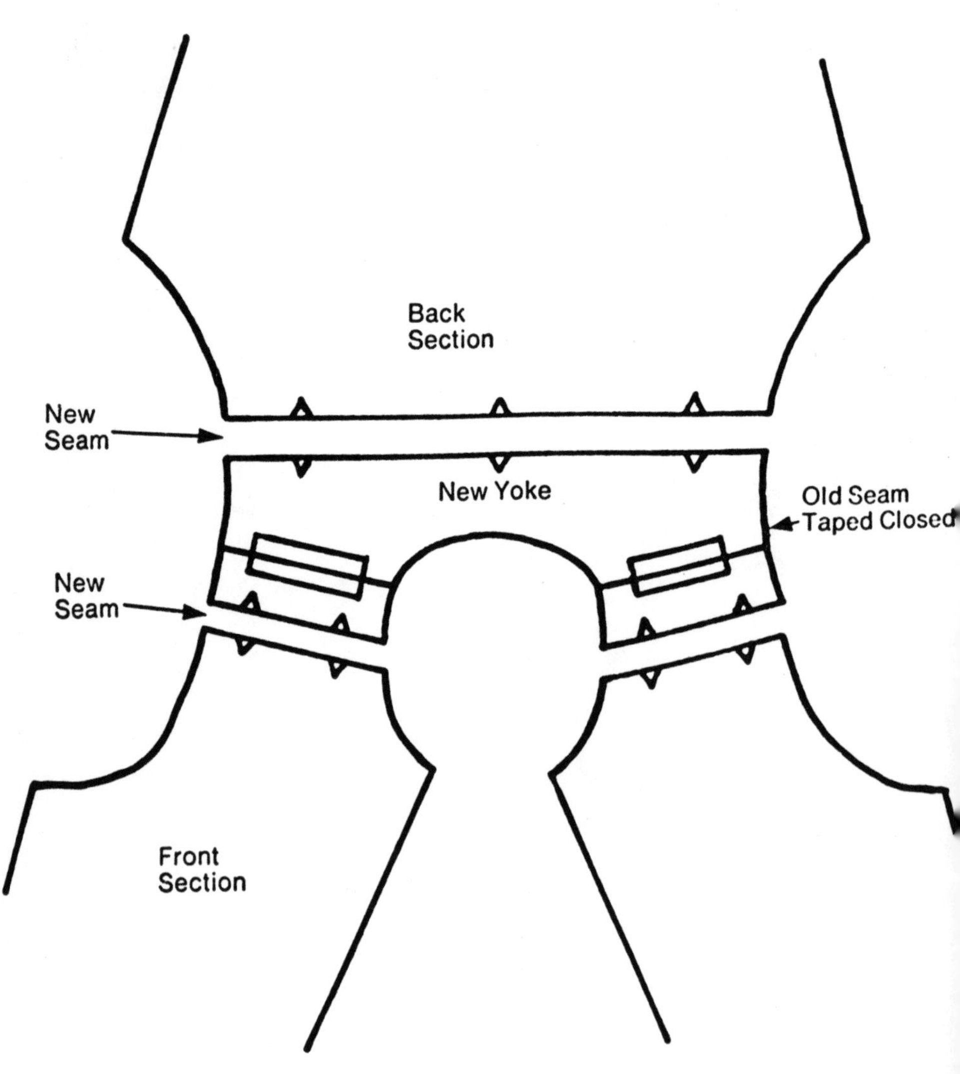

Figure 70

Step 4. Tape the section cut off the front to the section cut off the back at the normal seam line (Figure 70).

Step 5. Add seam allowances to the entire pattern.

Notches may be marked on the yoke seam lines before the pattern pieces are cut to clarify the final pattern. These notches will then be extended to the seam allowances before this final pattern is cut out.

Seams that do not affect the shape of a garment can be added anywhere, simply by cutting the pattern wherever the seam is to go. Seam allowances, however, must be added where the pattern is cut. Similarly, seams that are straight lines may be removed by taping the seams together where they would normally be sewn. Be careful that the actual seam lines are being taped together and not the seam allowance lines. Curved seam lines, on the other hand, may not be taped together to eliminate seams because the two edges will not coincide at all points when they are laid out flat. Figure 71 illustrates a side seam that cannot be eliminated by taping the seam lines together.

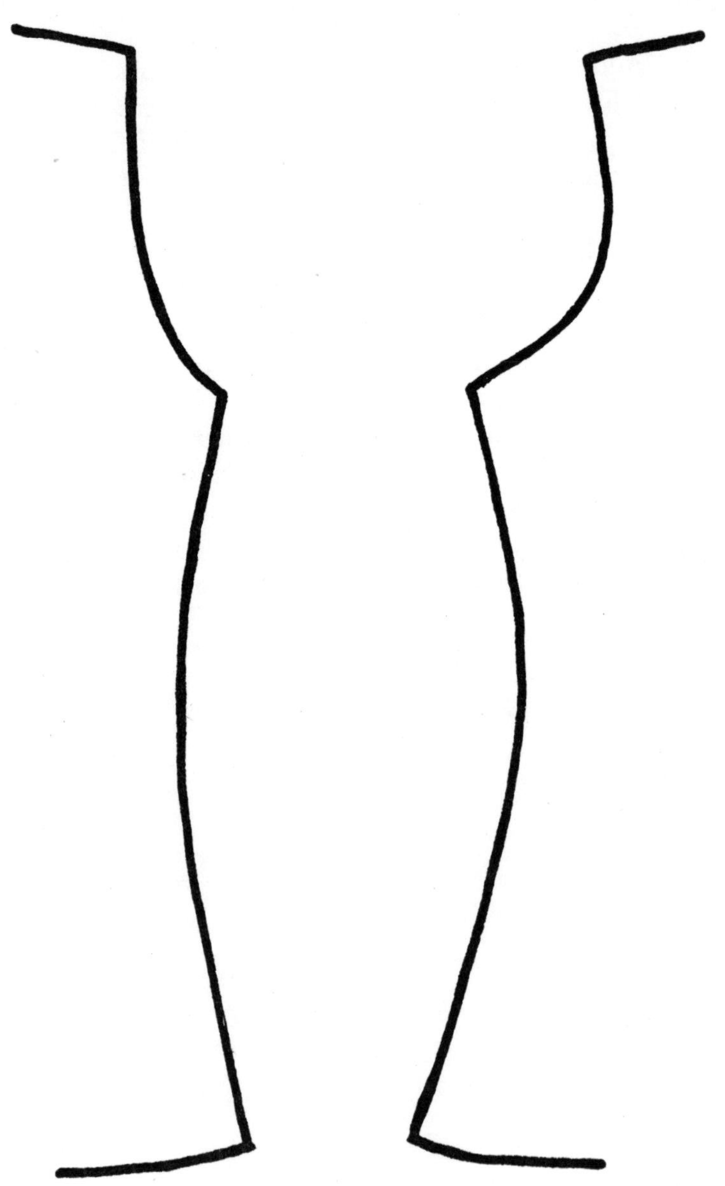

Figure 71

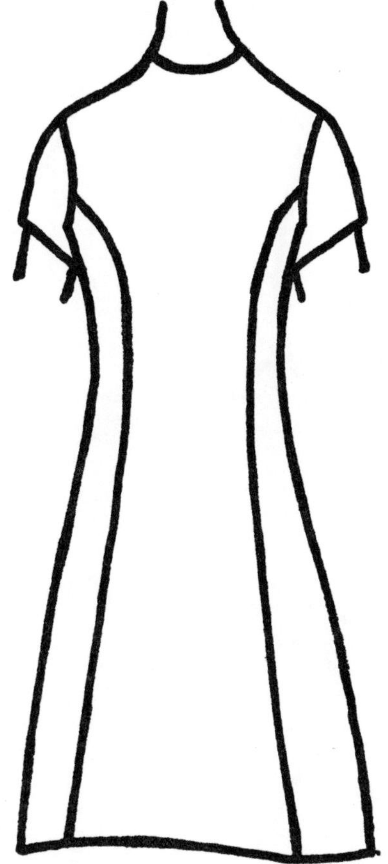

Figure 72

CHANGING A DART TO A SEAM

Darts can normally be changed to seams. One example that illustrates this is the dress shown in Figure 72. The shaping that would normally be done by the dart is being done by a side front seam. An alteration of the basic bodice will show how this can be achieved.

STEP 1. Trace the original Basic Bodice pattern onto a new sheet of paper, swinging the dart to the side seam.

STEP 2. Sketch a line where the side front seam is to go (Figure 73).

ALTERING A DART TO A SEAM (Steps 1 to 3)
Establishing the Seam Line

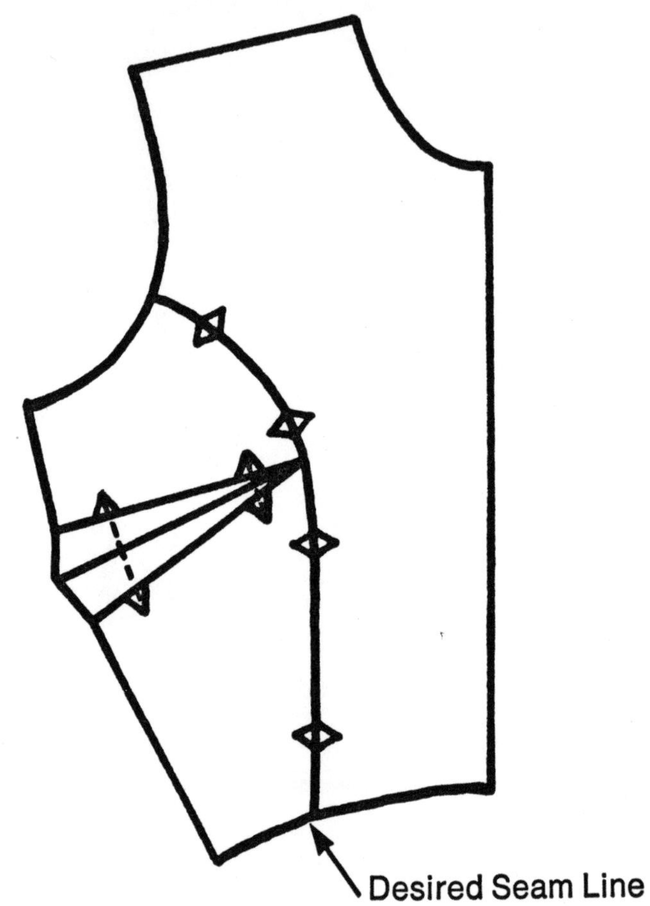

Figure 73

STEP 3. Mark notches along the new seam line and across the dart.

STEP 4. Cut the pattern along this new seam line (Figure 74).

STEP 5. Cut out the dart.

ALTERING A DART TO A SEAM (Steps 4 & 5)
Cutting The Pattern

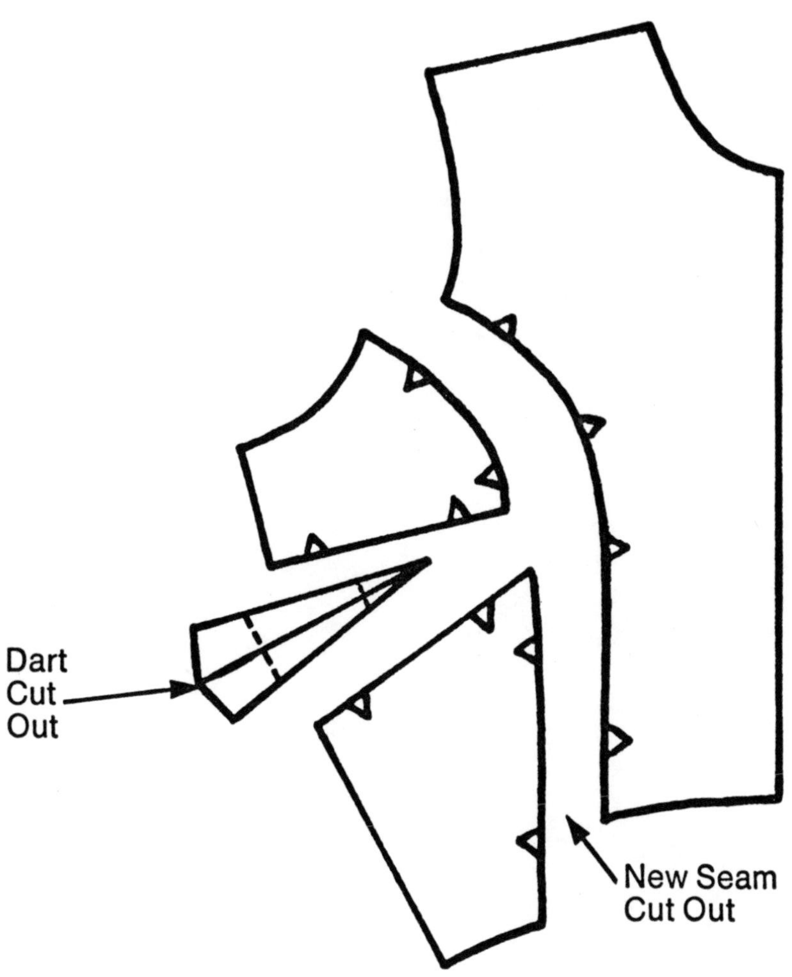

Figure 74

STEP 6. Tape the dart opening closed as if it were sewn (Figure 75).

STEP 7. Round the seam lines gradually into smooth curves.

STEP 8. Add seam allowances, extend the notches, and the pattern is complete.

ALTERING A DART TO A SEAM (Steps 6 & 7)
Removing the Dart

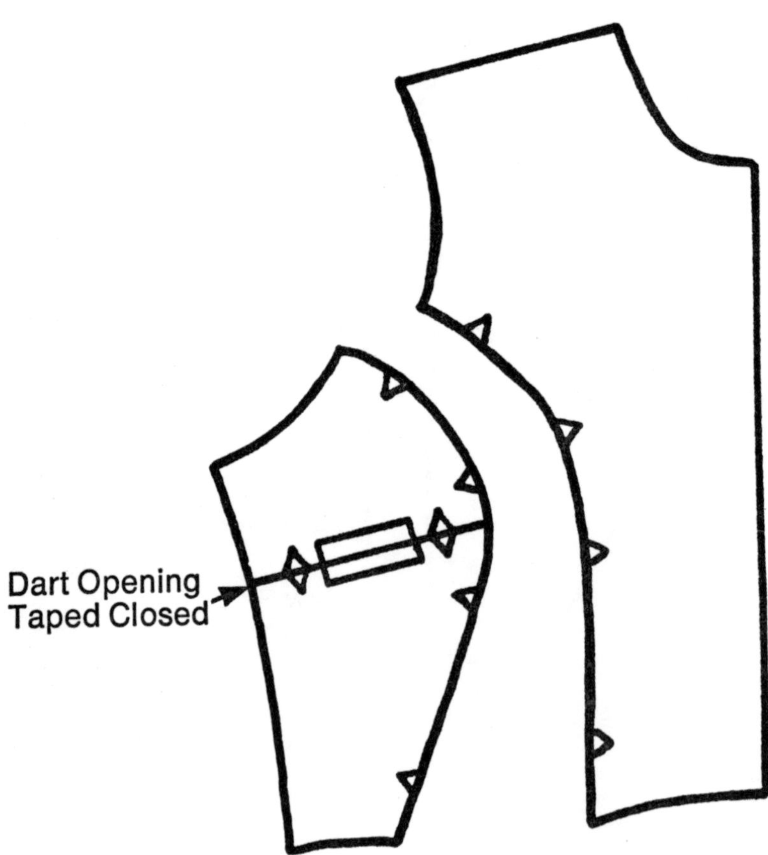

Figure 75

SIDE FRONT SEAM WITH DART

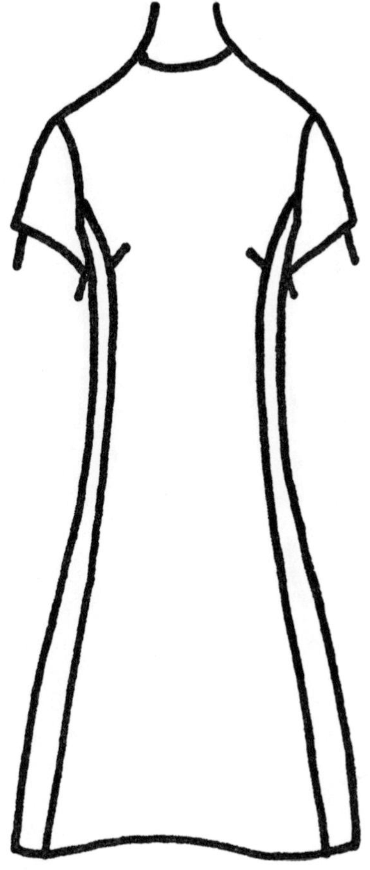

Figure 76

Sometimes the side front seam does not go directly over the bust point. If this is the case, a small portion of the dart will be left in for proper shaping, as in Figure 76.

FITTED SLEEVE EXPANDED AT SHOULDER

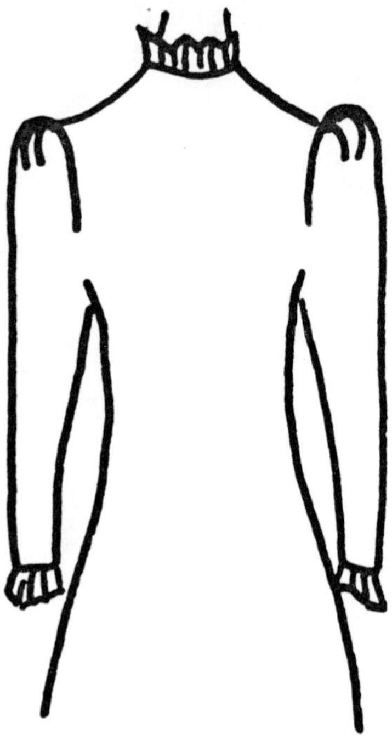

Figure 77

CHANGING THE SHAPE BY CUTTING

One of the most frequent steps a drafter must take is expanding a basic pattern to create fullness. Cutting the pattern and respacing it is one way of doing this. Figure 77 illustrates a sleeve with gathers at the shoulder point, and fullness at the upper arm—the traditional leg o'mutton sleeve. To achieve this effect, the sleeve pattern is cut and expanded in the following manner.

STEP 1. Trace the Basic Fitted Sleeve pattern on a sheet of paper.

EXPANDING BY CUTTING (Steps 1 to 4)

Cutting the Sleeve Cap

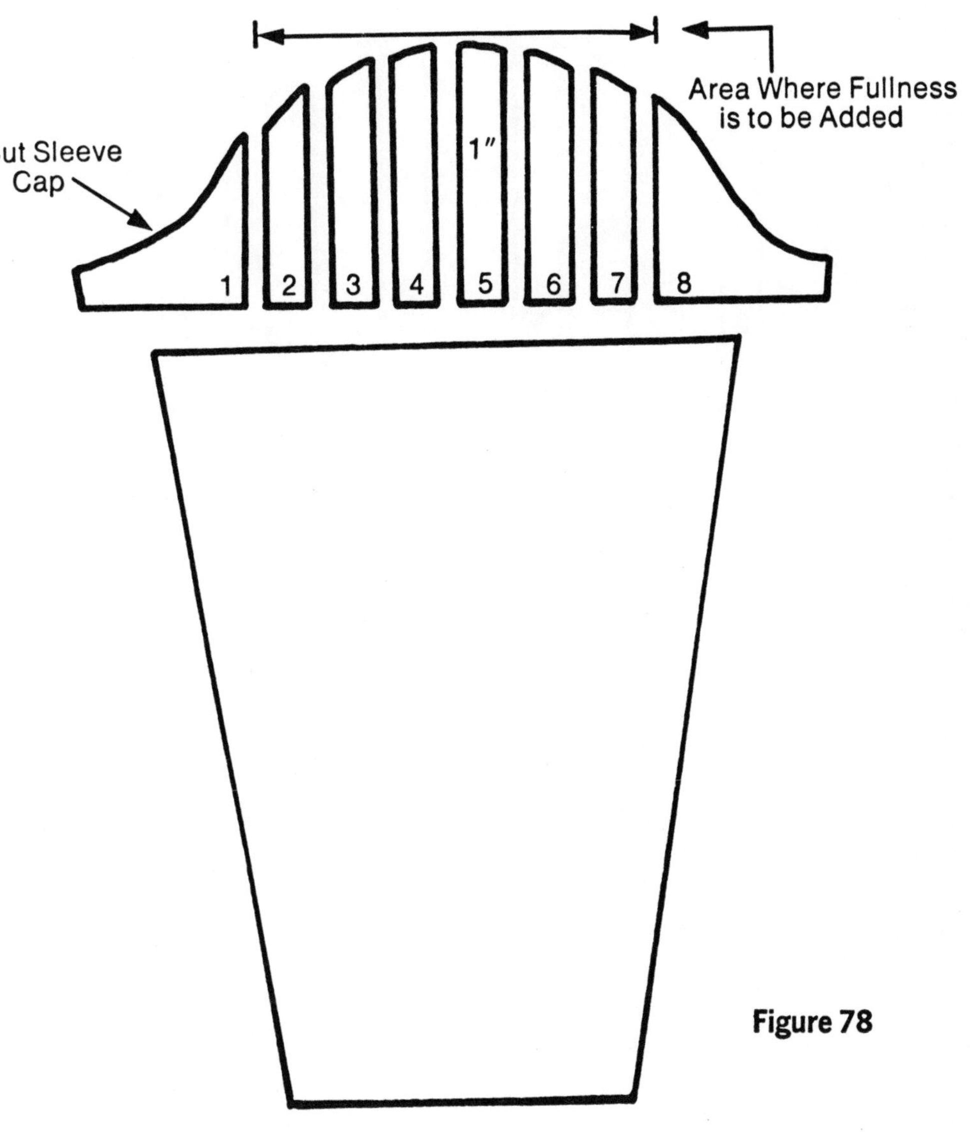

Figure 78

EXPANDING BY CUTTING (Step 6)

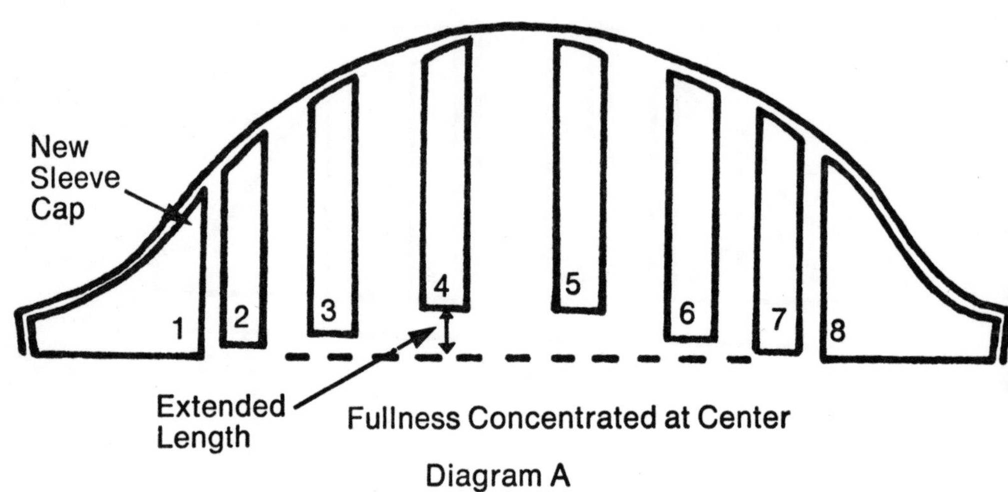

Fullness Concentrated at Center

Diagram A

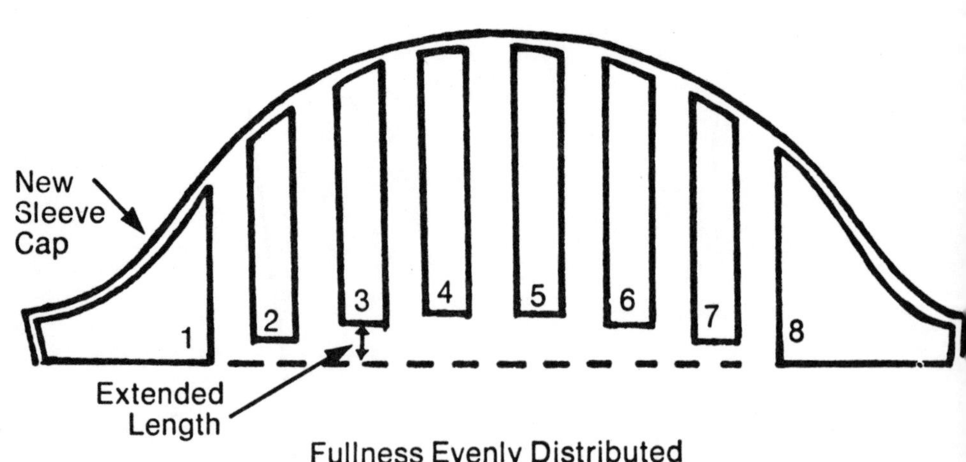

Fullness Evenly Distributed

Diagram B

Figure 79

STEP 2. Cut the sleeve cap off the traced pattern about an inch below the Biceps line (See Figure 78).

STEP 3. Determine where the gathers of the sleeve are to fall. (This is usually only in the center of the sleeve cap pattern.) Mark off the sleeve cap pattern into one-inch strips in this area and number the strips.

STEP 4. Cut the sleeve cap apart.

STEP 5. Retrace the arm portion of the sleeve pattern onto another sheet of paper.

STEP 6. At the top of the arm, lay out the numbered sleeve cap pieces in order, leaving space between the strips, as is shown in Figure 79. Note that the strips are raised above the original Biceps line, in order to add height as well as fullness. Increasing the fullness in many patterns requires expansion in both horizontal and vertical directions, as will be explained later in this section.

The amount of fullness and height which will be added to the original sleeve will be determined by the distance between the strips and their height above the original Biceps line as they are spread out on the new pattern. (Methods of determining how much fullness to add are discussed later in this section, on pages 159-160. Assume, for example, that 3″ are to be added to the width of the sleeve cap and 2″ to its height. To increase the width by 3″, extend the Biceps line 1½″ out to each side of the original sleeve pattern and place the ends of the sleeve cap at each end of this expanded Biceps line. To raise the sleeve cap by 2″, position the center strips of the sleeve cap 2″ above the Biceps line. The side strips should be placed progressively lower at each side, and the ends of the sleeve cap should be placed right on the Biceps line (See Figure 79).

The location of the added fullness is determined by the position of the strips. If the gathers are to be concentrated at the point of the shoulder and taper off at the sides, the sleeve cap will be laid out as in Diagram A of Figure 79. If the fullness is to be evenly distributed across the entire top of the sleeve cap, the pattern will be laid out as in Diagram B of Figure 79.

Step 7. Draw a new sleeve pattern by using the cut sleeve cap strips as a guide. Connect the expanded edges of the sleeve cap to the Wrist line to form the new Side Seams.

Step 8. Add seam allowances.

The basic principle for expanding a pattern by cutting is fundamentally simple—expand the pattern where the fullness is to occur in the finished garment.

In the pattern illustrated, for example, the width of the top of the sleeve is expanded, as well as the width of the sleeve cap. To add fullness to the cap alone, leaving the body of the sleeve fitted, the pattern pieces would be raised and spread at the top only, in a fan shape, keeping the width of the original Biceps line for the new pattern. In this manner, fullness would not be added to the arm of the sleeve (See Figure 80).

SLEEVE CAP FULLNESS

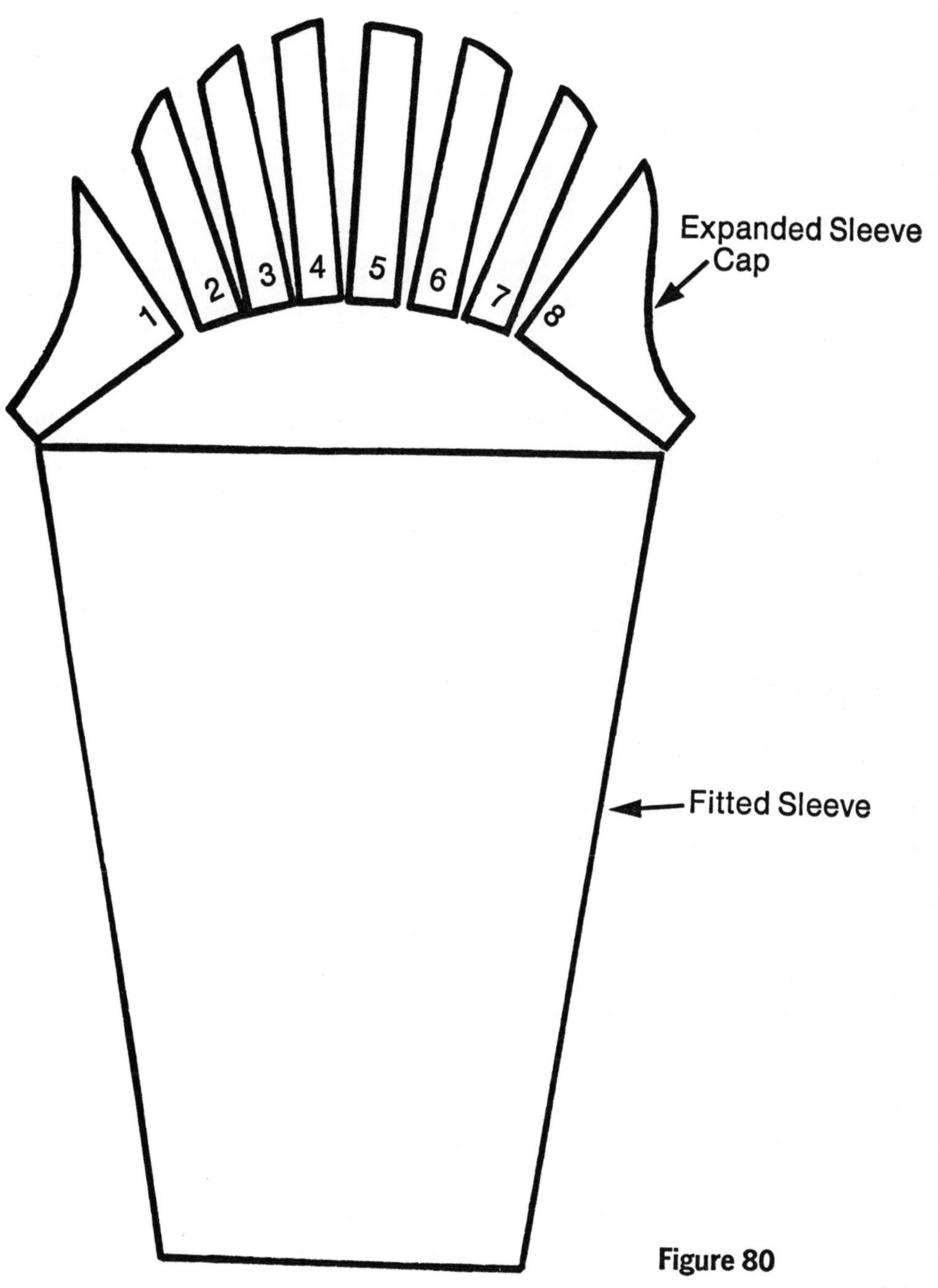

Figure 80

KNIFE PLEATS (Steps 1 to 4)

The Original Pattern

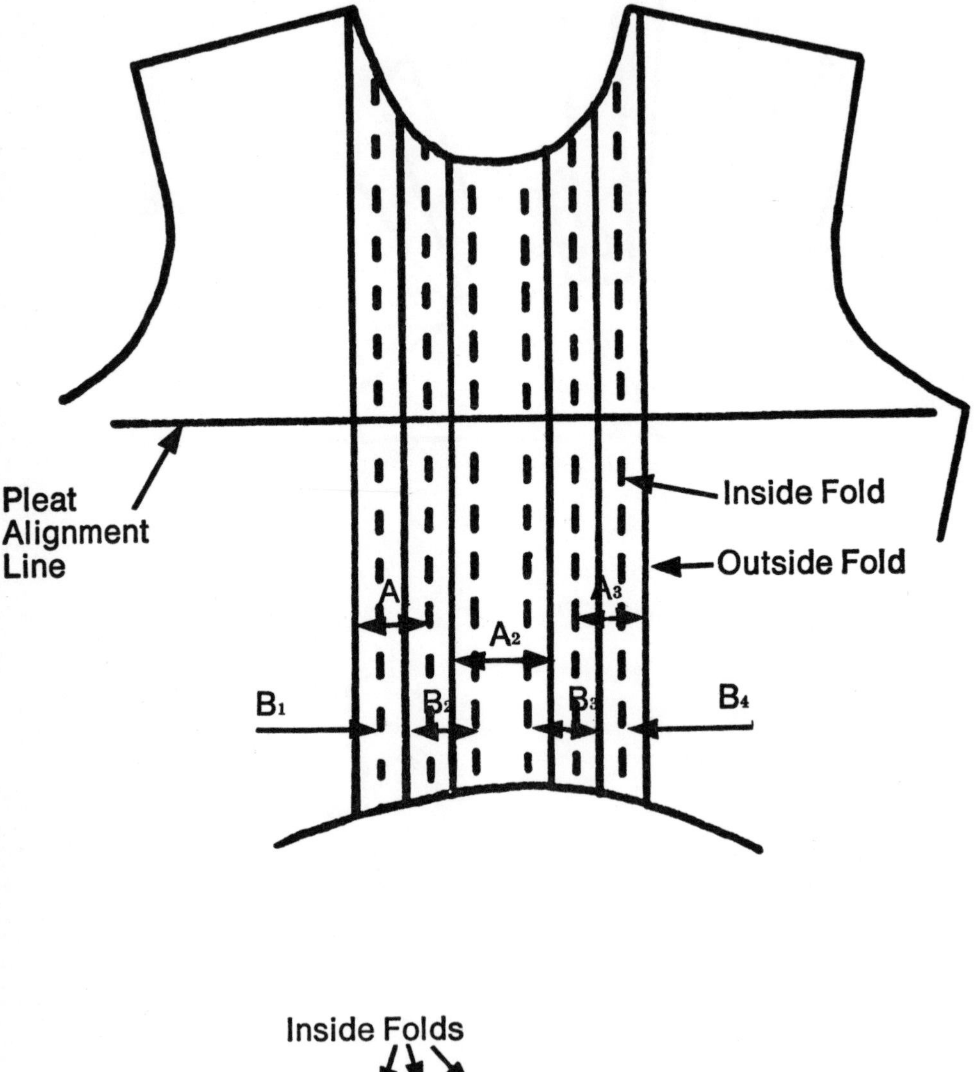

Pleat Alignment Line
Inside Fold
Outside Fold
A1
A2
A3
B1
B2
B3
B4

Inside Folds
Top View
Outside Folds

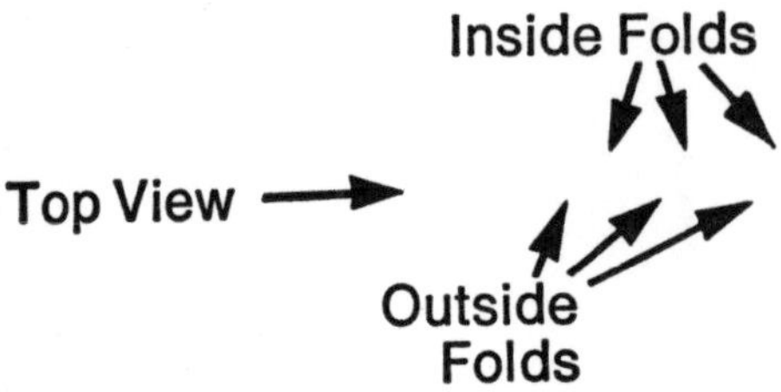

Figure 81

MAKING PLEATS

Making pleats is essentially the same process as expanding a pattern by cutting, except that it must be more carefully executed. The techniques of altering patterns for both knife pleats and box pleats are here described. The two pleats differ in that the box pleats alternate from one outside pleat to one inside pleat. Each pleat in the knife pleat, on the other hand, alternates from outside to inside. Compare Figures 81 and 83 for further clarification.

For the sake of clarity, the illustrations in this section show the full bodice front. However, the final bodice pattern should cover only the left half or the right half of the body, with the division at the Center Front line, to insure that the bodice will be symmetrical when it is cut out.

Knife Pleats

A knife-pleated bodice is illustrated in Figure 81. The solid lines indicate the outside folds and the dotted lines indicate the inside folds.

Step 1. Make two tracings of the front bodice pattern, swinging the dart allowance to the side seam.

Step 2. Draw a line straight across both patterns at the bottom of the armhole. These lines will be used to align the pleat strips.

Step 3. Using one of the tracings, cut out every other pleat strip as indicated by the "A's" in Figure 81. The center pleat strip goes from outside fold to outside fold. The other pleat strips go from an inside fold to an outside fold. Number the strips A1, A2, etc.

Step 4. On the other tracing, cut out the rest of the pleat strips (those indicated by the "B's"). Number these strips B1, B2, etc.

KNIFE PLEATS (Steps 5 to 7)
The Pleated Pattern

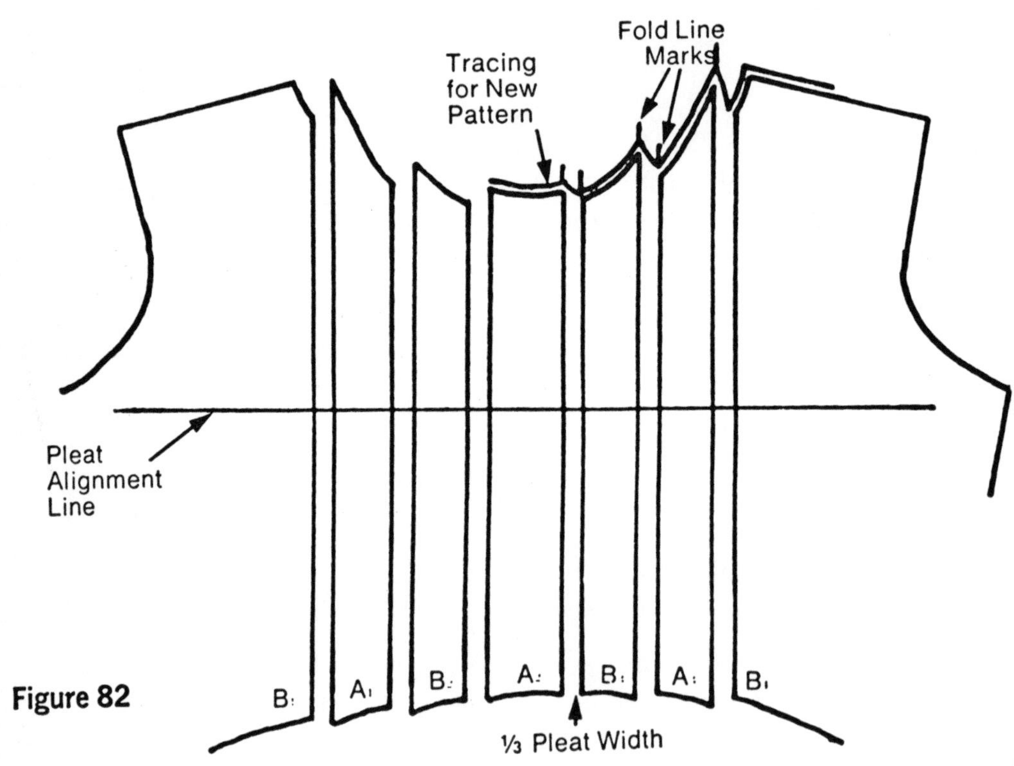

Figure 82

STEP 5. On a fresh sheet of paper, lay out the pleat strips in order (See Figure 82). Space them by the distance of the pleat fold which, in this case, is one-third the pleat width. Position the pleat strips vertically, using the Pleat Alignment line.

STEP 6. Trace around the pleat strips, following the contour carefully.

STEP 7. Mark the edges of the pleat strips on the pattern, as these will be the fold lines.

STEP 8. Add seam allowances and the pattern is complete.

BOX PLEATS (Steps 1 to 4)
The Original Pattern

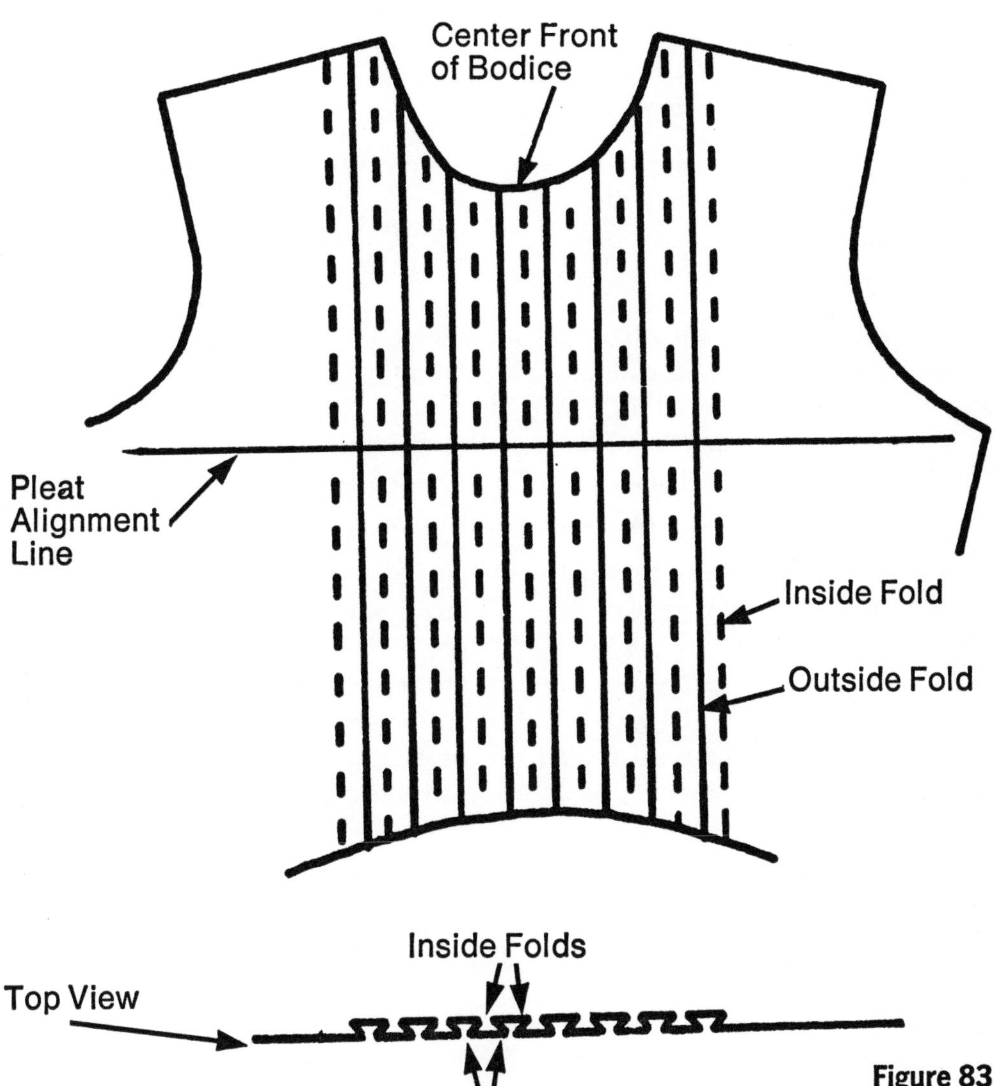

Figure 83

Box Pleats

Box pleats are drafted in almost the same way that knife pleats are.

STEP 1. Make two tracings of the bodice pattern, swinging the dart to the side seam position.

STEP 2. Draw a line straight across both patterns at the bottom of the armholes. This will be the Pleat Alignment line.

STEP 3. On one pattern, mark the outside pleats. These are represented by the solid lines in Figure 83. Number the pleats on the pattern to facilitate correct placement later. Also indicate in some way that these are outside pleats.

STEP 4. On the other pattern, mark the inside pleats. These are represented by the dotted lines in Figure 83. Number these strips and indicate that they are inside pleats.

Note in Figure 83 that the Center Front of the bodice falls on the center outside pleat. This outside pleat will therefore, be in the center of the new extended pattern (pleat number 5).

STEP 5. Cut the two patterns apart along the pleat lines and place the pleat strips so that they alternate, outside pleat to inside pleat, keeping them in the correct order (Outside 1, Inside 1, Outside 2, Inside 2, etc.). The inside pleats are represented by the shaded strips in Figure 84. All strips should be separated from each other by the distance of the pleat fold: In this case, this is one half a pleat width away. Make sure the pleat strips are lined up properly by using the Pleat Alignment line.

STEP 6. Trace around this pattern so that all the points are connected. Mark the edges of the pleat strips on the pattern, both top and bottom, to indicate the fold lines.

If there is any problem visualizing why these pleat patterns are drafted in this way, a sample pattern should be cut out and folded.

The preceding principles of pattern alteration have been described in relation to specific garments or specific parts of garments. Their application, however, need not be limited to these garments.

BOX PLEATS (Steps 5 & 6)
Drafting the Pleated Pattern

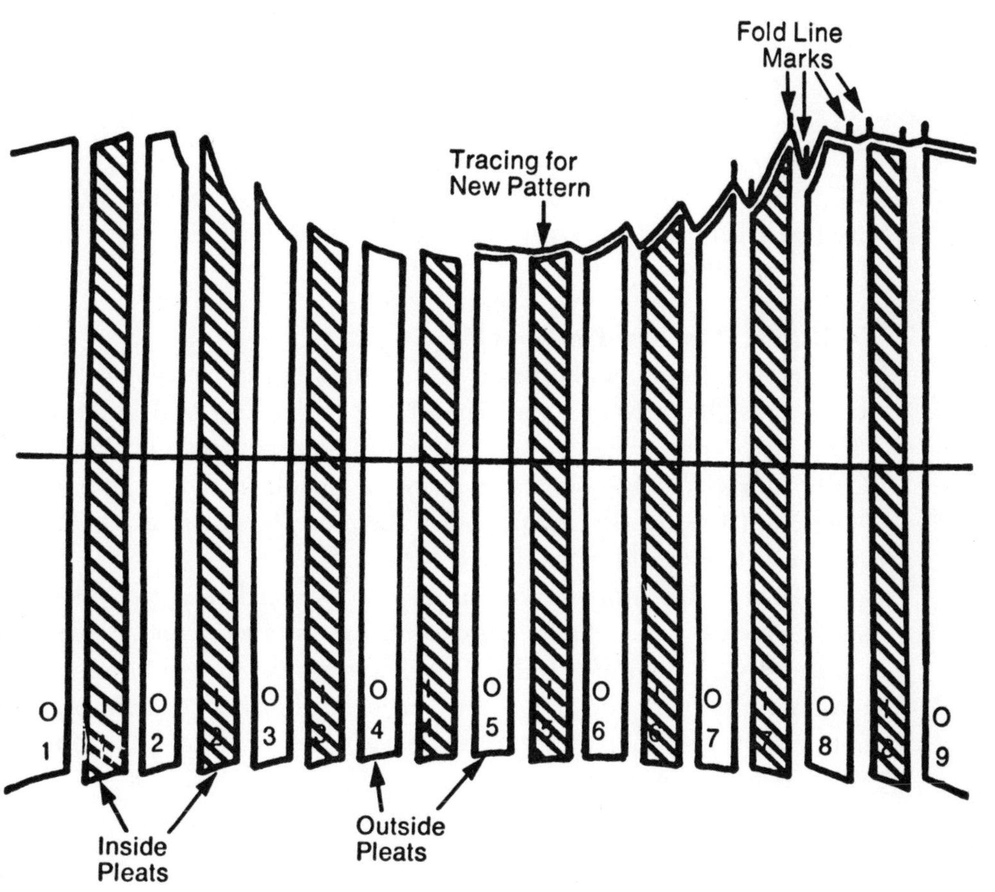

Figure 84

The important thing to remember is the concept behind the technique and not the specific illustration.

DETERMINING FULLNESS

The fullness of a garment and the shaping of patterns to attain fullness are governed by the following basic design principles, which are extremely important to the pattern drafter's work.

Essentially, clothes have two basic extremes to which they can go. One extreme is to be exceedingly close fitting, as with leotards. The other extreme is to be very full, as in a full, floor-length skirt. All garments will fall somewhere between these two extremes. One of the first features a pattern drafter should look for in a design is the degree of fullness it has.

Garments Hang On The Body

Basic to either the fitted or full look is the concept that garments must hang from some part of the body. The two basic areas of the body from which clothes hang are the shoulders and the waist. Coats, shirts, and blouses hang from the shoulders. Pants and skirts hang from the waist. Clothes must therefore be fitted at the waist and/or at the shoulders or they will fall off.

There are other points of the body which are also used as holding points for fullness. The wrist, for instance, can be used to hold up the bottom of a full sleeve if there is a fitted cuff. Similarly, the area just below or above the knees can be used to hold up the bottoms of knickers; and the ankles can be used to hold up the bottoms of harem pants.

The principle is that if a garment is going to be full it has to hang from a suitable part of the body. The bottom of a puffed sleeve cannot be held up at the three-quarter arm length because the cuff will slide down until the material is just hanging from the shoulder. In the same way, a skirt cannot be held up by the rib cage, because the weight of the material will pull it down to the waistline.

Designating The Amount Of Fullness

Fullness is normally measured by comparing the length of the material to the distance it is to be gathered into. If a 12″ length of material is to be gathered or pleated to 6″, this is referred to as double fullness.

Fullness And Material

The amount of fullness to be used in a garment is first and foremost dependent on the body of the material being used. To achieve a given shape, a material with substantial body will require less fullness than a lighter material.

Take the shape of the skirt in Figure 85 as an example. If a heavy quilted fabric is being used, less than double fullness would be sufficient. A medium weight fabric would require approximately triple fullness to achieve the same shape. If chiffon were being used, six times the material could be used and the shape of the skirt would still be narrower than the shape indicated in the figure. Hence, any design must always take into consideration the fabric in which it will be executed.

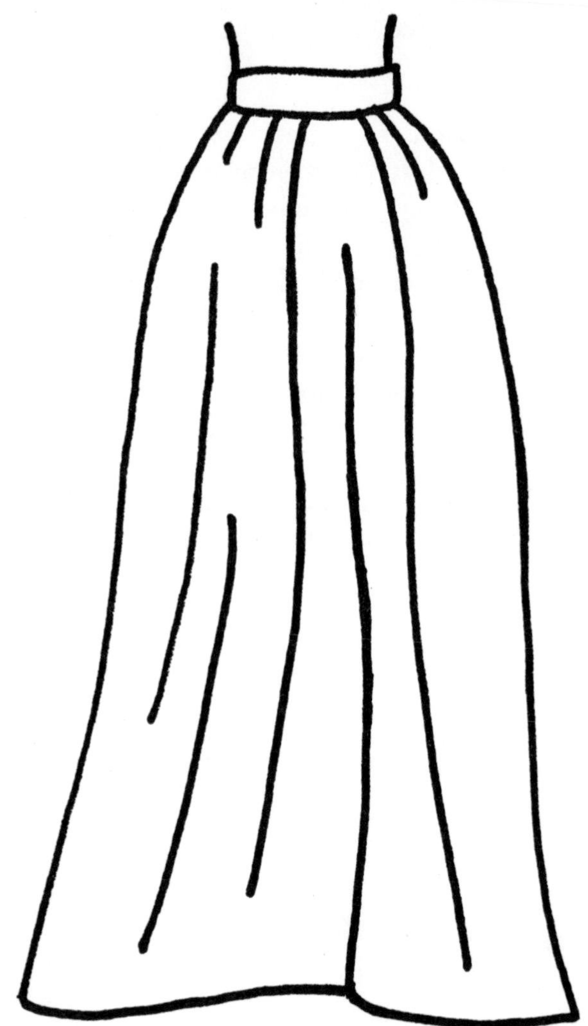

Figure 85

Fullness And Design

The amount of fullness which should be drafted will also depend on the design of the garment. The blouse in Diagram A of Figure 86 might only use the amount of fullness normally added by the dart-width allowance, or one-and-a-fourth to one-and-a-third fullness. The peasant blouse in Diagram B would use at least double fullness of a lightweight material.

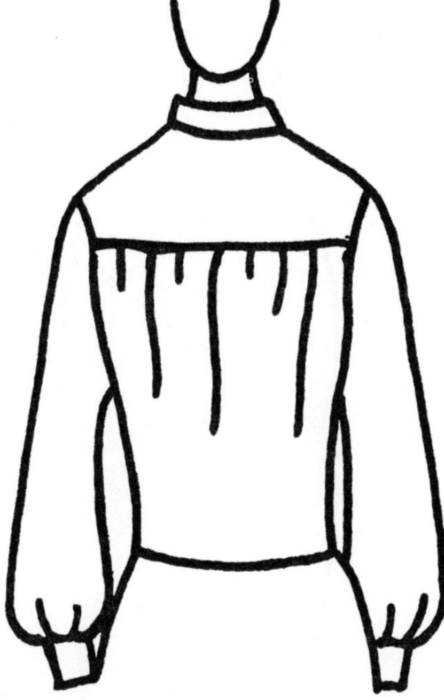

One and a Third Fullness

Diagram A

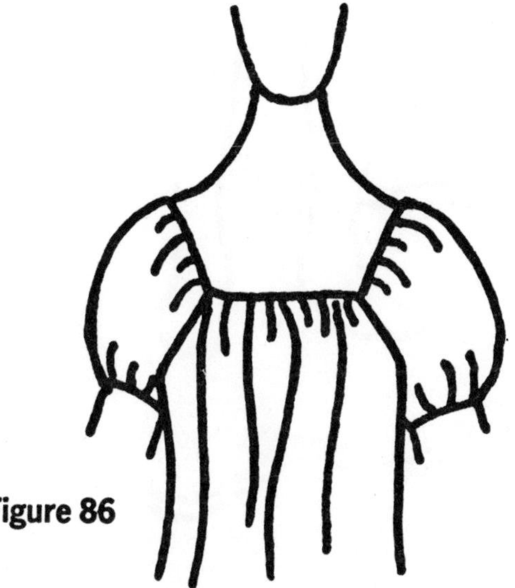

Figure 86

Diagram B

Double Fullness

MEASURING FOR FULLNESS
HEM CIRCUMFERENCE

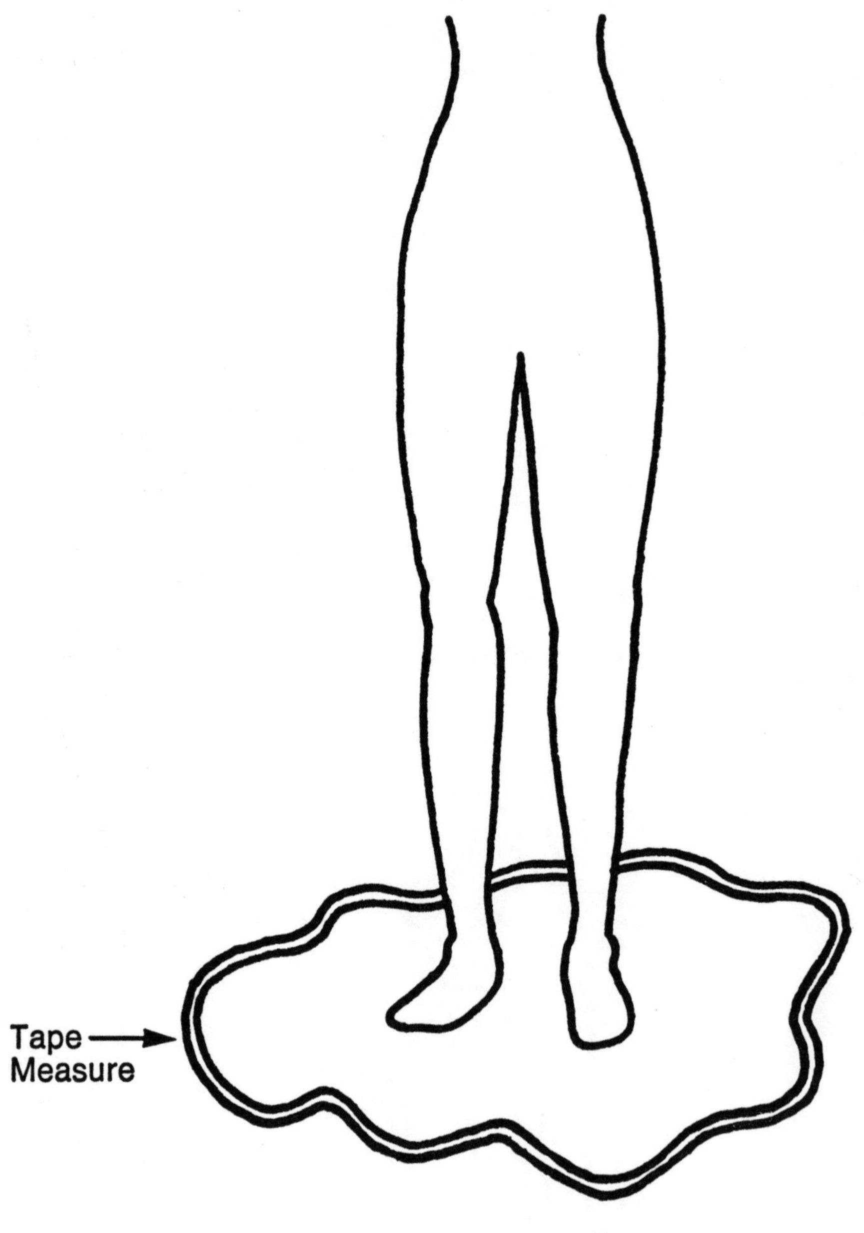

Figure 87

Measuring Fullness

Frequently, the amount of fullness to be used can be determined by measuring the shape of the desired garment. To determine the hem of the floor-length skirt in Figure 85 a tape measure may be placed on the floor to simulate the desired hem circumference (See Figure 87).

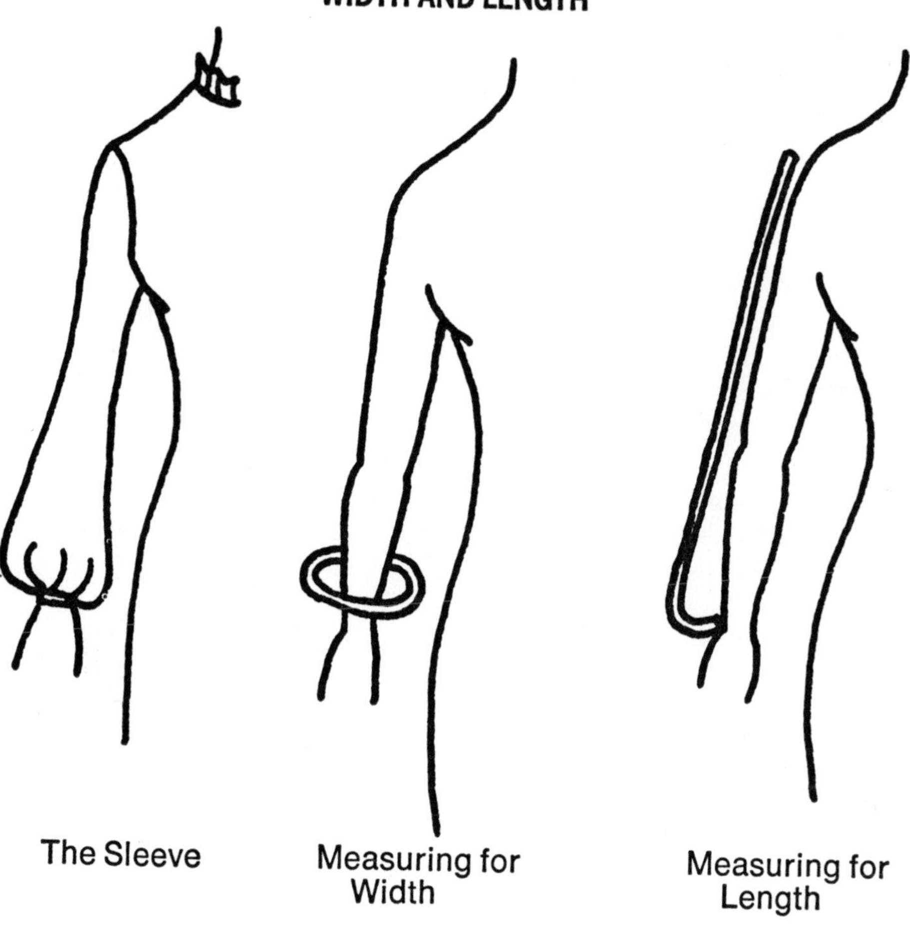

Figure 88

The full sleeve illustrated in Figure 88 is another example of how circumference is measured by simulating the desired shape with a tape measure. Notice that when a garment has extra fullness in circumference, it will also require extra fullness in length. The length measurement may also be taken by simulating the shape of the seam with a tape measure.

There are no quick and easy formulas for determining the amount of fullness that is going to be necessary. All of the factors described here will have to be taken into consideration. Every garment and every type of fabric will present different problems. The best rule to remember is: When in doubt, make it a little too large, because it can easily be taken in.

DETERMINING PATTERN SHAPES

Once the amount of fullness has been determined, it must be transferred to the patterns. The following items will govern this.

Expanding For Fullness

When patterns are expanded to accommodate for fullness, the fullness will occur where the patterns are expanded. Thus a sleeve will billow only to a certain degree when it is cut as a one-piece sleeve. It may be necessary to divide the sleeve pattern into two parts to achieve the desired shaping (See Figure 89).

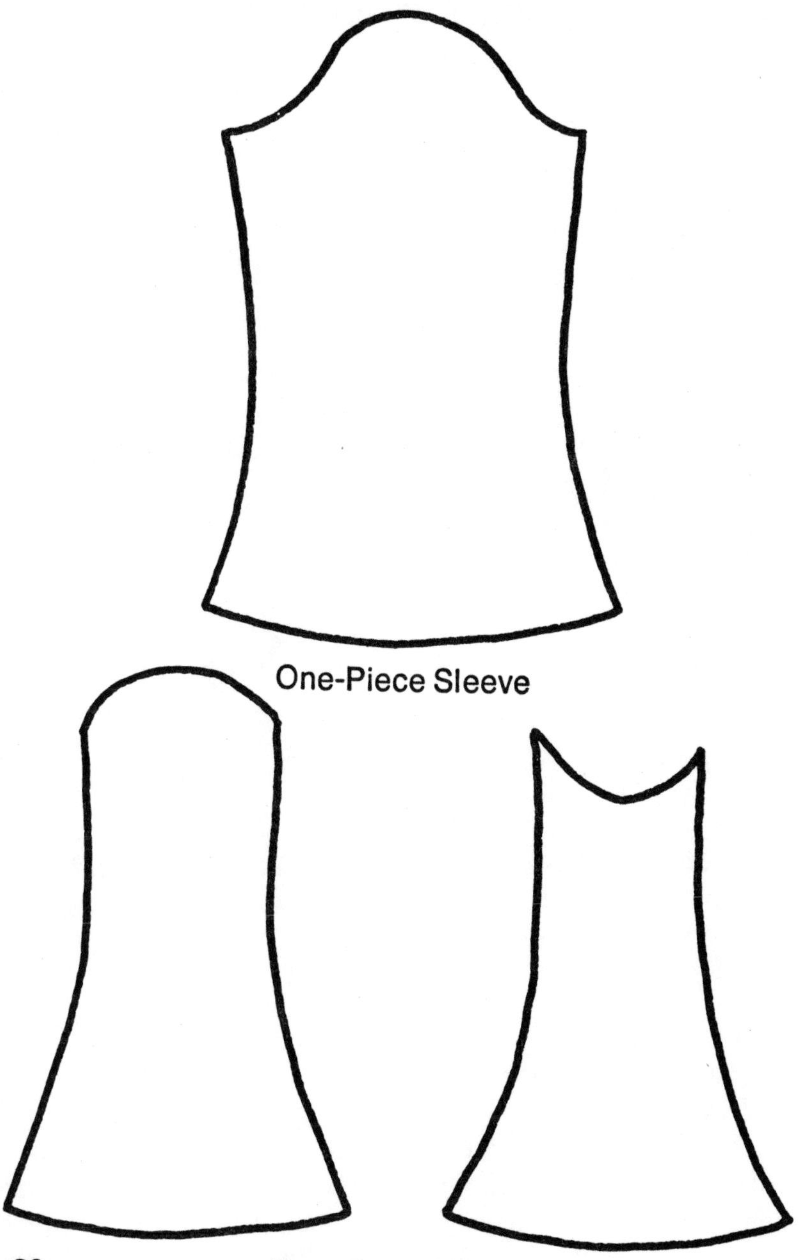

One-Piece Sleeve

Figure 89

Two-Piece Sleeve

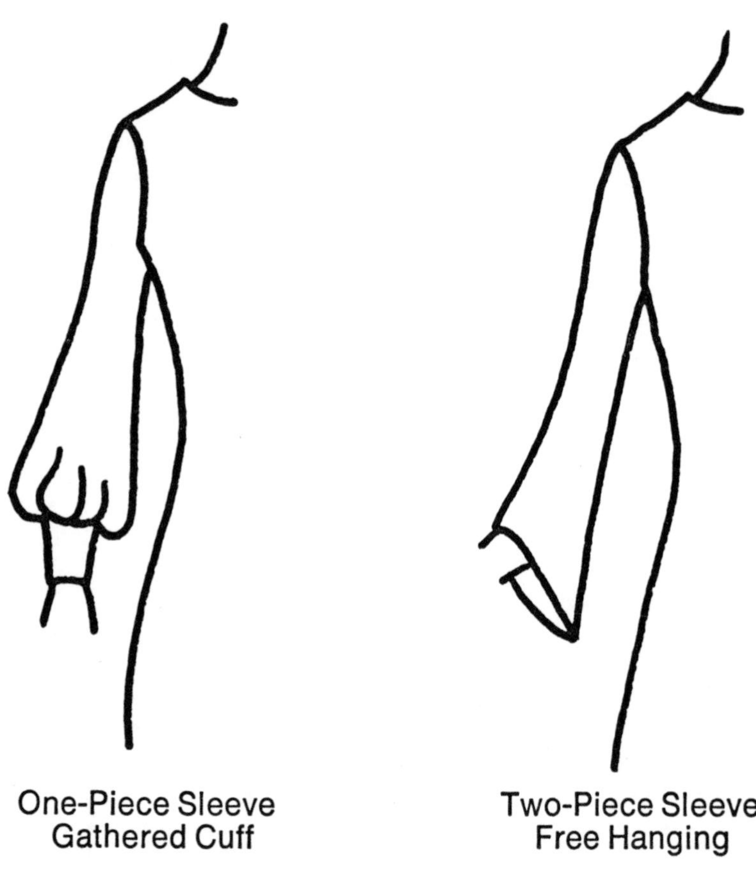

One-Piece Sleeve
Gathered Cuff

Two-Piece Sleeve
Free Hanging

Figure 90

Control Of Fullness

Another qualifying factor with fullness is in how it is to be controlled. A very full sleeve, for example, can be drafted in one piece if it is to be gathered into a cuff (Figure 90). The cuff will control the distribution of the fullness. On the other hand, a free-hanging sleeve with much less fullness may have to be cut in two pieces, because there is no means of controlling where the fullness will fall except by the placement of the seams.

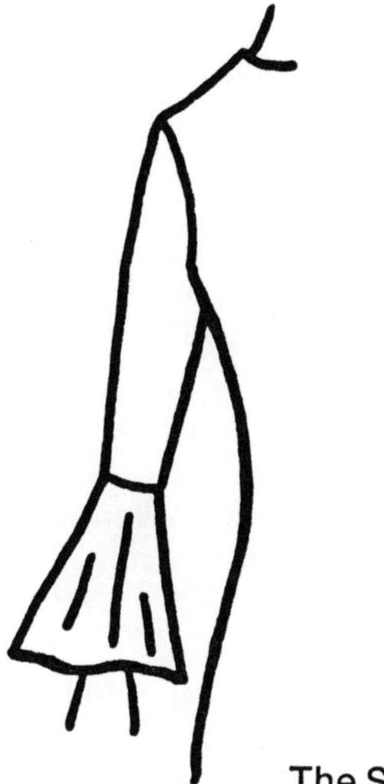

The Sleeve

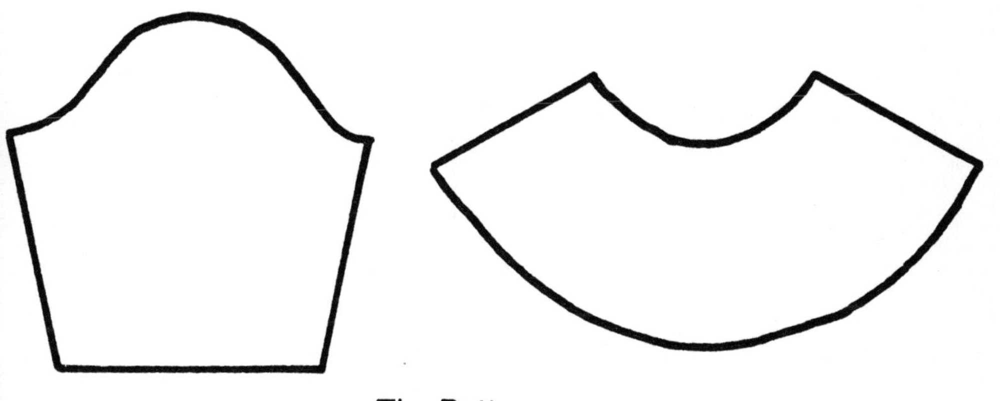

The Pattern

Figure 91

Transitions Between Fitted And Full

Material cannot be changed abruptly from close-fitted to full. The sleeve in Figure 91 must be drafted with two patterns in order to make the transition clear between the close-fitted section and the ruffle.

Using The Bias

The bias of the material must also be taken into consideration when the patterns are being drafted. Woven material that is cut on the bias will drape better than when it is cut on the straight. The biases of two sections which are to be joined together, however, must be cut on approximately the same bias angle, otherwise undesirable puckering may occur at the seam. Figure 92 illustrates a seam that has a bias-cut piece joined to a piece cut on the straight.

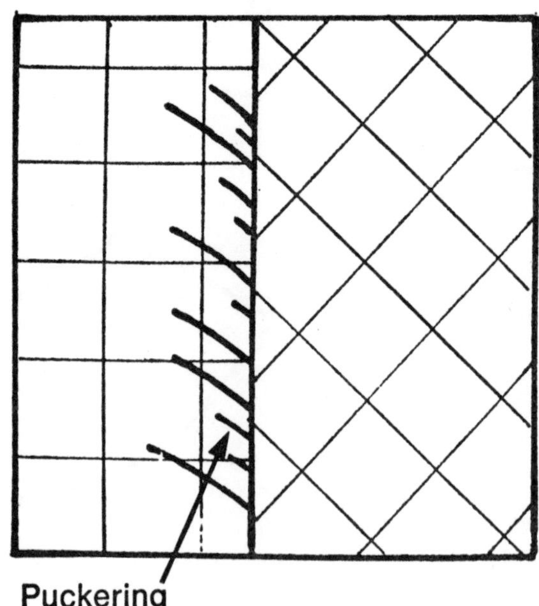

Figure 92

Selecting The Drafting Techniques

If a garment is to be closely fitted, the drafter should work with the basic patterns, altering them as necessary. This is the purpose of these patterns: to reflect the shape of the body on paper.

If, on the other hand, the garment is very full, the basic pattern may not be necessary. A full skirt, for instance, may be drafted by using only the Waist measurement, the Waist to Floor measurement, and the Hem Circumference measurement, as will be illustrated in the next section.

These applications of the drafting techniques should become clear as the development of the patterns is discussed in the next section.

Shaping During Fitting

A good deal of the shape of a design can be achieved by skillful drafting, but drafting by itself is not enough. It is also necessary to fit a newly created garment on the body of the prospective wearer in order to achieve first-rate results.

Fitting is more than making sure that the garment sits properly on the body. It is also the procedure by which the optimum shape of the desired design is developed. Each alteration in a pattern opens up new possibilities for developing this shape. Different seam placements and dart locations are not only able to provide variations in the external line of a garment—they may also affect a garment's final shaping and drape. These possibilities can only be developed and explored to their fullest in a fitting session.

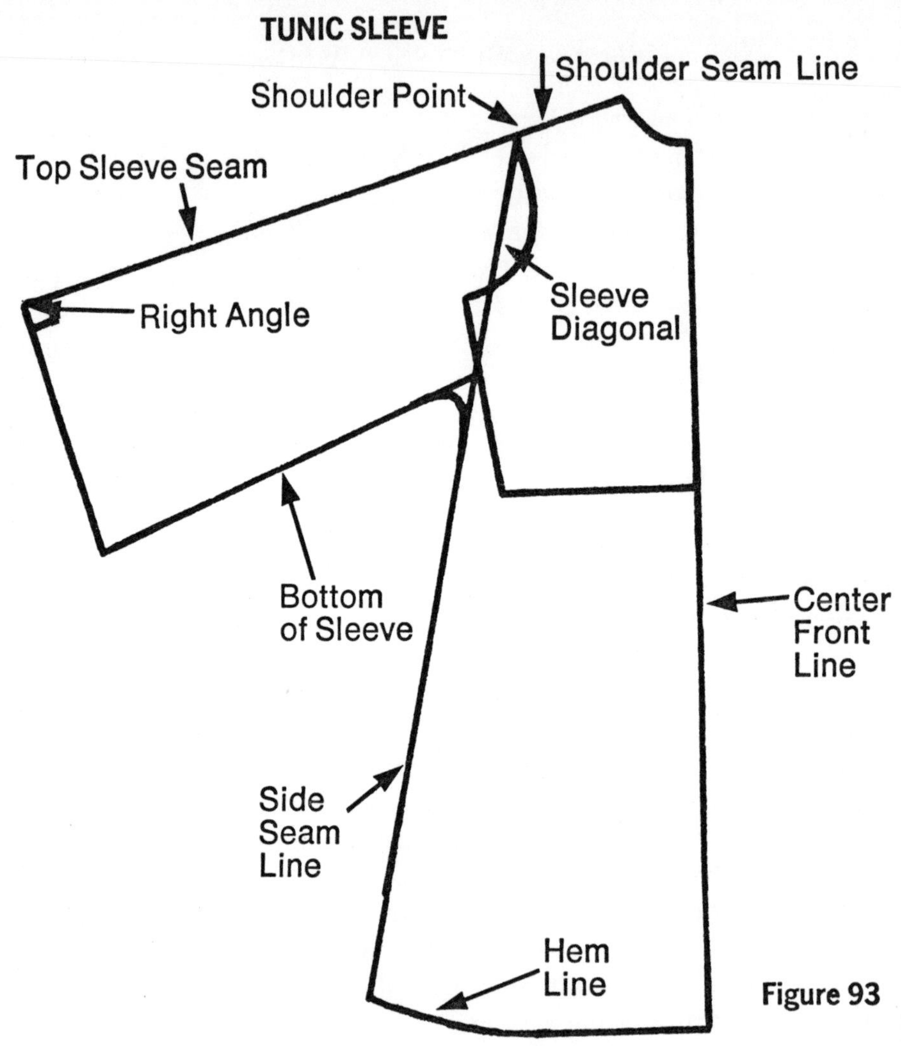

Figure 93

SLEEVE VARIATION I: THE TUNIC SLEEVE

The tunic sleeve is cut in one with the body of the garment. The basic bodice may be altered to achieve this effect by the following procedure.

STEP 1. Trace the Basic Bodice front onto a large sheet of paper.

STEP 2. Extend the Shoulder Seam line to form the top of the sleeve (see Figure 93).

STEP 3. Mark off the Shoulder to Wrist length on this extended line, starting at the point of the shoulder.

STEP 4. Measure the distance around the armhole curve and add 1″ to this. Draw a line of this length starting at the shoulder point, so that it intersects with the Side Seam line. This will be the Sleeve Diagonal.

STEP 5. Draw in the bottom seam of the sleeve starting at the bottom of the Sleeve Diagonal line. This line may be drawn in to any desired shape.

STEP 6. Extend a perpendicular line from the top of the sleeve to the bottom seam line to form the end of the sleeve.

STEP 7. Extend the Center Front line down to the desired Hem length and draw in the Side Seam line of the body to the desired shape. Darts can be omitted. Finally, curve the Hem. Add seam allowances and cut.

The back of the tunic is a duplication of the front, except for the neckline, which should be taken from the back bodice pattern. For women, the back of the tunic may be cut narrower than the front, if desired, by using the Back Bodice pattern as a basis for drafting the tunic back. The sleeves of the back pattern, in this case, should match the front sleeves. No center opening is needed for the back of the tunic because the front opening is cut large enough or is slashed for the head to pass through.

As has been mentioned earlier, the body and the sleeve of this style garment can be cut as one. In this case there is a seam at the top of the sleeve and another seam going around the bottom of the sleeve and down the side. If the material is not wide enough to achieve this effect, the sleeve may be cut separately by adding a seam line at the Sleeve Diagonal line. The configuration is still considered a tunic sleeve.

Another variation is to have the Shoulder Seam line and the top of the arm cut perpendicularly to the Center Front line.

PEASANT BLOUSE

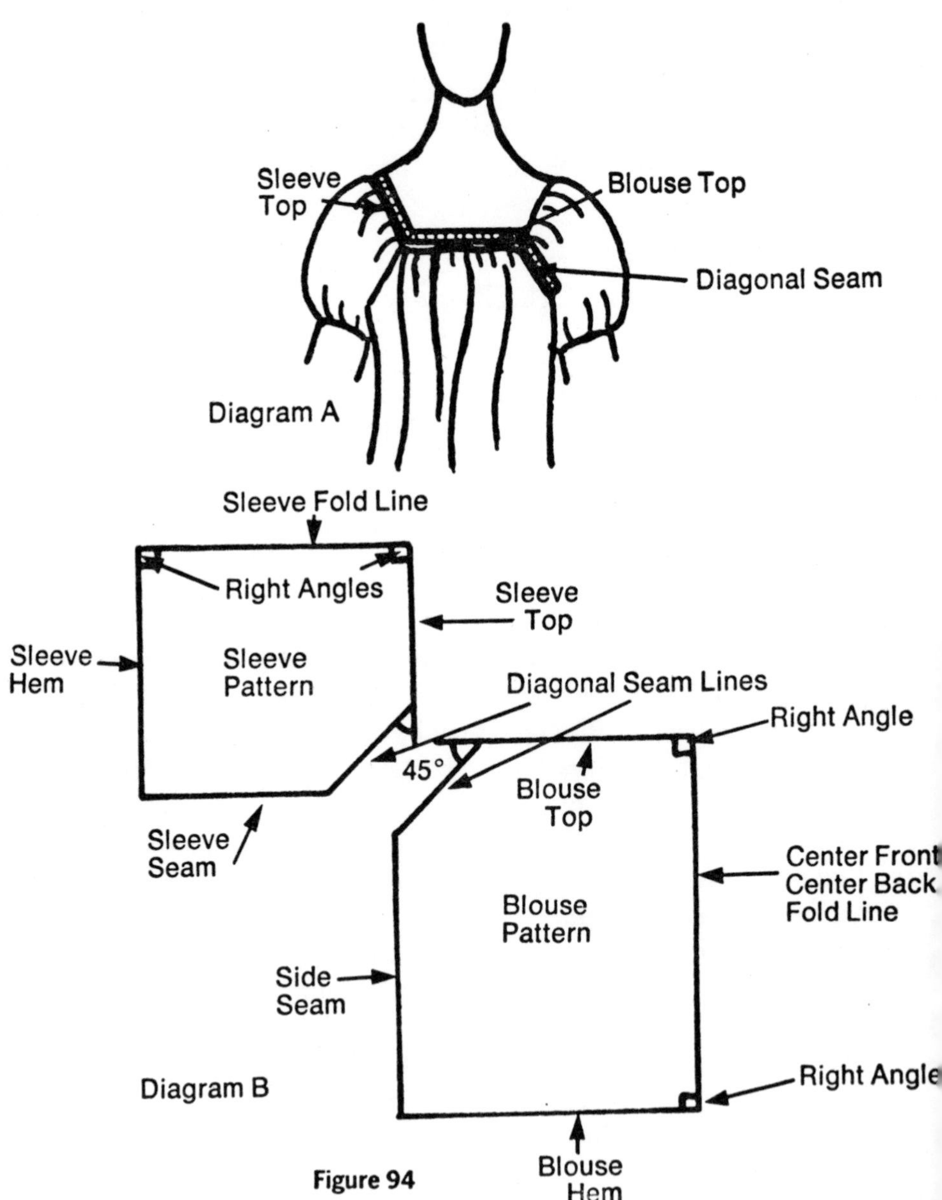

Figure 94

Figure 94

SLEEVE VARIATION II: THE PEASANT SLEEVE

The peasant sleeve and the body of the peasant blouse are drafted from a series of special measurements. This style of blouse and the location of the special measurements are illustrated in Diagram A of Figure 94. The pattern is illustrated in Diagram B.

Measurements:

The pattern for the peasant blouse is based on five measurements:

1. The finished length of the top of the sleeve.

2. The finished length of the top of the blouse. The finished neckline of this blouse is formed by the top of the blouse plus the top of the sleeve; therefore, the above two measurements taken together represent half the total length of the finished neckline.

3. The length of the diagonal seam which runs from the neckline to the underarm.

4. The length of the sleeve from neckline to sleeve hem, including any fullness.

5. The length of the body of the blouse, from neckline to hemline.

Drafting The Blouse

Step 1. Draw a line the length of the desired blouse (Measurement 5). This will be the Center Front/Center Back Fold line.

Step 2. Draw a line at right angles to the Center Front/Center Back Fold line, at the top of it. This will be the Blouse Top line.

Step 3. On the Blouse Top line mark off the entire Blouse Top measurement (Measurement 2).

The complete Blouse Top measurement is used for half the blouse pattern so that the blouse will have double fullness.

Step 4. Draw a line downward from the Blouse Top at a 45-degree angle, to make the Diagonal Seam (See Figure 94).

Step 5. Mark off the Diagonal Seam length (Measurement 3) on the Diagonal Seam line.

Step 6. At the end of the Diagonal Seam line, draw a line parallel to the Center Front/Center Back Fold line to create the Side Seam line.

Step 7. Connect the Side Seam line and the Center Front/Center Back Fold line to create the blouse Hem line.

Step 8. Add seam allowances, and the pattern for the body of the blouse is complete. Leave a large enough allowance at the top of the blouse to make a casing for a drawstring or an elastic. At the bottom of the blouse, leave a seam allowance sufficient for the desired width of the hem. The Side Seam and the Diagonal Seam need only the standard 5/8″ seam allowance.

Drafting The Sleeve

Step 1. Draw a line the length of the sleeve (Measurement 4). This is the Sleeve Fold line.

Step 2. At one end of the Sleeve Fold line, draw a line perpendicular to it. This will be the Sleeve Top line.

Step 3. Mark off the complete Sleeve Top measurement on the Sleeve Top line (Measurement 1). As with the blouse top, the complete measurement is used for half the pattern so that the sleeve will have double fullness when finished.

Step 4. Draw a line downward and to the left, at a 45-degree angle from the Sleeve Top line. This will be the Diagonal Seam line.

Step 5. Measure off the Diagonal Seam length on the Diagonal Seam line (Measurement 3). At this point, draw a line parallel to the Sleeve Fold line, to create the Sleeve Seam line.

Step 6. Draw a line connecting the Sleeve Fold line to the Sleeve Seam line, and running parallel to the Sleeve Top. This is the Sleeve Hem line.

STEP 7. Add seam allowances and the pattern will be complete. As with the Blouse Body pattern, be sure to allow a wide enough seam allowance at the Sleeve Top to make a casing for an elastic or a drawstring. Leave an appropriate allowance for a casing at the Sleeve Hem line also, as this will be gathered in the finished blouse. The Sleeve Seam and the Diagonal Seam need only the standard ⅝″ seam allowances.

CUTTING THE BLOUSE

To cut the blouse body: Place the Center Back/Center Front Fold line on the fold of the fabric, on the straight of the goods. Cut two, one for the blouse front and one for the blouse back.

To cut the sleeves: Place the Sleeve Fold line on the fold of the fabric on the straight of the goods. Cut two.

SEWING THE PEASANT BLOUSE

STEP 1. Sew the casings for the sleeve tops and hem and for the front and back blouse tops.

STEP 2. Join the sleeves and blouse sections on the Diagonal Seam lines, alternating blouse front, sleeve, blouse back, sleeve. The blouse top and sleeve top casings form the neckline of the blouse. This neckline will appear extremely wide until it is gathered by elastic or a drawstring, because it is cut double fullness. When sewing the diagonal seams, stop at the casings; do not sew them closed.

STEP 3. On each side, sew up the side seams and the sleeve seams in one long, continuous seam. Do not sew the casings closed.

STEP 4. Hem the blouse.

STEP 5. Insert elastic or drawstrings in neckline and sleeve casings, adjusting the final length of elastic to achieve desired neckline and sleeve widths. The points where blouse top and the sleeve top casings join at the neckline should be sewn closed by hand. Close the bottom sleeve casings by hand also.

SLEEVE VARIATION III: THE RAGLAN SLEEVE

The raglan sleeve, which is illustrated in Diagram A of Figure 95, may be drafted by altering the basic bodice pattern.

STEP 1. Trace the basic bodice front pattern and draw a line on the bodice where the sleeve seam is to go (See Diagram B of Figure 95). This usually intersects with the armhole just at the point where the armhole starts to curve to the side.

STEP 2. Cut on the line established in Step 1.

STEP 3. Follow the same procedure for the back pattern, using the basic bodice back pattern.

STEP 4. Attach the cut portions of the bodice to the fitted sleeve pattern by taping the armhole curve to the sleeve cap curve, as shown in Figure 95. Since the bodice curves will not match the sleeve cap edge exactly, the bodice sections will have to overlap the sleeve cap somewhat. The side point and the center point of the bodice section should coincide with the edge of the sleeve cap. The front and back bodice sections should meet at the center of the top of the sleeve.

The resultant sleeve has a shoulder dart, created by the original Shoulder Seam line. This dart ends at the point of the shoulder.

STEP 5. Trace the raglan sleeve pattern onto another sheet of paper, add seam allowances, and cut.

To avoid confusion in assembling the sleeve pieces, it is helpful to mark the front and back sections of the bodice before cutting them. Also mark the front and the back of the sleeve cap on the sleeve pattern.

RAGLAN SLEEVE

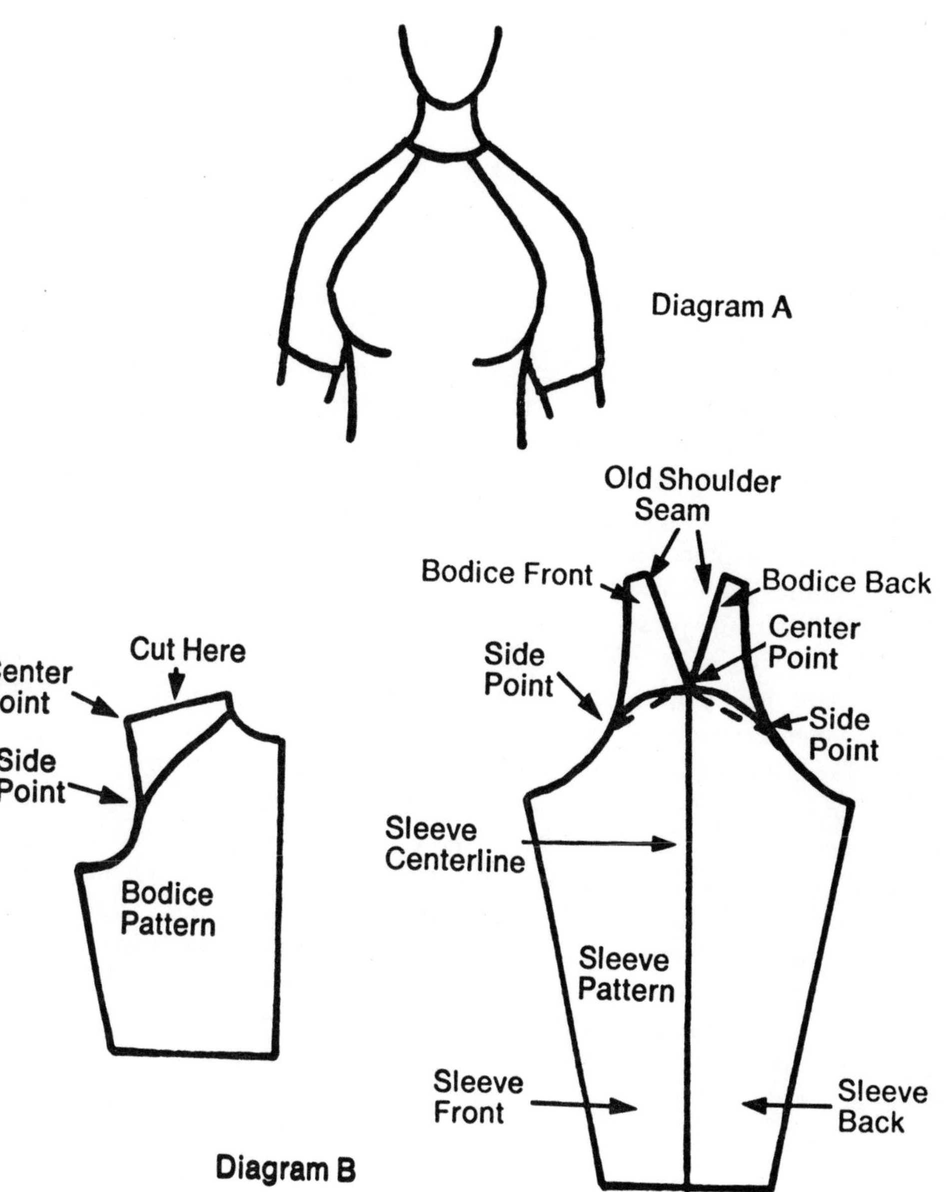

Figure 95

DEMONSTRATION LESSONS

THE READER BY NOW SHOULD HAVE a set of basic patterns and a general knowledge of the techniques used to adapt them to produce different patterns. In this section the application and adaptation of the fundamentals to the creation of contemporary clothes will be illustrated by a series of demonstration lessons. These demonstrations are meant to help the reader see how the different techniques are applied. Even if the reader has no intention of producing the actual garments, these chapters should be read carefully. The lessons go from the simpler problems to the more complex ones. They will build upon the skills already presented.

No book could possibly tell the reader how to draft every garment he could possibly conceive of. However, by observing how general techniques are applied to particular problems, the reader will begin to acquire a sense of how individual problems may be solved. In the end, it is this sense of how best to approach the drafting of a new design which constitutes the art and craft of drafting.

For those who have the time and strong enough interest, it is urged that each pattern described be drafted. Those who proceed from the pattern to make a trial muslin will gain the satisfaction and assurance of learning how the pattern works in fabric. If the reader lacks the time to draft full-size patterns, the techniques may be tried by making scaled-down patterns on 9″ × 12″ tracing paper. ¼″ = 1″ or ⅛″ = 1″ are good scales to use.

FLOOR LENGTH SKIRT

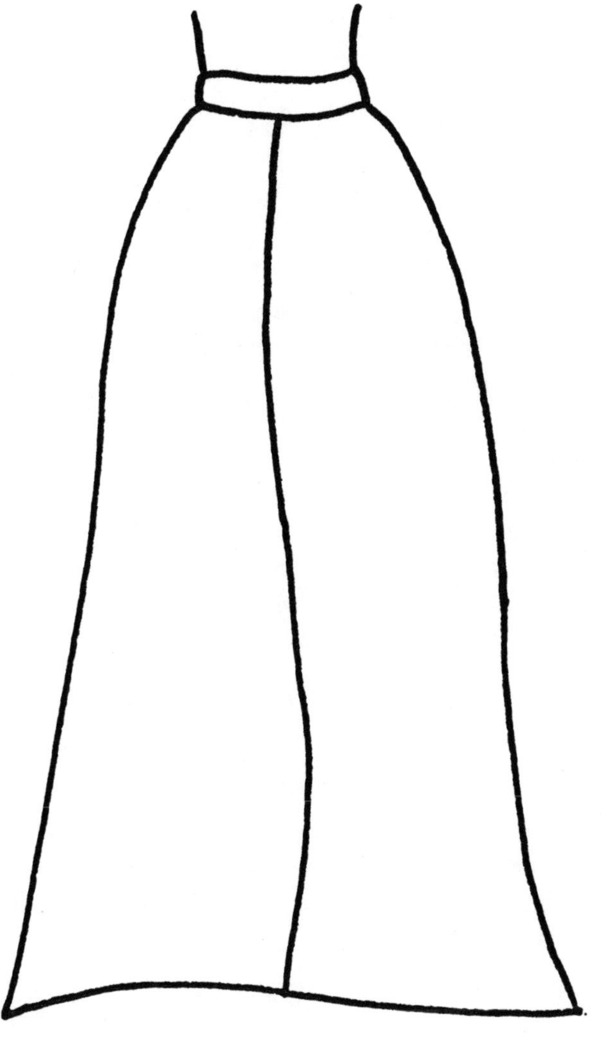

Figure 96

THE FLOOR-LENGTH SKIRT

The design illustrated in Figure 96 is a full, floor-length skirt that is not gathered at the waist. The fullness is achieved by the use of panels or gores which are wide at the bottom and taper to a fitted waist at the top.

This pattern can be drafted by using three basic measurements: the Waist circumference; the Waist to Floor measurement; and the Hem circumference. Effectively, these measurements will create a cone. The regularity of this shape will enable each of the panels to be cut from the same pattern. This is a very simple type of pattern to draft; the method can be applied to a short skirt as well as a long one. The degree of flare will be determined by the circumference of the Hem.

The demonstration pattern will be drafted for four gores, but a skirt might have almost any number. The one factor which determines the minimum number of gores is the width of the fabric from which the skirt will be cut. For example, if the material is 36″ wide, no gore could be wider than 34″ at the bottom (with 2″ for seam allowances). Thus, a four-gore skirt made with 36″ fabric could not have a Hem circumference wider than 136″ (4 gores x 34″= 136″).

Step 1. Draw a vertical line using the Waist to Floor length. This will be the Center Front/Center Back line (Figure 97).

Step 2. At the top of this line, draw a second line at right angles to the Center Front/Center Back line and mark off one-fourth of the Waist measurement on it. (This would be one-fifth for a five-gore skirt or 2 times one-fourth the Waist for a four-gore skirt gathered with double fullness.)

Step 3. At the bottom of the Center Front/Center Back line draw another perpendicular line and make this one-fourth the Hem circumference measurement. (One-fifth for a five-gore skirt.)

SKIRT PATTERN (Steps 1 to 6)
The Basic Shape

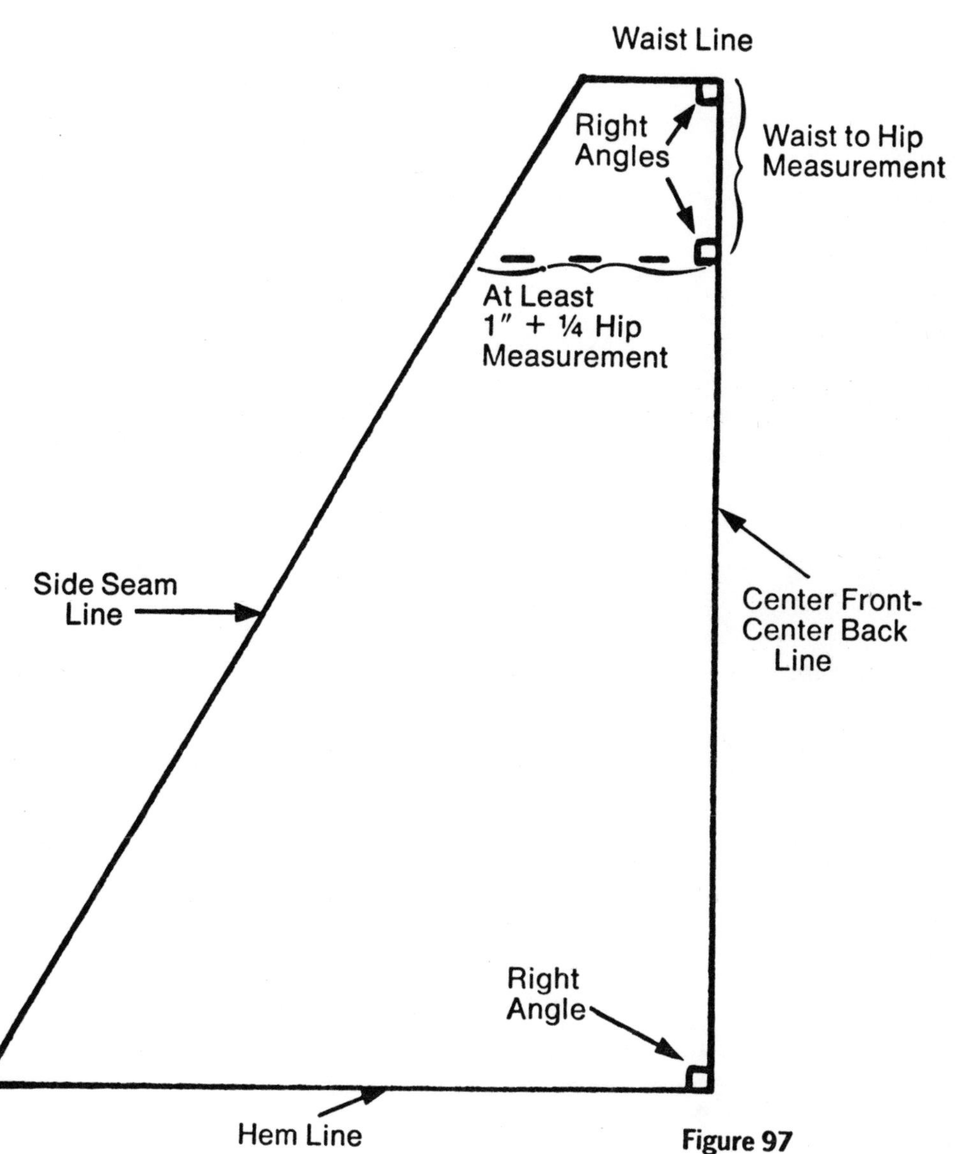

Figure 97

SKIRT PATTERN (Steps 7 to 11)

Curving the Seams

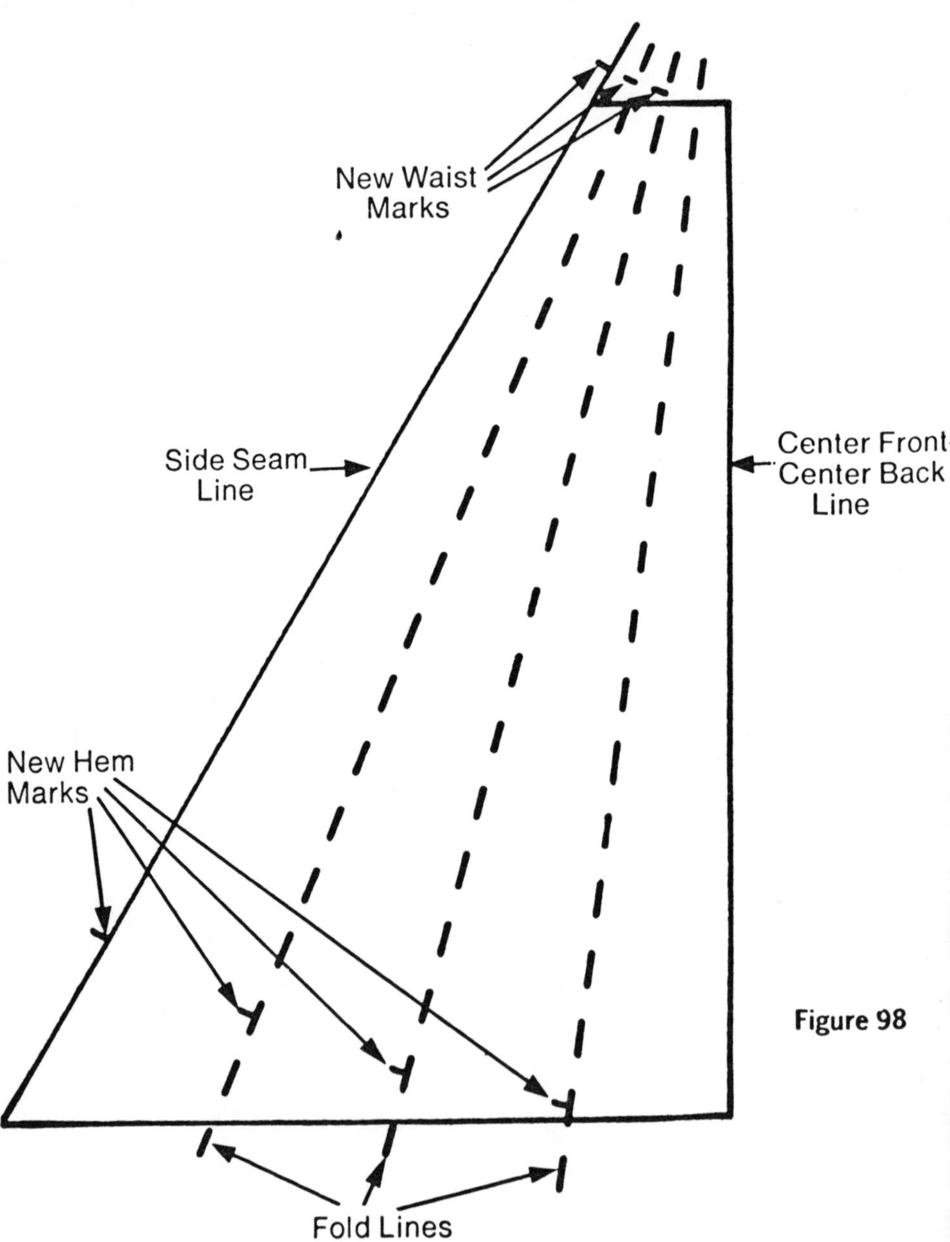

Figure 98

STEP 4. Connect the end of the Waist line to the end of the Hem line. This will form the Side Seam line.

At this point the pattern is checked to make sure that there is sufficient girth at the hips.

STEP 5. Measure down the Center Front/Center Back line the distance of the Waist to Hip measurement.

STEP 6. Measure across the pattern from this point to the Side Seam line with the measuring stick parallel to the Waist line. This measurement should be at least 1″ plus one-fourth the Hip measurement. If this is not the case, the pattern will have to be altered by extending the Side Seam to this distance.

The curve of the Waist and the Hem must now be determined (Figure 98). The procedure for doing this is the same as the procedure for curving the seam lines of the Mandarin collar.

STEP 7. Fold the Center Front/Center Back line to meet the Side Seam line. The gore pattern is tapered at Side Seam; therefore the Center Front/Center Back line will coincide with the Side Seam line above the original Waist and Hem lines.

STEP 8. Mark the new Hem and Waist points onto the Side Seam line taking them from the Center Front/Center Back line.

STEP 9. Fold the pattern in fourths.

STEP 10. Move the Center Front/Center Back line so that it intersects with the fold lines created by Step 9. Mark the Waist and Hem points on each of these folds.

STEP 11. Connect these points to create a curved Waist and Hem line (See Figure 99).

SKIRT PATTERN (Steps 12 to 14)
The Finishing Touches

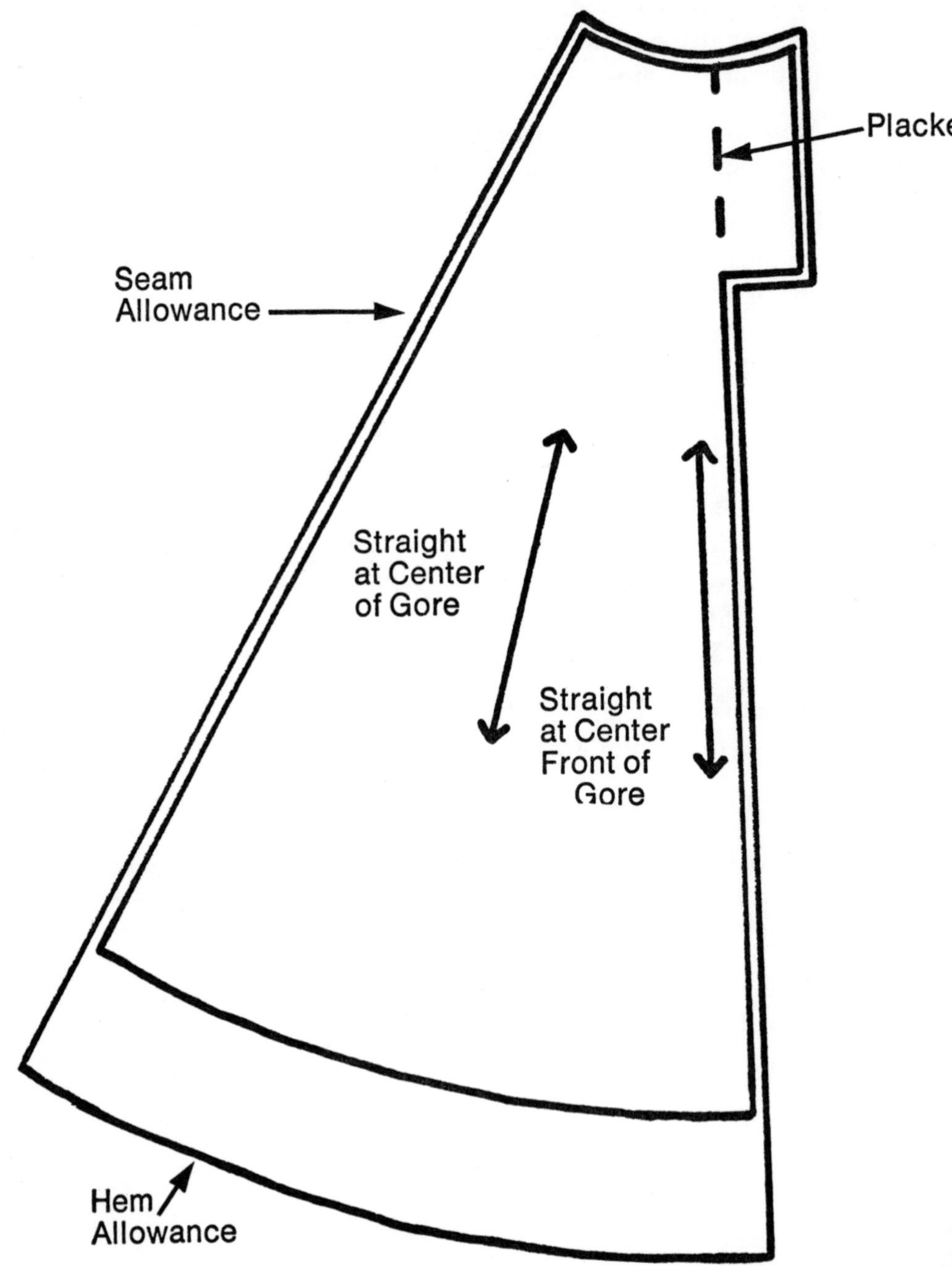

Figure 99

Step 12. Add a placket to the Side Seam line or to the Center Back seam.

Step 13. Add seam and hem allowances (Figure 99).

Step 14. The straight of the goods of the gore should now be determined. It is possible to place the straight on the center of the gore. This will distribute the fullness evenly around the skirt. Or the straight may coincide with the Center Back and the Center Front seams, which will cause the fullness to fall primarily towards the sides of the skirt.

Step 15. Draft a waistband.

The skirt pattern is now complete.

Figure 100

PATTERN FOR FITTED TOP (Steps 1 to 6)
Drawing the Shape

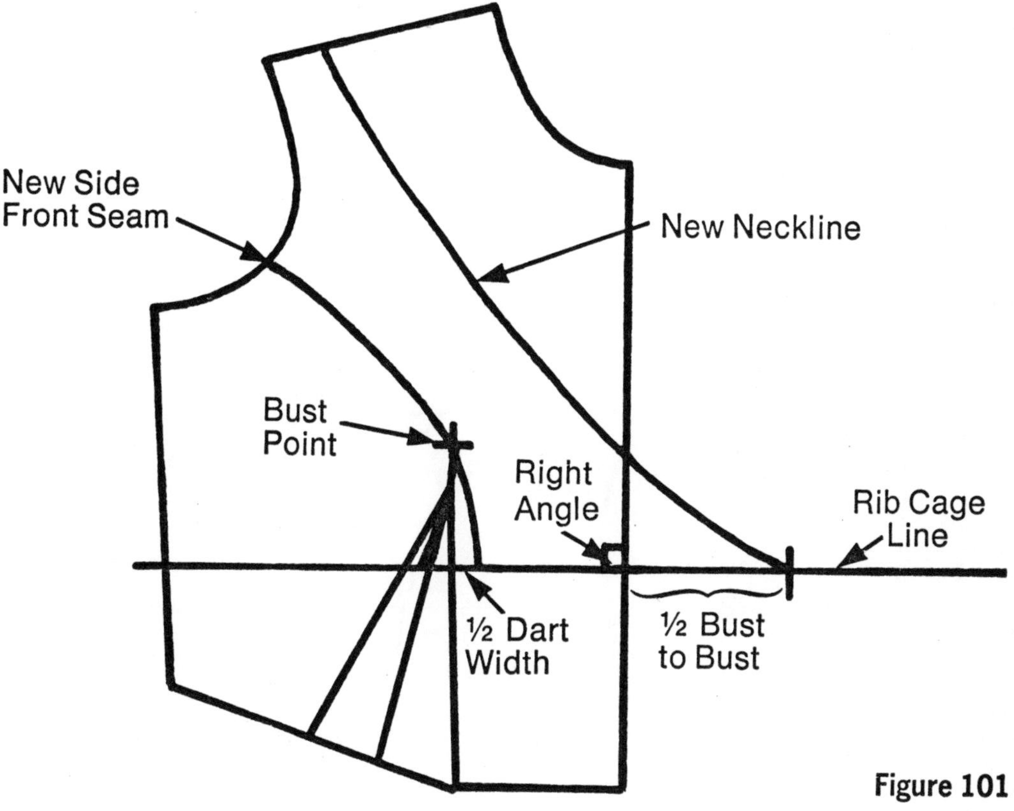

Figure 101

THE HIGH-WAISTLINE FORMAL

The dress illustrated in Figure 100 has a fitted top and a full skirt combined in a single garment. The top will be drafted by adapting the basic bodice pattern. This section will then be fitted. The skirt will be drafted using the fitted-top pattern as a reference.

The closure for this gown is made on the wrap-around principle, with the right side of the garment overlapping the left side.

Front Pattern For The Fitted Top

The basic bodice pattern will be used for drafting the top sec-

Cutting the Pattern

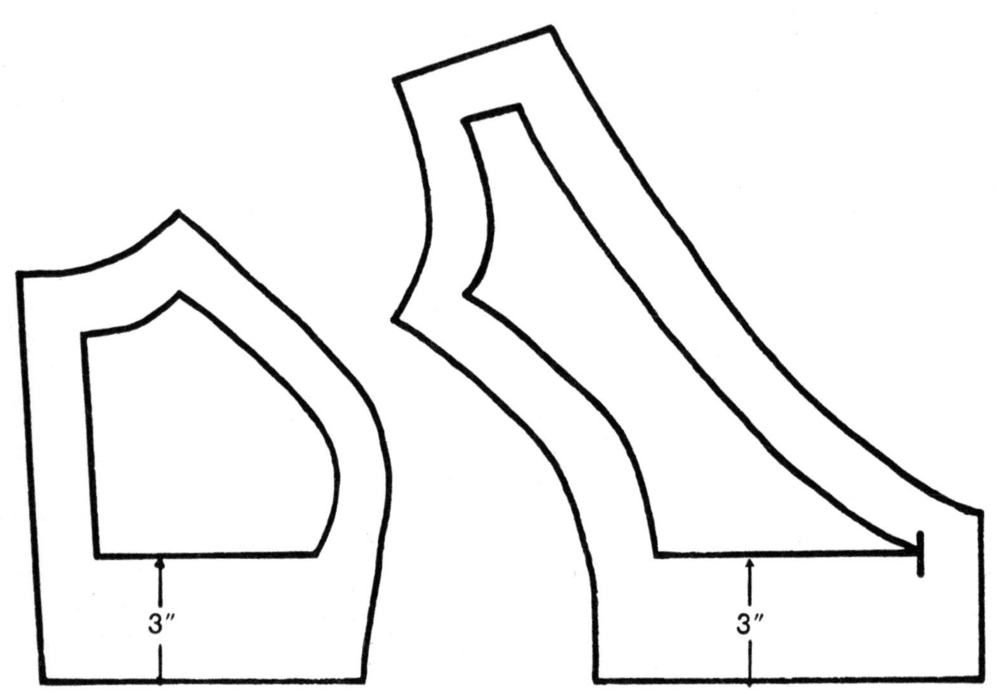

Figure 102

tion. This pattern will supply certain reference points which will then be adapted to achieve the desired design.

STEP 1. Trace the Basic Bodice Front pattern onto a new sheet of paper, marking the Bust Point and Dart onto the new pattern.

STEP 2. Measure down from the neck along the Center Front line the Neck to Rib Cage measurement and mark this point (Figure 101).

Step 3. Draw a line at right angles to the Center Front line at the Rib Cage point. This line should extend to both sides of the Center Front line because of the wrap-around feature of the dress.

Step 4. On the Rib Cage line mark a point one-half of the Bust to Bust measurement to the right of the Center Front line. This is the reference point for the opening of the garment.

Step 5. Sketch in the neckline of the dress, following the neckline of the design.

Step 6. Sketch in the Side Front seam. The inside portion of the seam passes through the Bust Point and intersects with the Rib Cage line one-half the Dart Width to the right of the dart. The other seam passes through the Dart Centerline. The correct Dart Width at the Rib Cage line is maintained in this way.

Step 7. Cut out the pattern at the Side Front seam. Trace the two parts of the front pattern on another sheet of paper and add seam allowances (Figure 102). A 3″ or 4″ seam allowance should be added at the raised waistline.

Back Pattern For The Fitted Top

The back pattern can be drafted using the bodice pattern for the back. Two alterations will be necessary.

Step 1. Alter the neckline (Figure 103). Be sure the Shoulder Seam for the back is the same length as the Shoulder Seam for the front.

Step 2. Mark in the new raised waistline at the Rib Cage length.

Step 3. Add seam allowances and cut the pattern out.

Fitting The Top

The top section of this particular design is meant to be carefully fitted. For this reason, and because of the extreme adaptation of the basic pattern, it is suggested that a trial muslin copy be cut out,

PATTERN FOR FITTED TOP (Steps 1 to 3)

The Back Section

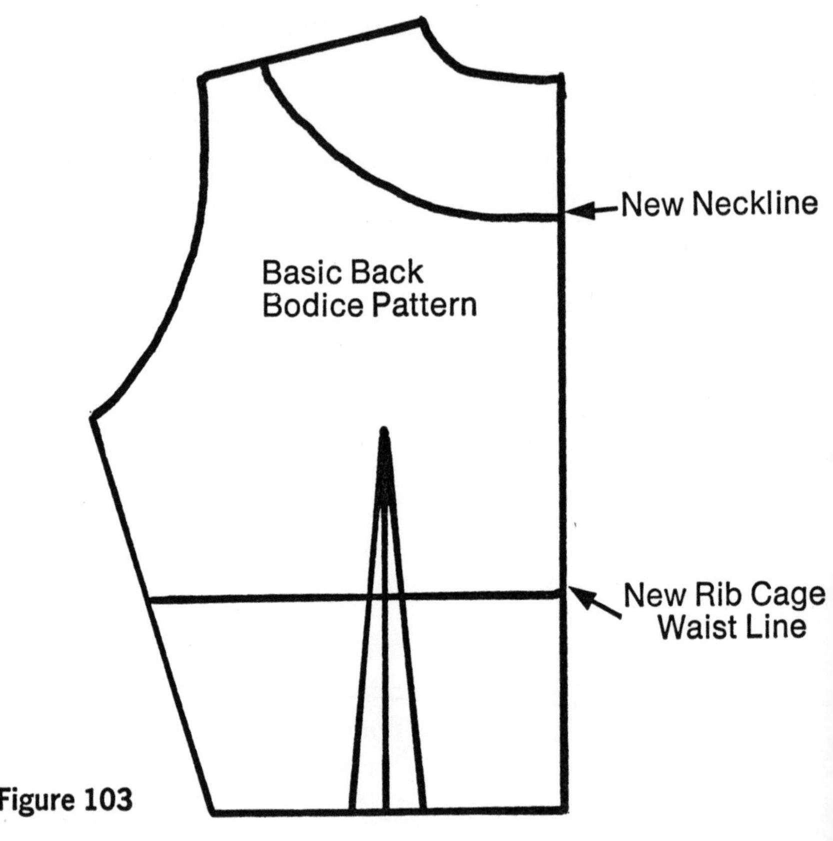

Figure 103

sewn and fitted. Sew all the seams and pin the opening closed for the fitting.

The normal fitting adjustments should be made at the shoulder seam and the side seams. Great care should be taken with the side front seam as this is the unique aspect of this particular design. Care should also be taken with fitting the waistline of this garment. It is meant to fit the rib cage snugly, otherwise the skirt will not hang properly. Some allowance will have to be left at the waistline for the fullness of the skirt when it is added. It is best to leave adequate seam allowances at the side to adjust for this.

FRONT PATTERN FOR SKIRT (Steps 1 to 8)

The Basic Dimensions

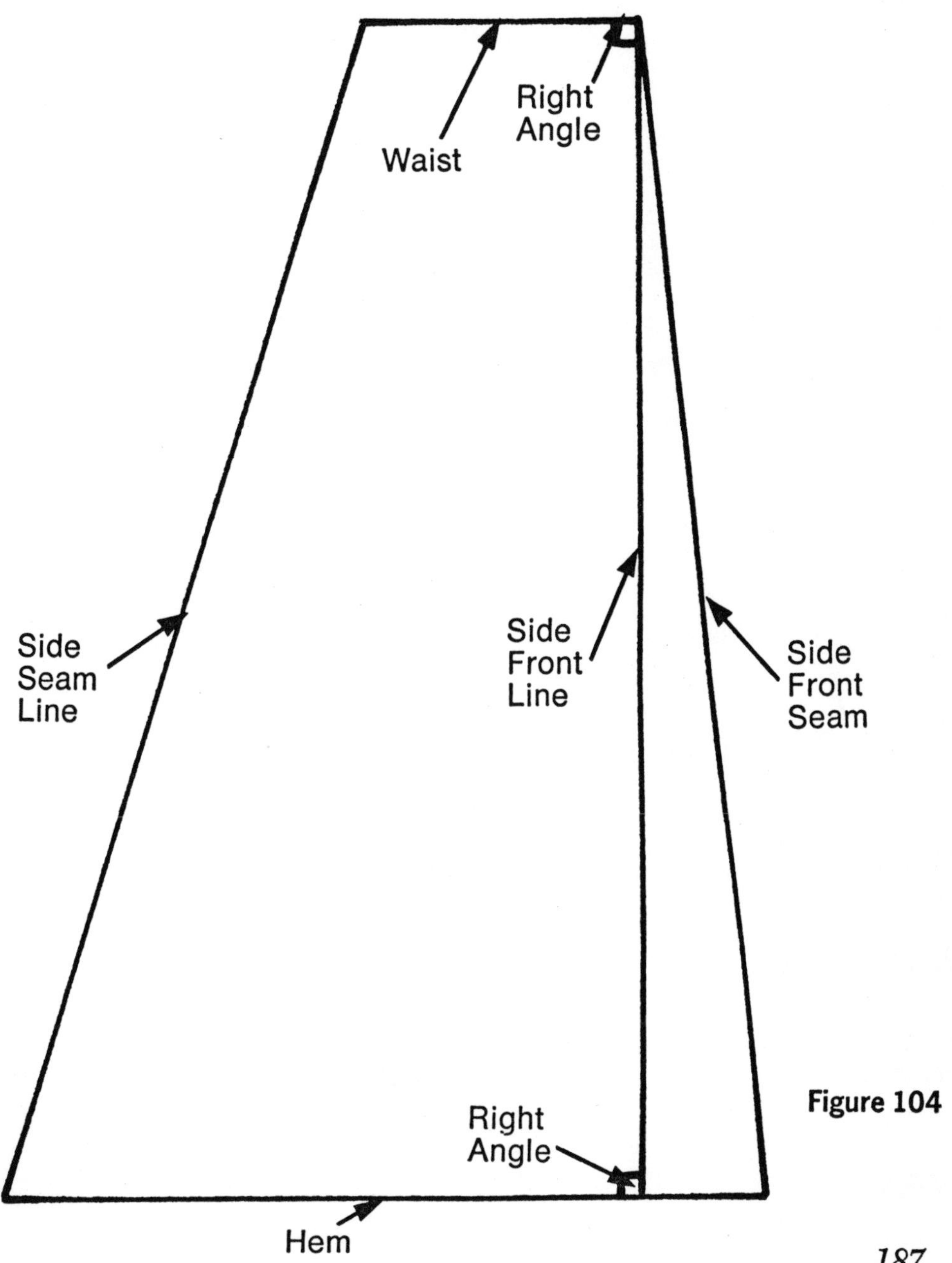

Figure 104

BACK PATTERN FOR SKIRT (Steps 1 to 4)

The Basic Dimensions

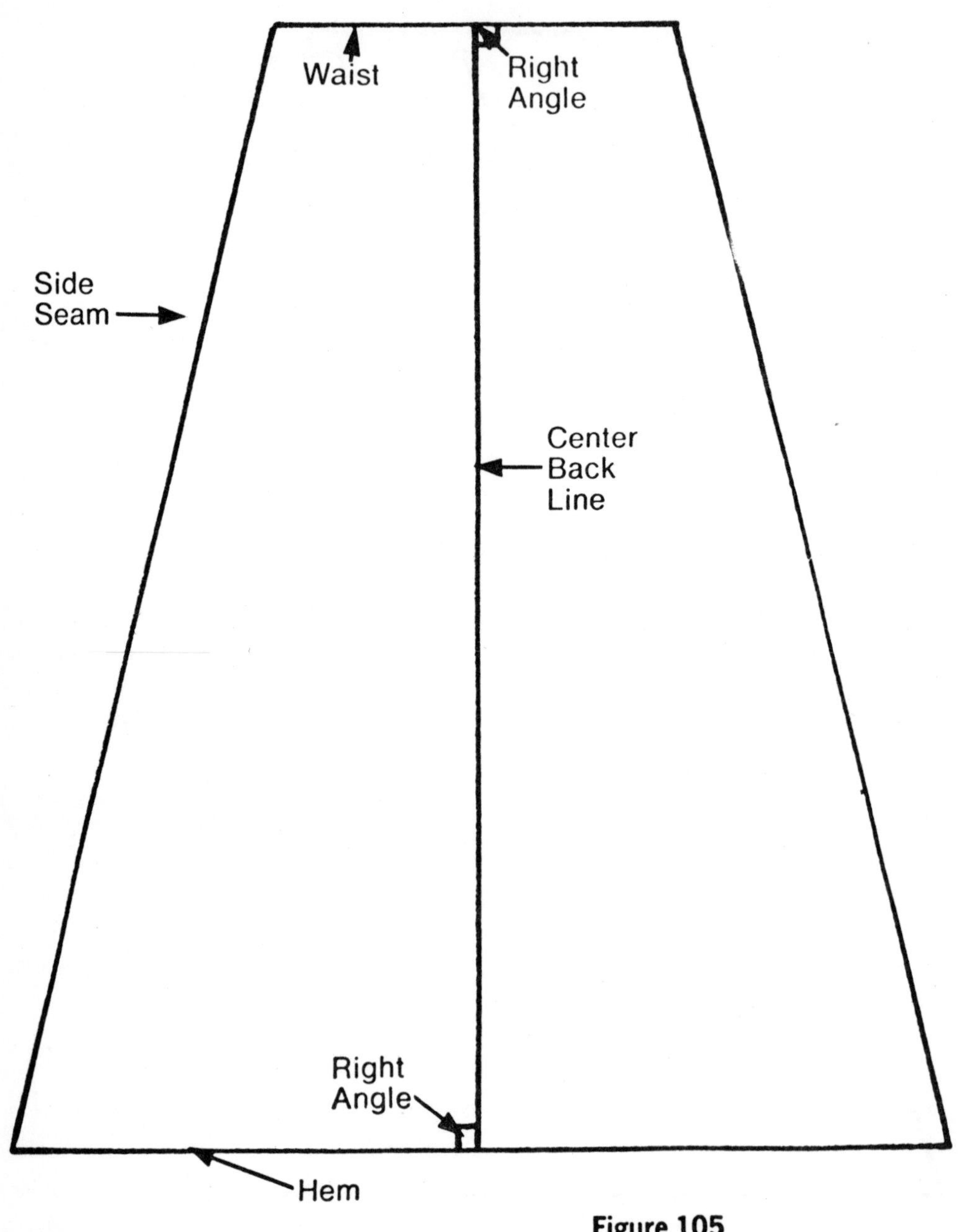

Figure 105

Front Skirt Pattern

After the top has been drafted and fitted, the skirt may be drafted to fit onto it at the raised waistline.

Step 1. Measure the front of the top section where the skirt is to be attached. This should be measured while the Side Front seam is still sewn closed.

Step 2. Draw a horizontal line of this length (Figure 104). This will be the Waist line.

Step 3. Draw a vertical line down from the right end of this line. This will be the Side Front line.

Step 4. Mark the Rib Cage to Floor distance on this line.

Step 5. At the bottom of the Side Front line draw a line parallel to the Waist line. This will be the Hem line.

Step 6. Slope the Side Front seam slightly to the right of the Side Front line, as shown in Figure 104.

Step 7. From the intersection of the Side Front seam and the Hem line measure off the desired Hem circumference for the front. Some alteration to this measurement may be necessary if the pattern does not look right.

Step 8. Draw in the Side seam.

Step 9. The Waist line and the Hem line may now be curved (See pages 178-179.)

Step 10. Add seam allowances and hem allowances. A five- or six-inch facing allowance may be added to the Side Front seam or this may be cut separately. The pattern is now ready to be cut.

Back Skirt Pattern

The back pattern is drafted in essentially the same manner as the front pattern. The only difference is that the Center Back line will be used as a reference line rather than the Side Front.

STEP 1. Measure the back of the top section where the skirt is to be attached. This gives the width of the Waist for the back of the skirt. Draw a Waist line of this length.

STEP 2. Draw the Center Back line at right angles to the Waist line. Extend the Center Back line down to the Hem length.

STEP 3. Draw a Hem line of the desired length, as shown in Figure 105.

STEP 4. Draw in the Side Seams.

STEP 5. Curve the Waist line and the Hem line.

STEP 6. Add seam allowances and cut. The Center Back line may be used as a fold line for this pattern.

THE A-LINE DRESS

The patterns drafted so far have illustrated the technique of drafting a pattern from a few basic measurements (the floor-length skirt), and the technique of adapting the basic pattern to create an original design (the formal dress). The next garment to be considered will demonstrate how the drafting process may be combined with the draping process to achieve a given design.

The body of the dress illustrated in Figure 106 has a fitted top from the shoulder to just below the bust. The rib cage to waist area is nipped but does not fit as tightly as the fitted bodice. The top of the skirt section leaves a sufficient allowance for the movement of the hips without being too full. The bottom of the skirt flares out from the hips. The opening is a zipper in the Center Back seam.

The sleeves are fitted down to the elbow. From there, they flare out slightly to the wrist.

A-LINE DRESS

Figure 106

Front Pattern For The Dress

The front pattern of this dress will be partly drafted and partially draped. It will be drafted to just below the underarm dart. The rough proportions for the rest of the dress will then be drawn in. The actual shape will be determined by draping it.

Step 1. Trace the Basic Bodice pattern, pivoting half of the dart to the underarm seam.

Step 2. Extend the Center Front line down to the desired Hem length.

Step 3. At the bottom of the extended Center Front line draw a perpendicular line for the Hem line. Mark off one-fourth of the desired Hem circumference.

Step 4. Connect the bottom of the Armhole curve to the side of the Hem line.

Step 5. Extend the end of the dart to the Side Seam line. Do not worry about shaping the point of the dart at this time as this can be done during the fitting.

Step 6. Measure down the Waist to Hip length on the Center Front line.

Step 7. Measure out from this point to the Side Seam, keeping the yardstick parallel to the Waist line. This measurement should be at least 2″ plus one-fourth of the Hip measurement. If it is not, extend the Side Seam so that it will be.

Step 8. Draw in the desired neckline.

Step 9. Add seam allowances and cut the pattern out. The Center Front line will be a fold line.

FRONT DRESS PATTERN (Steps 1 to 8)

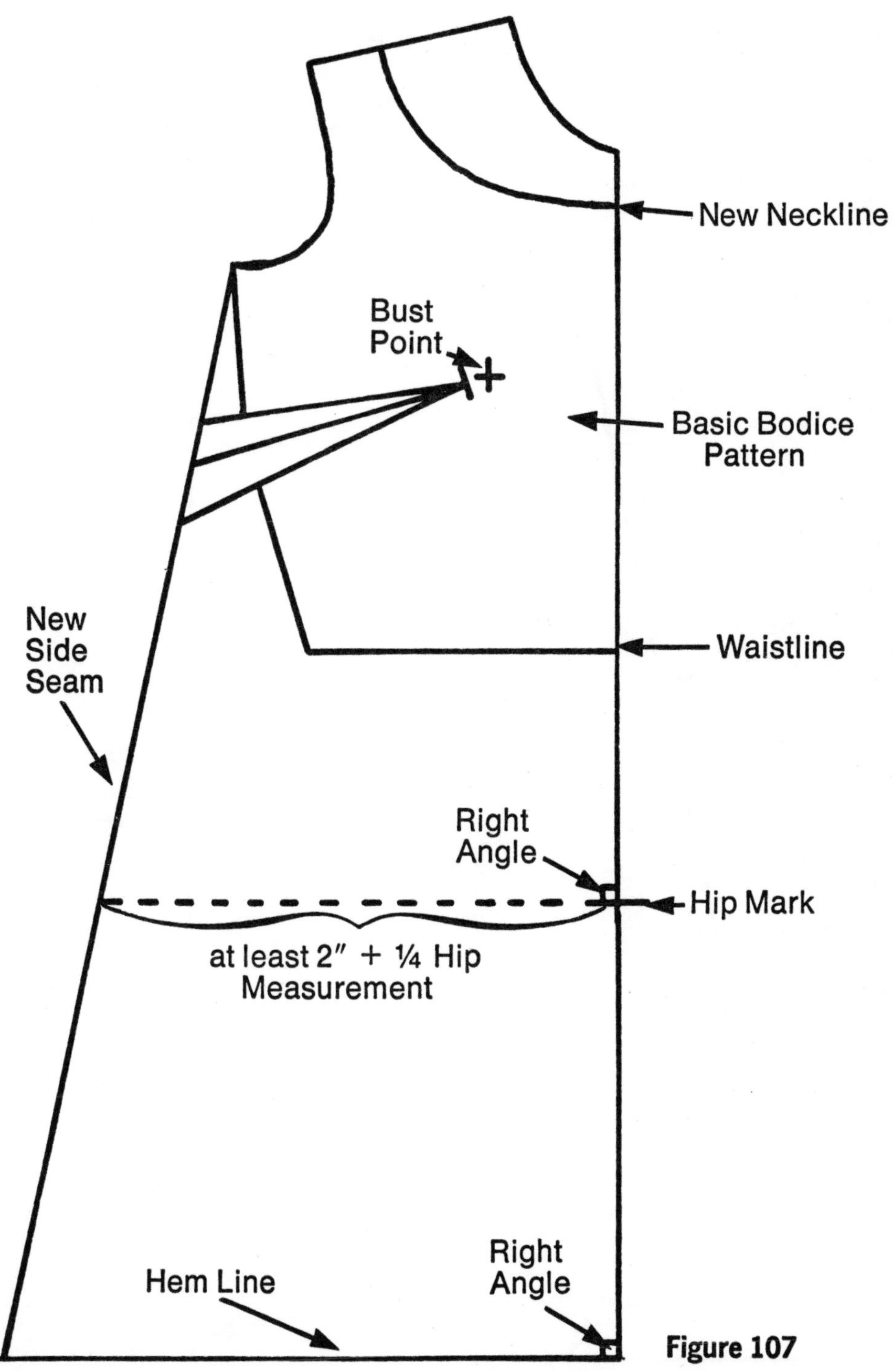

Figure 107

BACK DRESS PATTERN

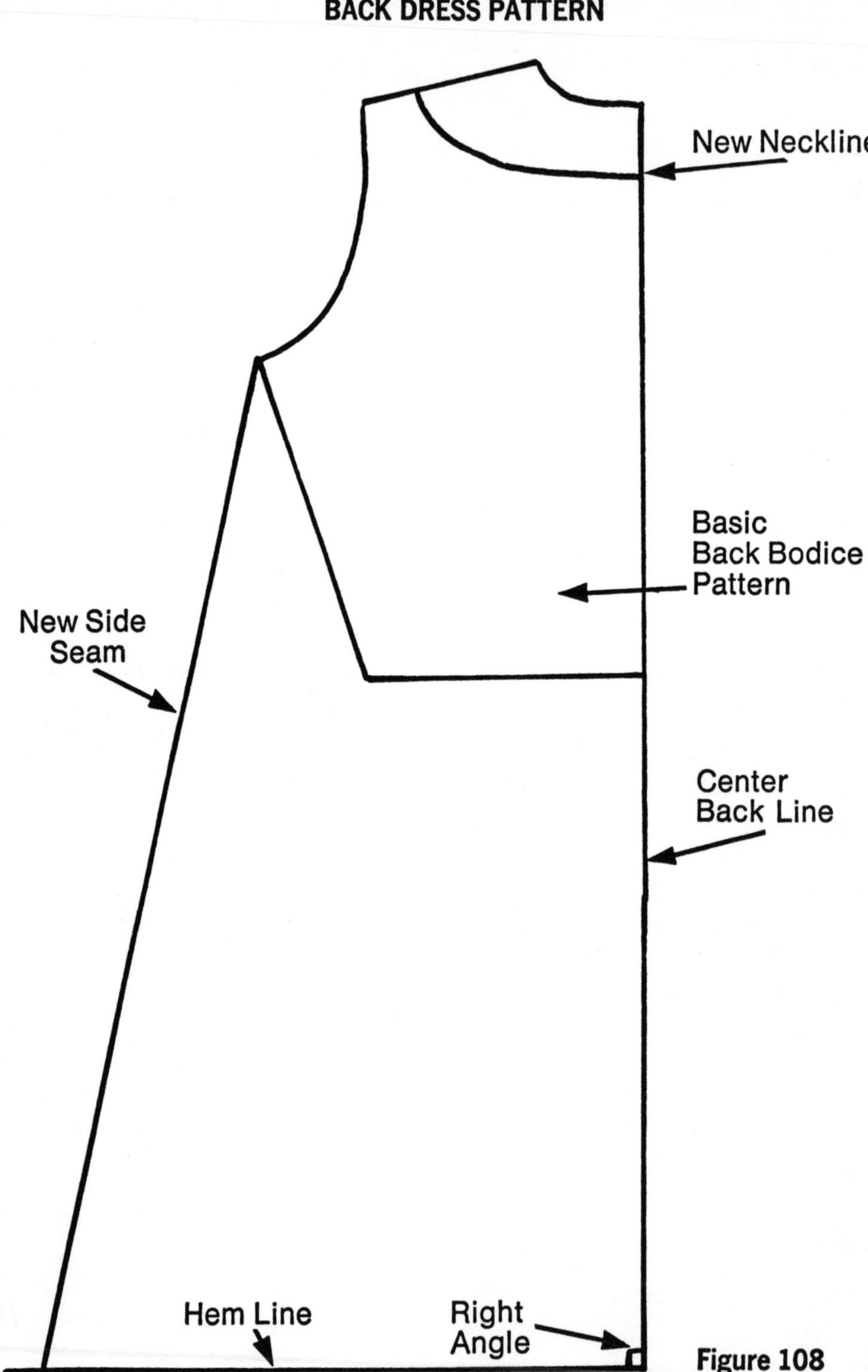

Figure 108

Back Pattern For The Dress

Step 1. Place the Basic Bodice Back pattern on a large sheet of paper and trace around it. This design may or may not include a back dart. If it is to have a back dart, this will be added during the fitting. Do not try to draft it.

Step 2. Measure down the Center Back line the required distance to the hem.

Step 3. Draw a line perpendicular to the Center Back line from this point. This will be the Hem line.

Step 4. Mark on the Hem line one-fourth of the Hem circumference.

Step 5. Connect the bottom of the Armhole curve to this point. This will be the new Side Seam line.

Step 6. Redraw the back neckline so that the width of the shoulder seam is the same width in the back as it is in the front. The back neckline should dip approximately 2″ below the shoulder of the dress.

Step 7. Add ample seam allowances and a hem allowance. It is always best to have an excessively large hem allowance for a dress since it may easily be shortened.

Fitting The A-Line Dress

Cut out the dress in muslin. Mark the Side Dart and pin it closed. Pin the Shoulder Seam and the Side Seams to just above the dart. The back seam will be pinned once the dress has been put on for the fitting.

Step 1. Check the top of the dress for the correct fit. Adjust the side dart so that the fabric fits from the shoulder to the chest area.

Step 2. Draw in the desired neckline. The muslin neckline may be cut to the desired finished shape, but mark this carefully so that seam allowances can be added later.

Once the upper portion of the dress has been fitted, the lower portion may be draped to the desired design.

STEP 3. Adjust the diagonal dart so that the front of the dress shapes in from the chest to the waist. This dart may be either straight or curved. It should end at the Side Waist point. A back dart may be added if desired.

STEP 4. Pin the front half of the dress to the back half, adjusting the seams to the desired fit.

STEP 5. Mark the seam lines and dart lines carefully with a felt-tip pen. Mark the end of the dart for the correct shaping.

STEP 6. The dress may now be taken off and unpinned.

STEP 7. Go over the marks carefully and machine baste the muslin together. The Center Back seam may be sewn to just above the hips. The rest of the seam will have to be pinned temporarily.

STEP 8. Try the dress on for a final fitting and correct as necessary.

STEP 9. Trace the corrected muslin onto paper to make a final pattern. Be sure the neckline has the correct seam allowances added. Change the other seams to a standard size. The final hem line does not need to be marked until the actual dress is sewn together.

THE SLEEVE PATTERN

The fitted sleeve can be used as the basis for this pattern.

STEP 1. Trace the fitted sleeve pattern onto a new piece of paper (Figure 109).

STEP 2. Measure the desired circumference of the bottom of the sleeve.

STEP 3. Mark this measurement on the bottom of the sleeve.

STEP 4. Reshape the side seams.

SLEEVE PATTERN (Steps 1 to 5)

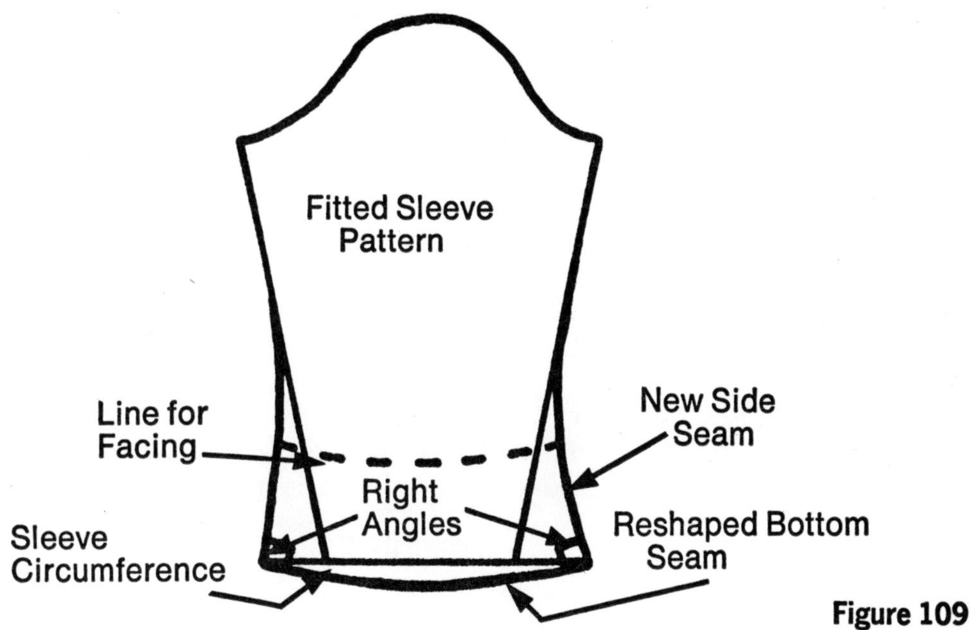

Figure 109

Step 5. Reshape the bottom of the sleeve in a gentle curve so that the bottom of the sleeve meets the side seams at right angles.

Step 6. Add seam allowances and cut.

Facings

Facings will be required for both the neckline and the bottom of the sleeves.

Step 1. Trace the neckline and the shoulder seams of both the front and the back patterns onto a sheet of paper.

Step 2. Remove the paper and draw a second curve 3″ in on the pattern. This pattern will be the facing for the neckline.

Step 3. Follow the same procedure for a facing for the bottom of the sleeve. It will probably be necessary to make a 5″ or 6″ facing for the sleeve.

All facings are made on this principle: a flat duplication of whatever curve is to be faced.

THE FULL-SLEEVED SHIRT

Shirts such as the one illustrated in Figure 110 are the same shape as the basic bodice pattern except that they are expanded in width. They may have a close-fitting waist or they may hang straight down from the chest. In any case they are extended to hip length so that they may be tucked into pants.

The sleeve for this design is the basic fitted sleeve which has been expanded at the bottom and gathered into a cuff. The collar is a version of the basic shirt collar pattern.

Pattern For The Body

The bodice pattern will be used as the basis for the shirt pattern. The following alterations will have to be made.

THE SHIRT

Figure 110

SHIRT PATTERN (Steps 1 to 8)

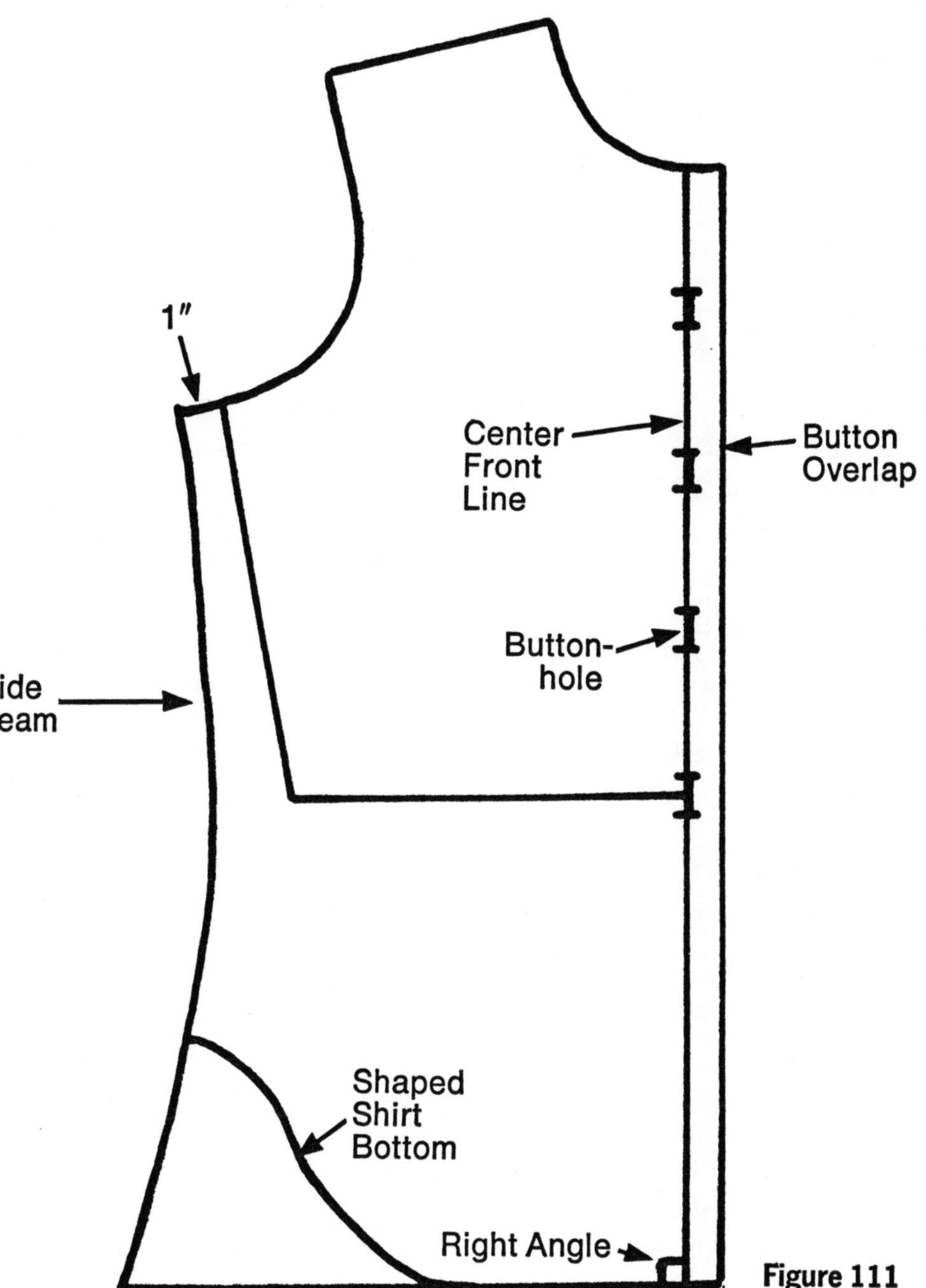

Figure 111

STEP 1. Trace the Basic Bodice Front pattern onto a new sheet of paper.

STEP 2. Extend the Center Front line down to 2″ beyond the Waist to Hip measurement (See Figure 111). Draw a perpendicular line at this point for the bottom of the shirt.

STEP 3. Mark off 2″ plus one-fourth the Hip measurement on the bottom of the shirt.

STEP 4. Extend the Side Seam out 1″ at the bottom of the Armhole curve.

STEP 5. Draw in the Side Seam line from the Armhole curve to the bottom of the shirt with the desired shape.

STEP 6. The shirt will stay tucked into the pants better, if the bottom of the shirt is shaped as indicated in Figure 111. This curve starts on the Side Seam line halfway between the waist and the bottom of the shirt. It curves to a point on the bottom of the shirt that is one-half the Across Shoulder measurement from the Center Front line.

STEP 7. Extend a line parallel to the Center Front line ¾″ away. This will be the button overlap.

STEP 8. The buttons and buttonholes are spaced with one at the collar, one at the waist, and one halfway between these two. Two more buttons are added halfway between these three buttons.

STEP 9. Add seam allowances to all the seams and a 1″ to 1½″ facing allowance to the Button Overlap line.

The back section may be drafted by following the same procedure using the Basic Bodice Back pattern. The main difference is that the Center Back line will be a fold line.

A yoke may be added to this shirt.

If this shirt is being drafted for a woman, the front dart should be pivoted to the side seam.

COLLAR PATTERN (Steps 1 to 3)

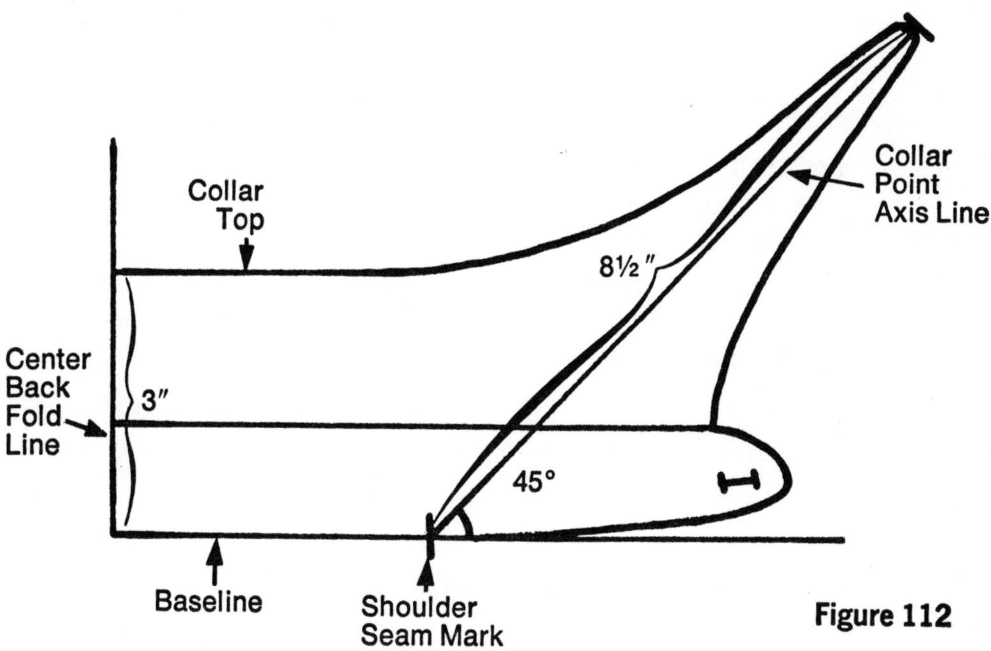

Figure 112

The Collar

The basic part of the collar may be drafted using Steps 1 to 9 for the shirt collar. (See pages 79-83.) The following steps will be needed to finish it.

Step 1. Mark the top of the collar on the Center Back Fold line 3″ from the Baseline (Figure 112).

Step 2. Mark the point of the collar 8½″ from the Baseline following the Collar Point Axis line.

Step 3. Draw in the desired collar shape.

Step 4. Add a ⅝″ seam allowance to all edges and cut out the pattern.

The Sleeve Pattern

For this design the basic sleeve pattern is adapted in the following manner.

Step 1. Trace the Basic Sleeve pattern onto another sheet of paper.

Step 2. Expand the sleeve cap 1″ to either side of the Side Seam line to compensate for the expanded chest width on the body of the shirt (Figure 113).

The bottom of the sleeve must be expanded in length and width so that it will be full at the bottom. In this case the sleeve is lengthened 4″ and the Wrist line is expanded for a total Width of 20″.

Step 3. The sleeve is to be set into a 4″ cuff. The Wrist line of the fitted sleeve is the correct length therefore for the bottom of the new sleeve. (The sleeve is shortened 4″ for the cuff, then lengthened 4″ for fullness.)

Step 4. Expand the Wrist line to 20″.

Step 5. Curve the Side Seam line of the sleeve from the Sleeve Cap to the bottom of the sleeve as illustrated in Figure 113.

Step 6. Curve the bottom of the sleeve.

In this design the sleeve is to be gathered into a cuff. The cuff will control the distribution of the fullness. If this sleeve were to be freehanging, the sleeve would be divided into two sections so that the fullness would be more evenly distributed.

Step 7. Add seam allowances and cut.

The Shirtsleeve Cuff

Shirtsleeve cuffs can come in a variety of different lengths. The short ones that are approximately one inch wide may be drafted following the simple waistband pattern. Wider cuffs, such as the one used in this shirt, should be drafted by the following technique.

SLEEVE PATTERN (Steps 1 to 7)

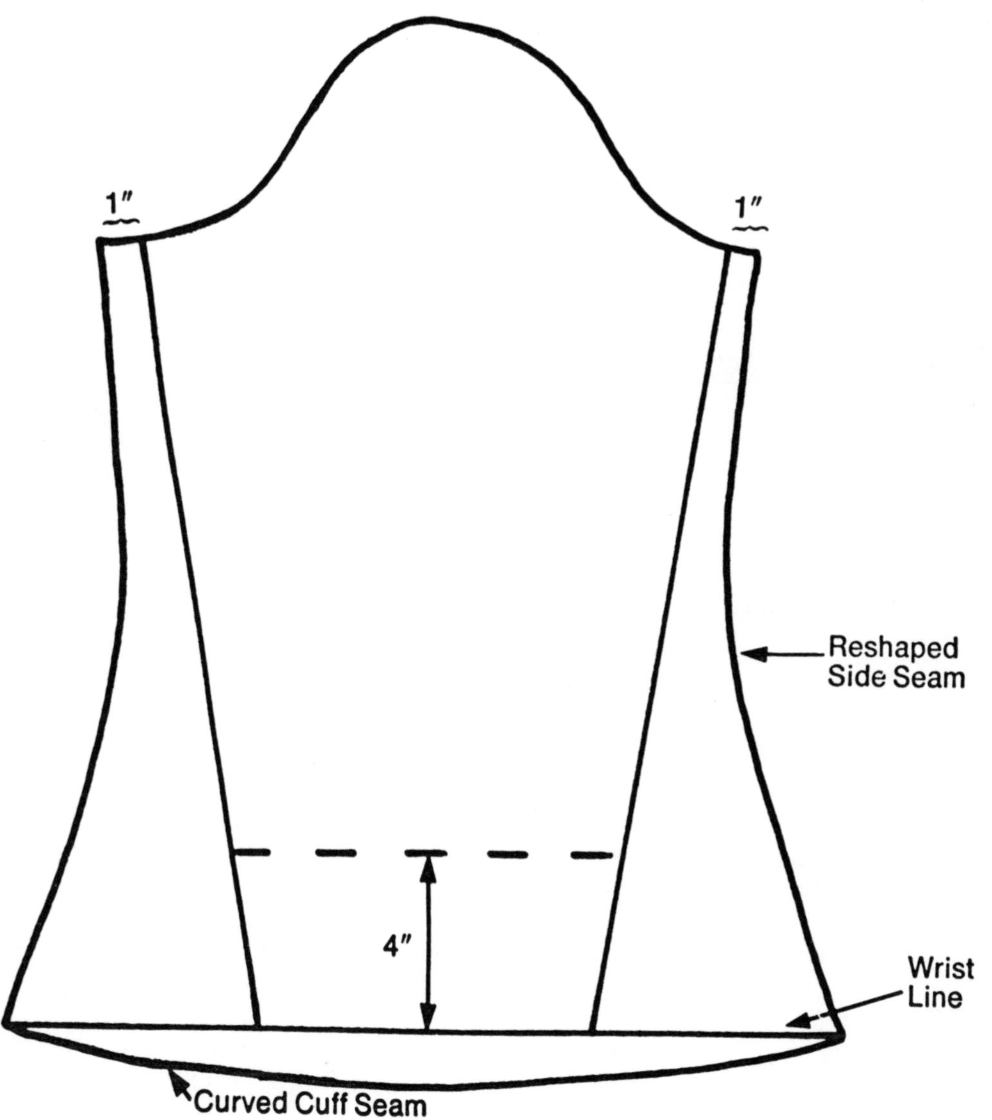

Figure 113

THE CUFF PATTERN (Steps 1 to 7)

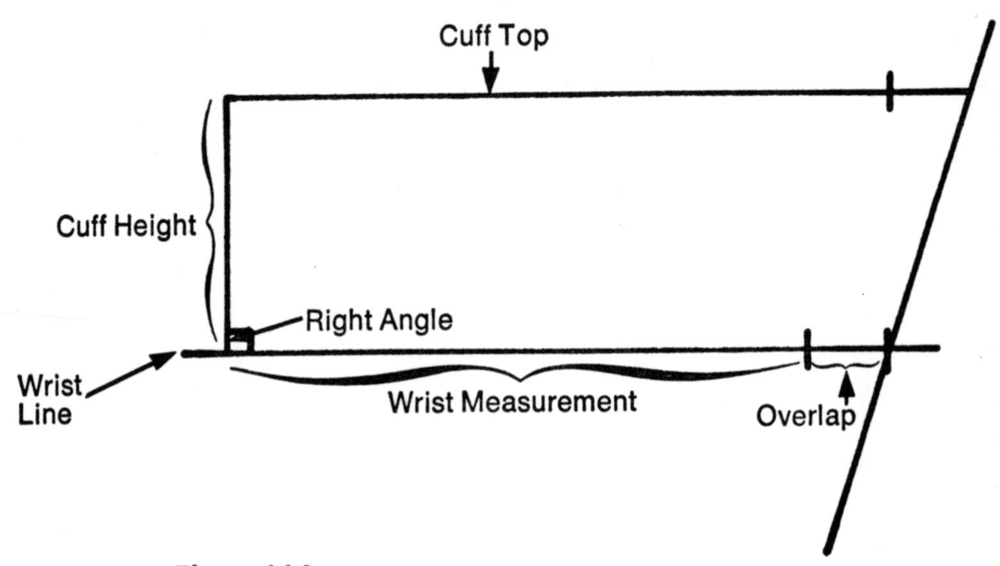

Figure 114

Step 1. Measure the arm of the person who is to wear the cuff, at the desired cuff height. This measurement should be taken over the sleeve which is to be sewn into the cuff. The material for a very full sleeve may add as much as 1″ to this measurement and an allowance for this fullness must be included. The resultant measurement will be the Cuff Top measurement.

Step 2. On a sheet of paper draw a horizontal line. This will be the Wrist line (Figure 114).

Step 3. On the Wrist line mark off a measurement which is the sum of the Wrist length and the desired amount of Cuff Overlap. The Cuff Overlap is usually ¾″ to 1″, depending on the size of the button.

Step 4. On one end of this line, draw a perpendicular line which is the desired height of the cuff. In the case of this shirt, this is 4″.

Step 5. Draw a line parallel to the Wrist line at the top of the cuff. This will be the Cuff Top line.

Step 6. Mark off the Cuff Top measurement (Step 1) plus the desired amount of Cuff Overlap on the Cuff Top line.

Step 7. Connect the end of the Wrist line to the end of the Cuff Top line.

Step 8. Curve the seam lines by the pattern-folding procedure that was described for the Mandarin Collar (pages 86-91). The pattern will look like Figure 115.

Step 9. Add ⅝″ seam allowances and cut the pattern out.

Two of these cuff patterns will be cut for each sleeve. The cuff is sewn down one side seam, across the Wrist line and up the other side seam, and then turned inside out.

THE CUFF PATTERN (Step 8)
Curving the Seam Lines

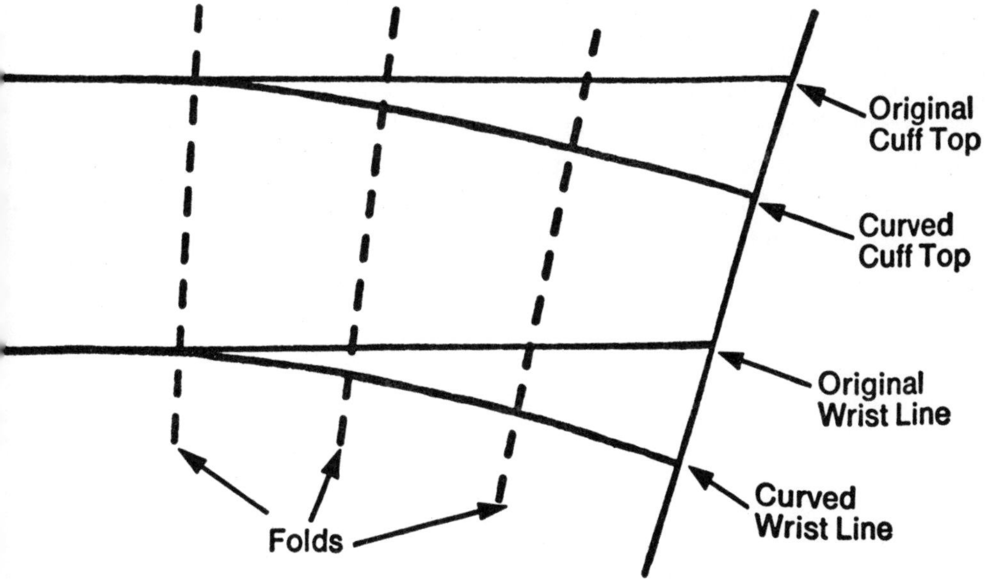

Original Cuff Top

Curved Cuff Top

Original Wrist Line

Curved Wrist Line

Folds

Figure 115

FITTED CUFF

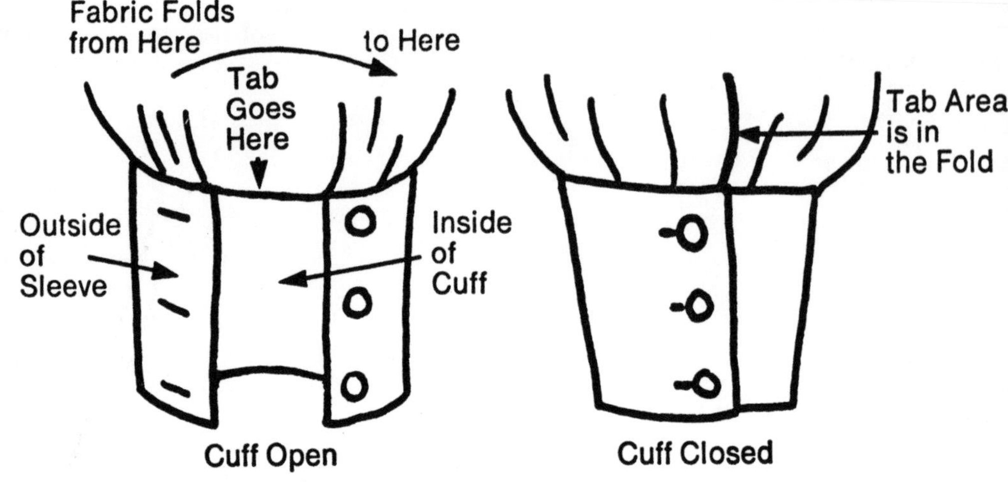

Figure 116

The Facing For The Cuff Opening

Before the sleeve can be sewn into the cuff, a provision for opening the cuff must be included (Figure 116). This is done by facing a short portion of the back of the sleeve (Figure 117). The sleeve will be set into the cuff, starting at one side of this opening, going around the sleeve and stopping at the other side of the opening. This opening will allow one side of the cuff to overlap the other side.

To insert the tab, stitch it to the right side of the sleeve hem, as shown. Clip into the corners and turn it to the inside of the sleeve as if it were a facing. Hem this tab.

CUFF OPENING

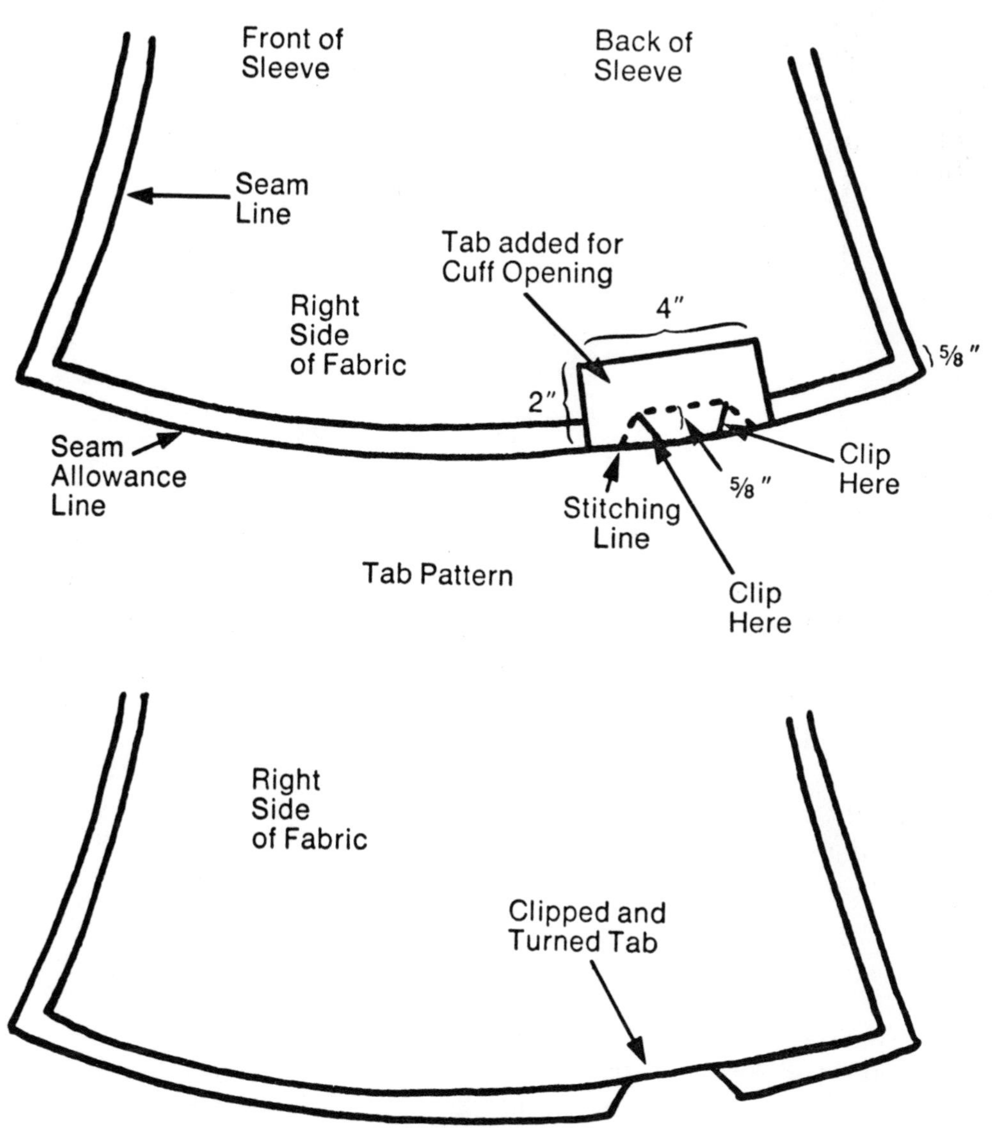

Figure 117

FLARED PANTS

Figure 118

FLARED PANTS

None of the designs illustrated so far have used decorative seams. The seams have been used primarily for shaping the garment. The flared pants in Figure 118 have decorative seams at the sides. The shape of the pants follows the basic fitted pattern down to just below the knees. From this point they flare. The decorative seams create an inset panel at the side of the pants where the side seam would normally be. This panel is 1½″ wide from the bottom of the waist-

PANTS PATTERN (Steps 1 to 6)

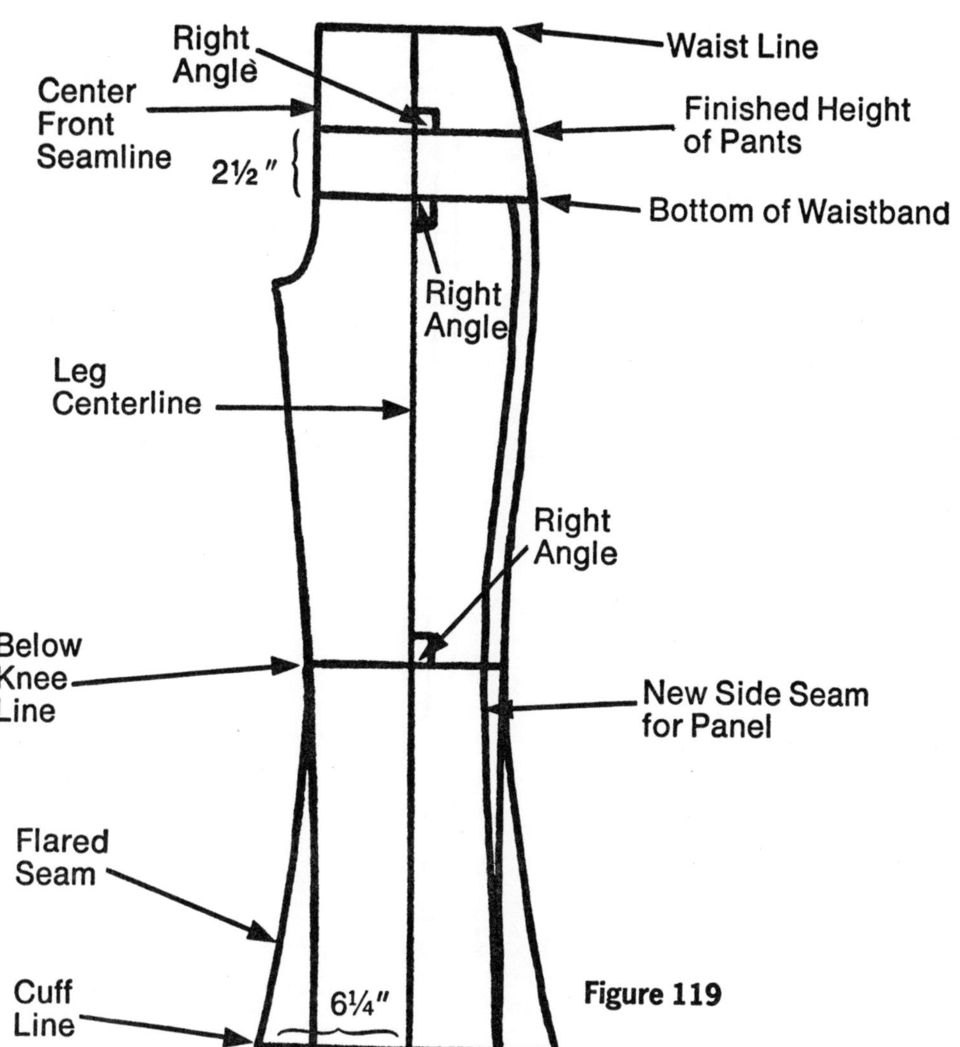

Figure 119

band to the point where the pants start to flare. The panel at this point flares to a final width of 4½" at the cuff. The waistband is the hip-hugger style.

The Pants Pattern

The following steps may be used to alter the fitted pants pattern.

SIDE PANEL PATTERN

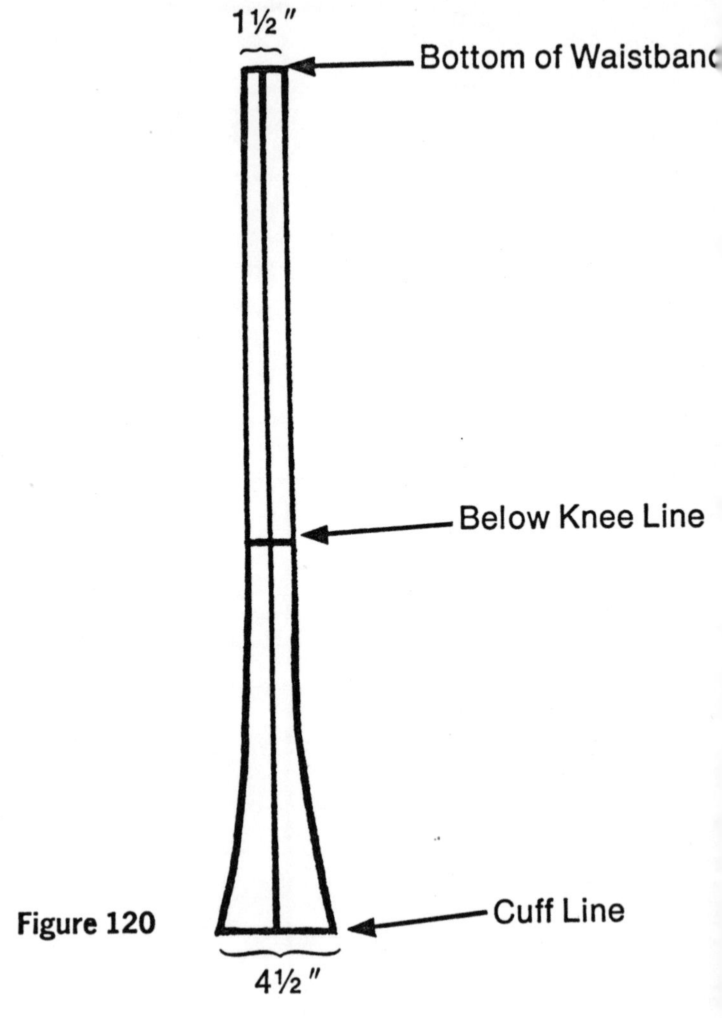

Figure 120

STEP 1. Trace the Basic Pants Front pattern onto a new sheet of paper. Indicate the Leg Centerline position at the cuff (Figure 119).

STEP 2. Draw a line at the desired height of the lowered Waist line. In this case, this line is 4″ below the natural waistline, and parallel to it.

Step 3. Draw a second line parallel to the top of the pants, 2½″ below the new Waist line. The 2½″ is the width of the waistband. This line represents the bottom of the waistband.

Step 4. Measure down from the waist to the Below the Knee measurement and draw a line parallel to the Waist line. This is the Below the Knee line.

Step 5. The final circumference of the pants at the cuff will be 25″; 12½″ of this is in the front. Divide this width equally on both sides of the Leg Centerline, placing 6¼″ on either side. Flare the Inseam and the Side Seam line from below the knee to the cuff.

Step 6. Draw in one-half of the side panel on the pattern. This is ¾″ wide from the bottom of the waistband to below the knee. From there, it widens to 2¼″ at the Cuff line.

Step 7. Draft a placket on the Center Front Seam line starting from the original (natural) Waist line.

The original Waist line is used to draft the placket in order to get the correct placement of the bottom of the placket on the pants. The correct height of the placket will be determined when the waistband is cut. The inside section of the waistband will have to be extended to cover the width of the placket.

Step 8. Trace the inside portion of the placket to make a pattern for the facing.

Step 9. Cut the trouser and waistband sections apart at the bottom waistband line. Save the waistband pieces to use when drafting the complex waistband described below.

Step 10. Add seam allowances to the finished seams of this section of the pants and cut the pattern out.

The back pants pattern may be altered the same way the front pattern was altered.

Pattern For The Side Panel

The side panel is cut separately, according to the measurements used for trimming down the side seam of the pants.

Step 1. Draw a vertical line the distance between the bottom of the pants waistband and the Cuff line (Figure 120).

Step 2. Draw a perpendicular line at the top and bottom of this line and at the Below Knee measurement.

Step 3. Draw in the shape of the panel. This is 1½" from the top to the Below Knee measurement, flaring to 4½" at the Cuff line.

Step 4. Add seam allowances and cut.

Notice that the cutting technique of altering seam locations was not used in this alteration. The side seam of these pants has a curved seam that makes it impossible to apply that technique here.

The Complex Waistband

The complex waistband utilized in these pants is drafted to fit the contour of the body. It cannot be a straight waistband because this style would not fit the contour of the hips.

Step 1. Cut out the front and back waistband sections of the pants pattern. On the front section, be sure to include the allowance for the top of the placket. On the back section, include the dart (Figure 121).

These pattern pieces set the size for the waistband. Two techniques will now be used to curve the waistband.

COMPLEX WAISTBAND PATTERN (Step 1)
Tracing the Pants Pattern

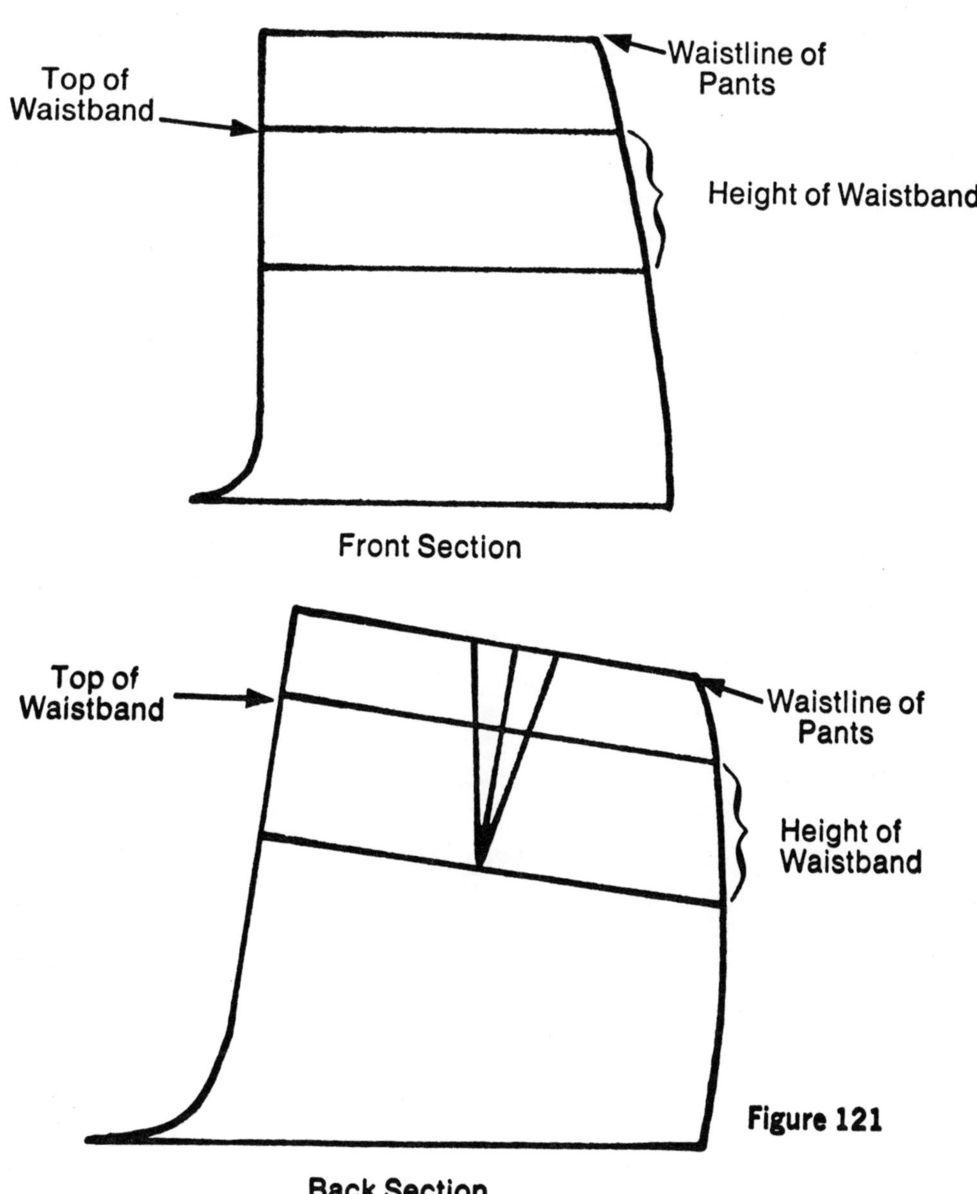

Back Section

COMPLEX WAISTBAND PATTERN (Steps 2 to 5)
Curving the Waistband

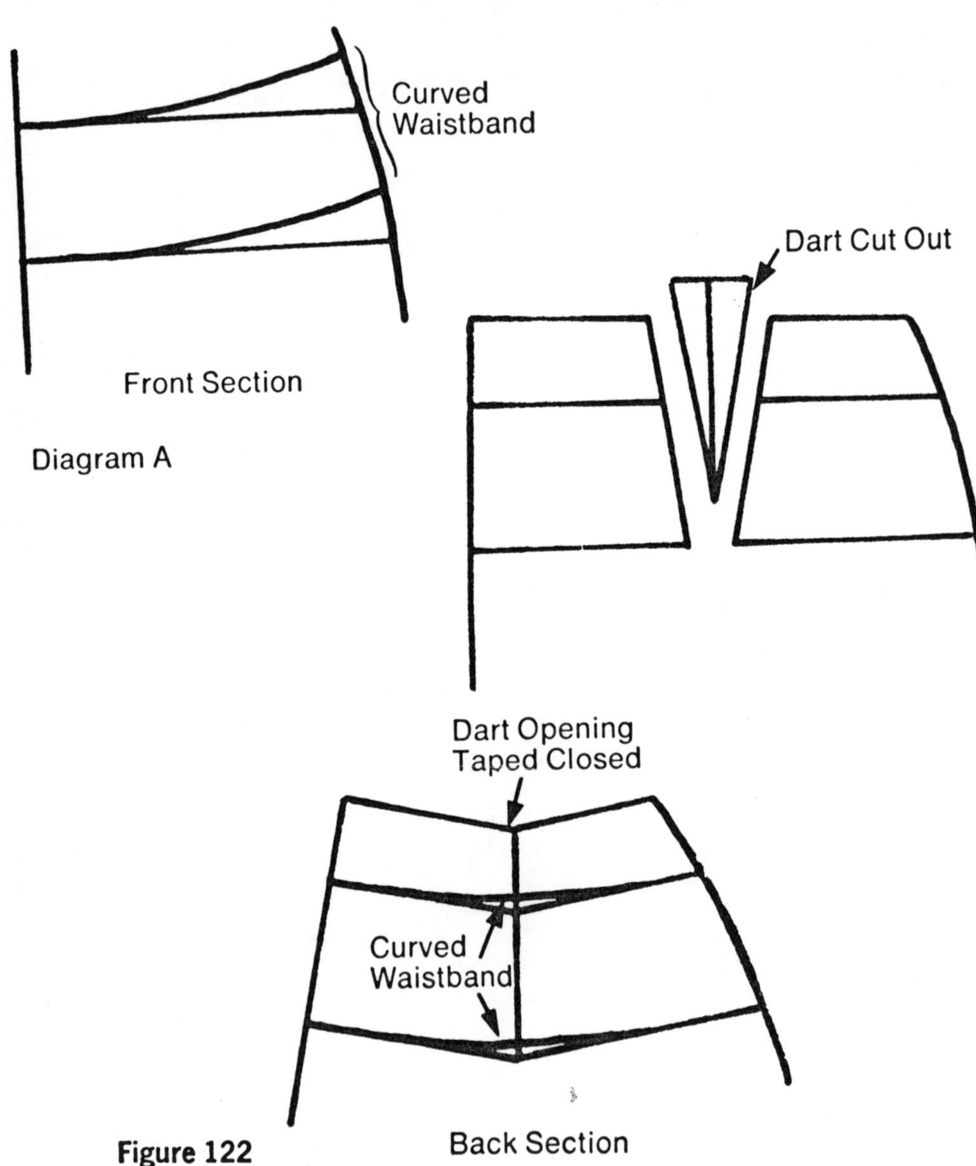

Figure 122

Diagram B

STEP 2. For the front section, curve the waistband using the folding technique described for the Mandarin Collar. See Diagram A of Figure 122.

STEP 3. For the back section, cut out the dart and tape the two dart edges together as if they were sewn. See Diagram B of Figure 122.

STEP 4. Correct the back waistband curve freehand.

STEP 5. Add ⅝" seam allowances to all the edges. The Center Back may be a fold line, but there should be a seam at the sides.

THE JUMP SUIT

The jump suit pictured in Figure 123 requires a fairly extensive adaptation of the basic patterns. It is cut in four sections with two front sections and two back sections. The upper body and the pants are cut in one piece. The waistband illustrated in the design is appliqued after the garment is finished.

The Front Section

The jump suit pattern is drafted by using the bodice pattern as the starting point. The lower portion of the suit is drafted by adapting the pants measurements.

Step 1. Trace the basic bodice pattern onto a fresh sheet of paper (Figure 124).

JUMP SUIT

Figure 123

FRONT PATTERN (Steps 1 to 10)

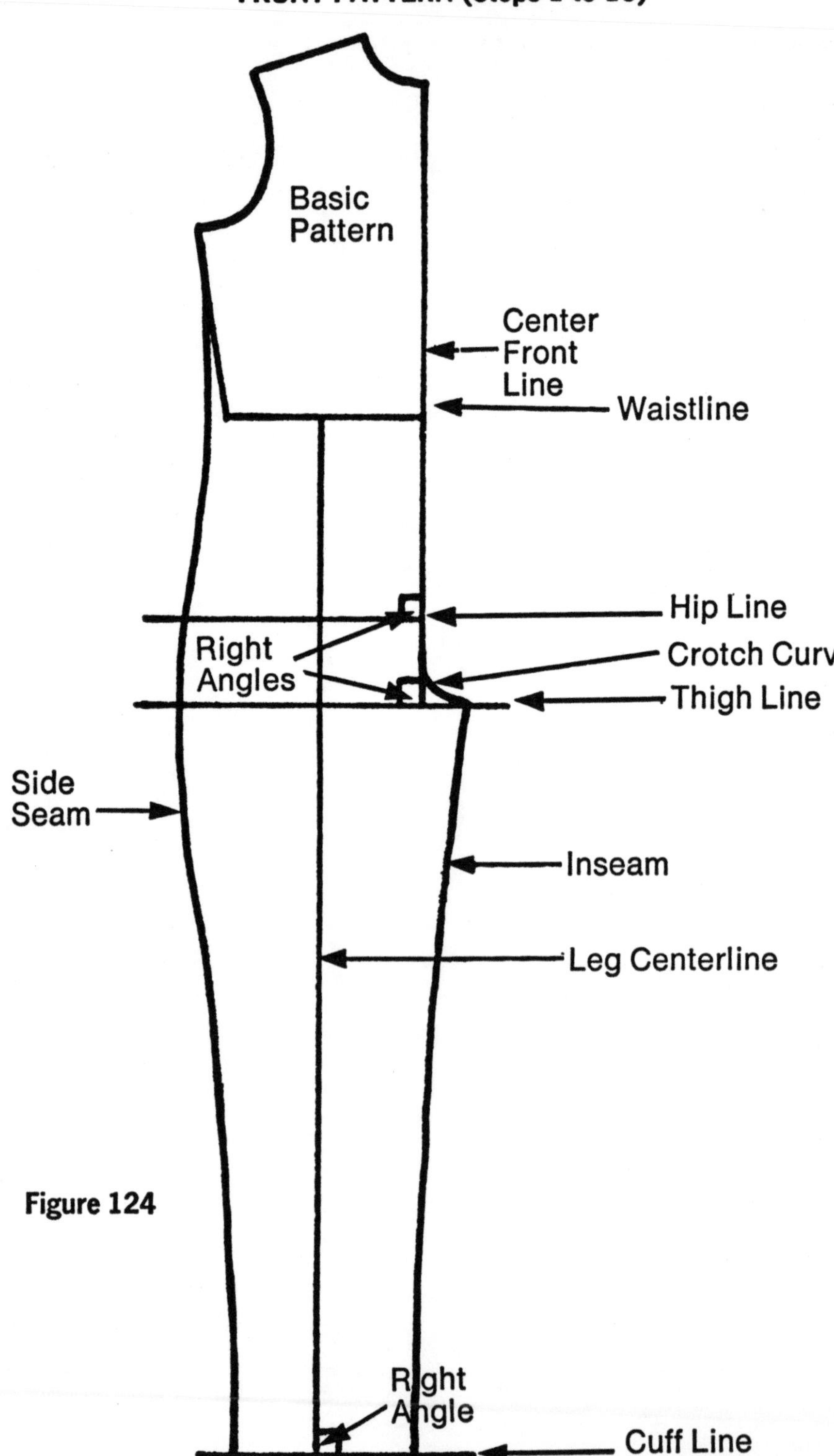

Figure 124

STEP 2. Extend the Center Front line.

STEP 3. Mark off the Waist to Hip length on the Center Front line and draw a perpendicular line from this point. This is the Hip line.

STEP 4. Mark off 1″ plus one-fourth of the Hip measurement on this line.

STEP 5. Subtract the Inseam length from the Waist to Floor measurement. Add 2″ to this and mark this length on the Center Front line measuring down from the Waist line. Draw a perpendicular line at this point. This is the Thigh line.

The Waist to Floor measurement, minus the Inseam, gives the length of the crotch; 2″ are added to this as an allowance for the movement of the body, particularly when sitting.

STEP 6. Divide the pattern Waist line in half and draw a line from this point parallel to the Center Front line. This is the Leg Centerline.

STEP 7. Mark off the Inseam length on the Leg Centerline, starting from the Thigh line. Draw a perpendicular line at this point. This is the Cuff line.

The basic axes for the suit have now been established.

STEP 8. On the Thigh line mark off ¾″ plus one-fourth the Leg, Highest Point measurement to either side of the Leg Centerline.

STEP 9. Mark off 4″ on each side of the Cuff line.

STEP 10. Draw in the Side Seam line, Inseam line, and the Crotch curve, as shown in Figure 124.

STEP 11. Add seam allowances and cut.

THE BACK SECTION

To draft the back section, a tracing is made of the front section. The following modifications will be necessary.

BACK PATTERN (Steps 1 to 3)

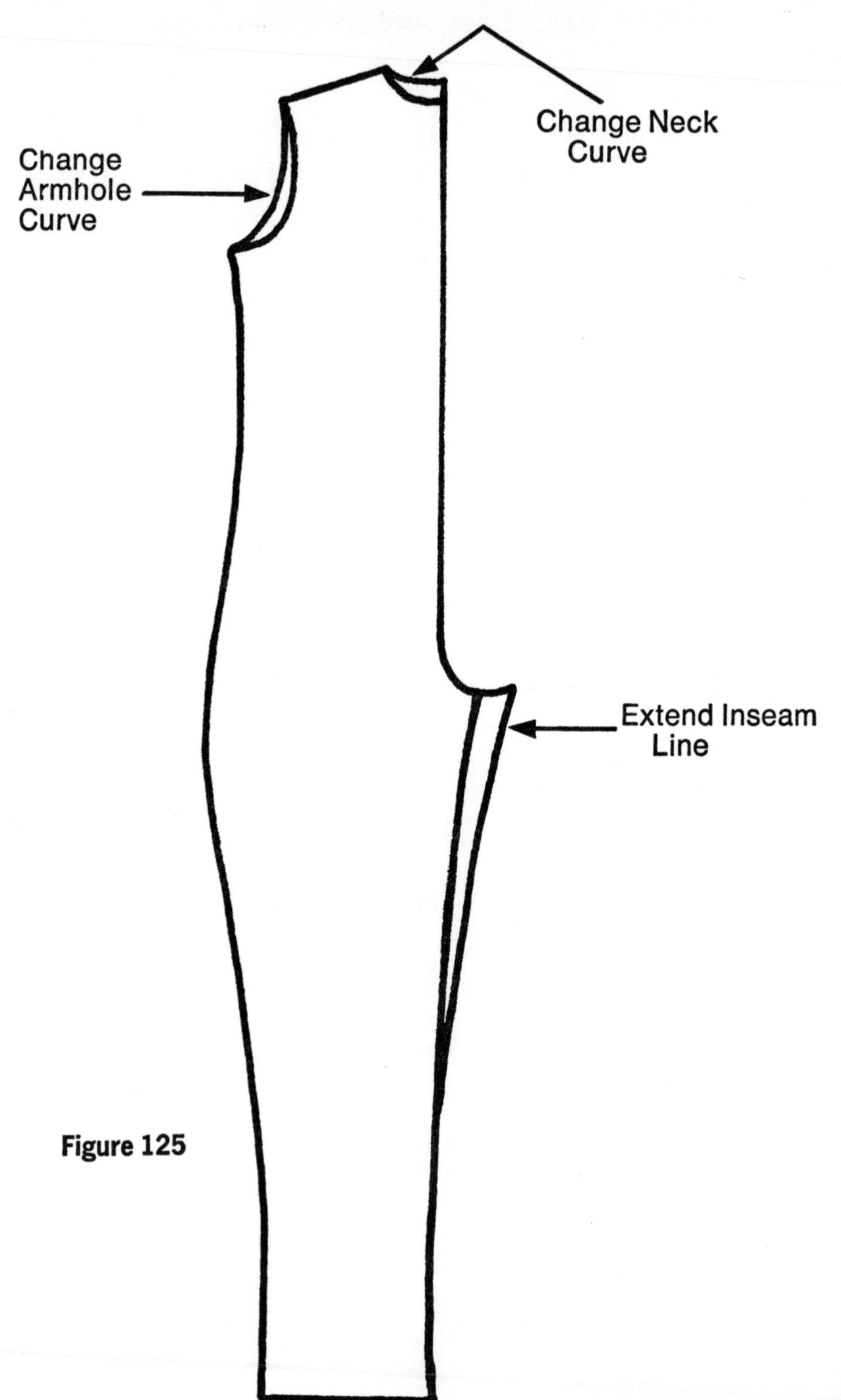

Figure 125

STEP 1. Redraw the Neck curve (Figure 125).

STEP 2. Redraw the Armhole curve.

STEP 3. Add 1½″ to the Thigh line and redraw the Inseam line.

STEP 4. Add seam allowances and cut.

Any style collar or sleeve may be added to the jump suit.

FITTING THE JUMP SUIT

To fit the jump suit, the person who is to wear it should sit. As he is sitting, adjust the Shoulder Seam so that the jump suit fits the upper part of the body snugly but comfortably. Next, have the wearer stand as the rest of the suit is being fitted. The cuff length should be set with the wearer bending over at the waist. This will pull the pants legs up to their highest length. Set the hem and have the wearer straighten up. Check the length.

GUSSETS

A gusset may be added at the crotch to reduce the strain on the crotch seam. This is particularly advisable if the jump suit is going to be used for any strenuous activity. The gusset with the pertinent measurements is shown in Figure 126. Add seam allowances.

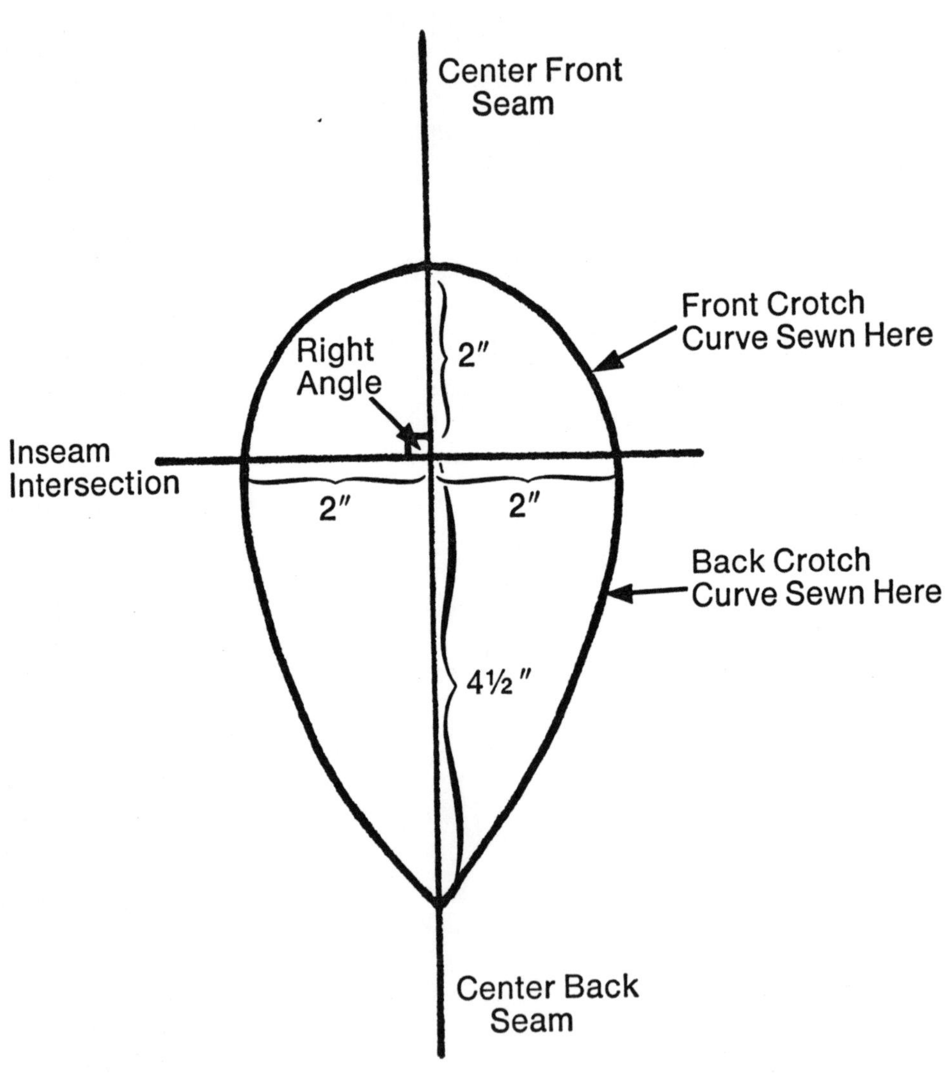
Center Front
Seam
Front Crotch
Curve Sewn Here
Right
Angle
2″
Inseam
Intersection
2″
2″
Back Crotch
Curve Sewn Here
4½″
Center Back
Seam

Figure 126

SLEEVE GUSSET

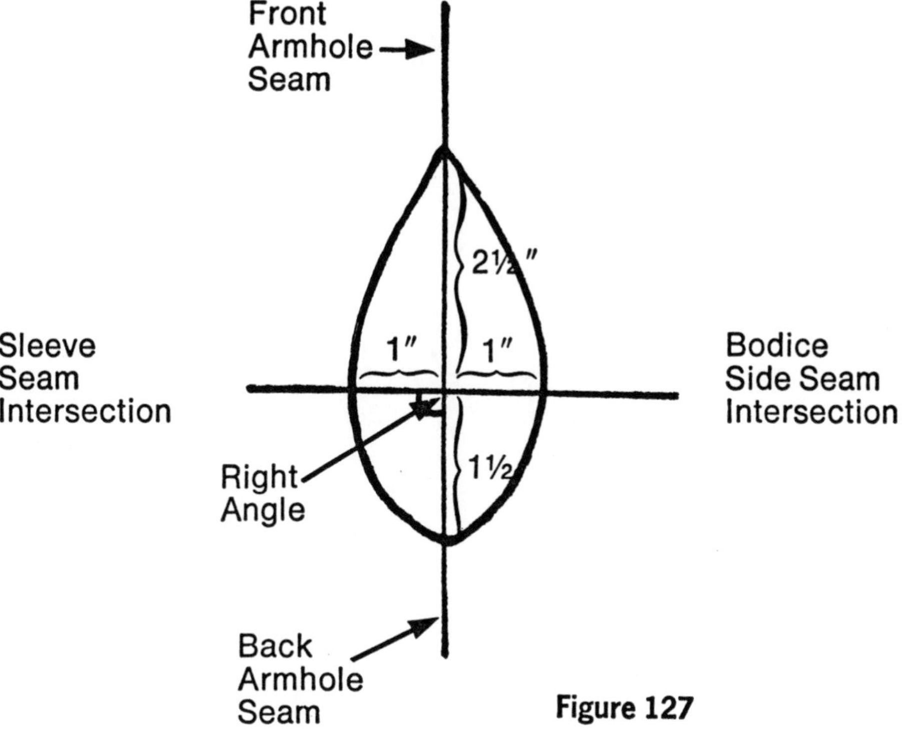

Figure 127

Gussets of this type may also be added to the underarm seam of sleeves. A sleeve gusset is illustrated in Figure 127. Seam allowances will have to be added.

The gusset is sewn in by pinning the short axis of the gusset to the appropriate seam. The crotch gusset is pinned at the Inseam line and the sleeve gusset is pinned at the Side Seam and Sleeve Seam line. The gusset is then eased in from these points to the long axis of the gusset. This axis is the Center Front/Center Back seam of the Crotch gusset and the Armhole seam of the sleeve gusset.

Figure 128

THE SUIT COAT

The suit coat is perhaps the acme of the pattern drafter's art. It must fit well and hang with a pleasingly flat finish. Drafting the collar and lapel also requires special care. The procedure for drafting the double-breasted coat illustrated in Figure 128 will be described.

FRONT PATTERN (Steps 1 to 6)
The Basic Dimensions

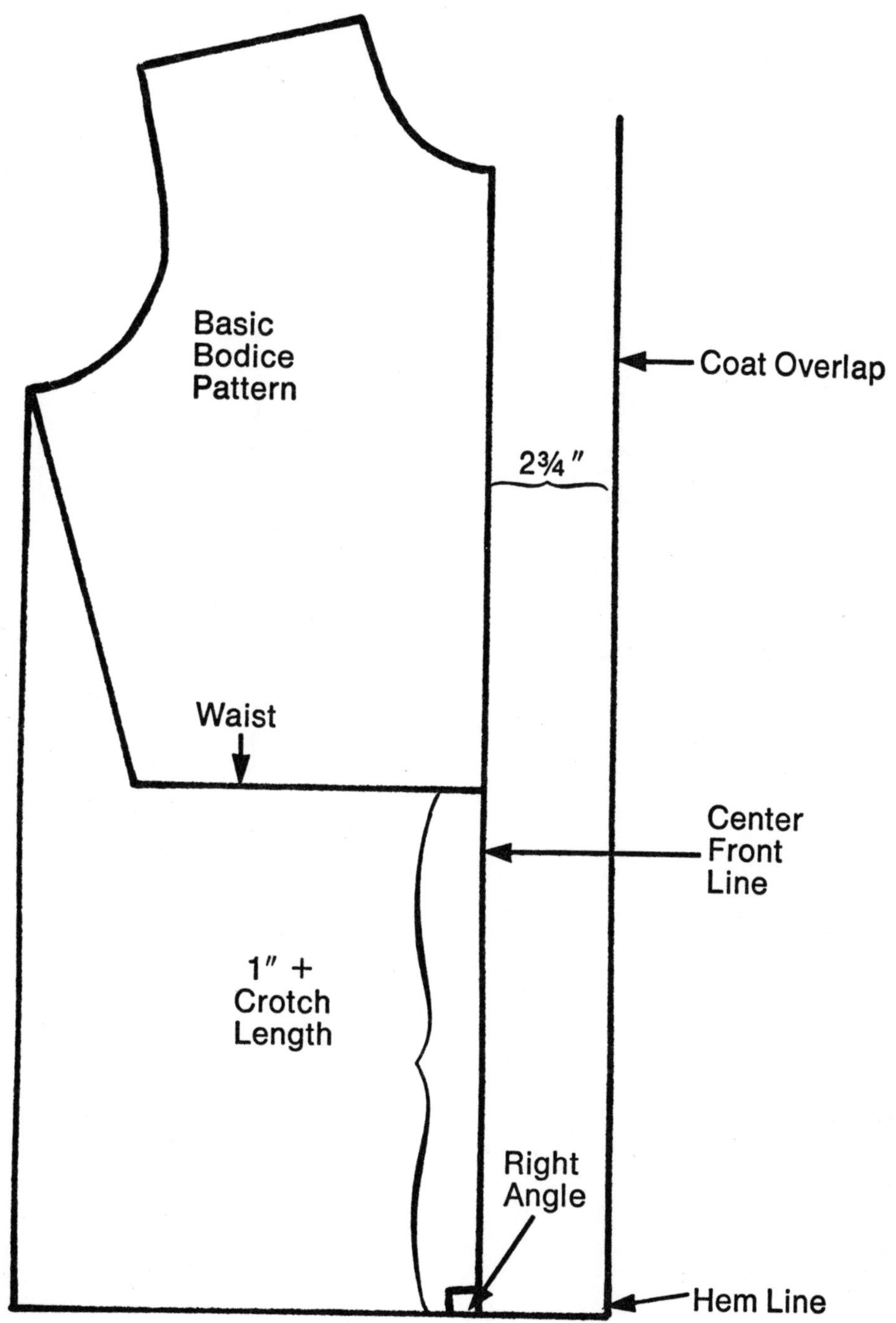

Figure 129

BUTTON OVERLAP

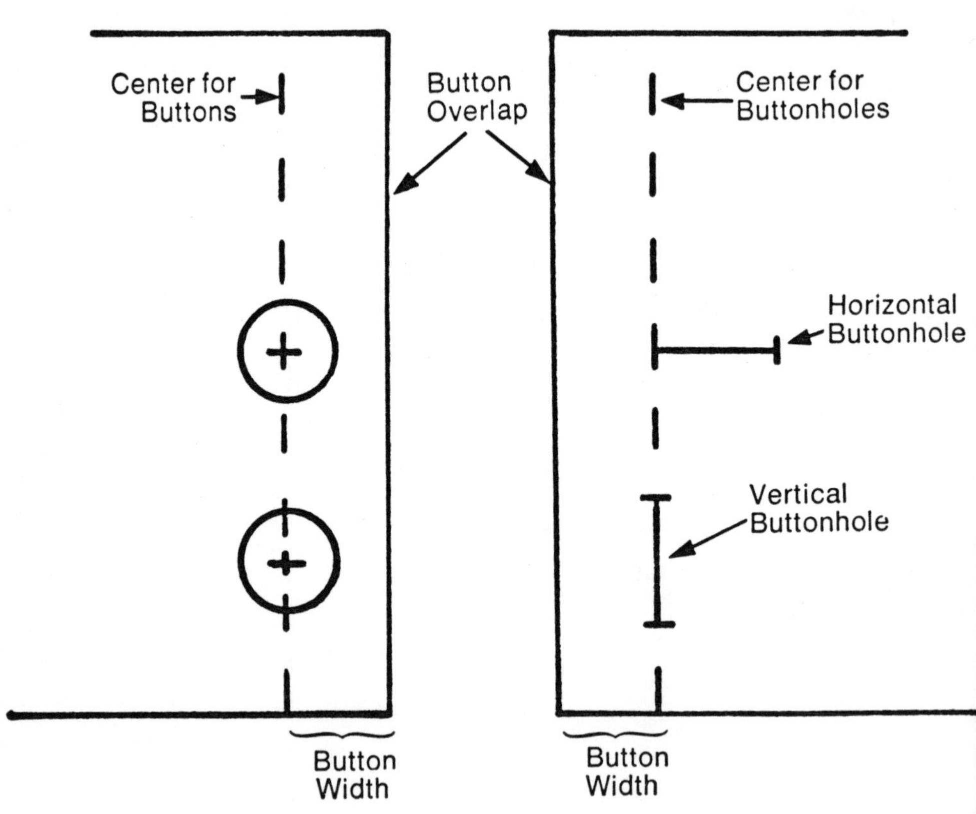

Figure 130

The first steps that must be taken to draft this coat are to establish the basic shape. The length is extended to just below the crotch. The side seam is moved to the back of the armhole. A center back seam is included, and the overlap for the front of the coat is added. After this, the shape of the lapel and the collar are drawn. The sleeve is drafted last.

The Front Pattern

Step 1. Trace the Basic Bodice Front pattern onto a larger sheet of paper.

Step 2. Extend the Center Front line down (see Figure 129).

Step 3. Subtract the Inseam measurement from the Waist to Floor measurement to determine the Crotch length. Add 1″ to this measurement. Mark this length on the Center Front line measuring down from the Waist line. Draw a perpendicular line at this point. This is the Hem line.

Step 4. Mark off 1″ plus one-fourth the Hip measurement on the Hem line.

Step 5. Draw a line straight down from the bottom edge of the armhole to the point just marked on the Hem line.

Step 6. Draw a line parallel to the Center Front line 2¾″ to the right. This line establishes the edge of the coat.

The overlap of the coat is 2¾″ from the Center Front line because the buttons are centered 2″ from the Center Front and ¾″ are added for the button overlap.

The button overlap is normally calculated by adding the width of the button to the Center line for the buttons (See Figure 130). In this case the buttons will be ¾″.

The Back Pattern

The back pattern may be drafted by tracing the front section. The following alterations will have to be made.

BACK PATTERN (Steps 1 to 4)

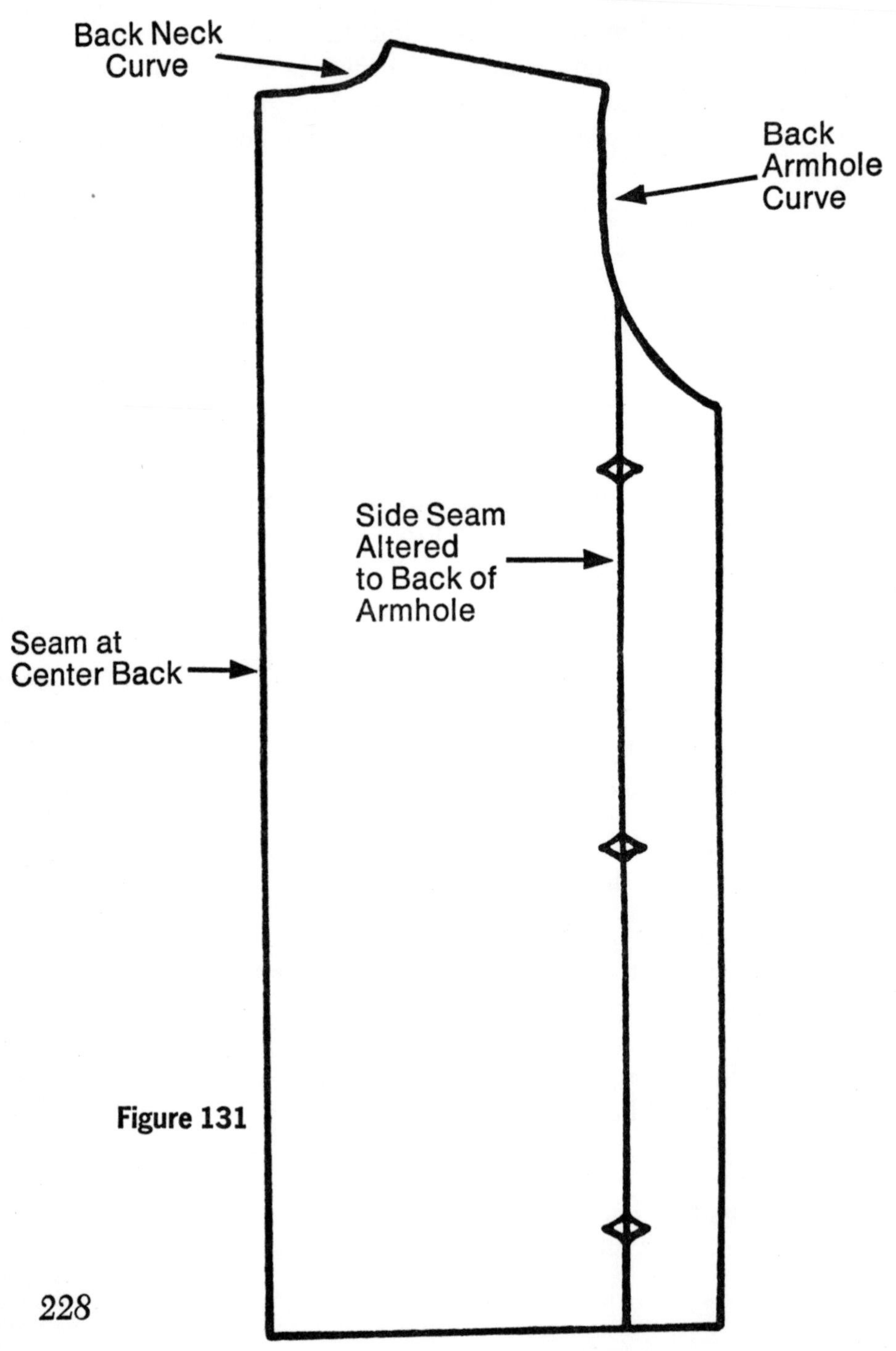

Figure 131

CHANGING THE SIDE SEAM (Step 5)

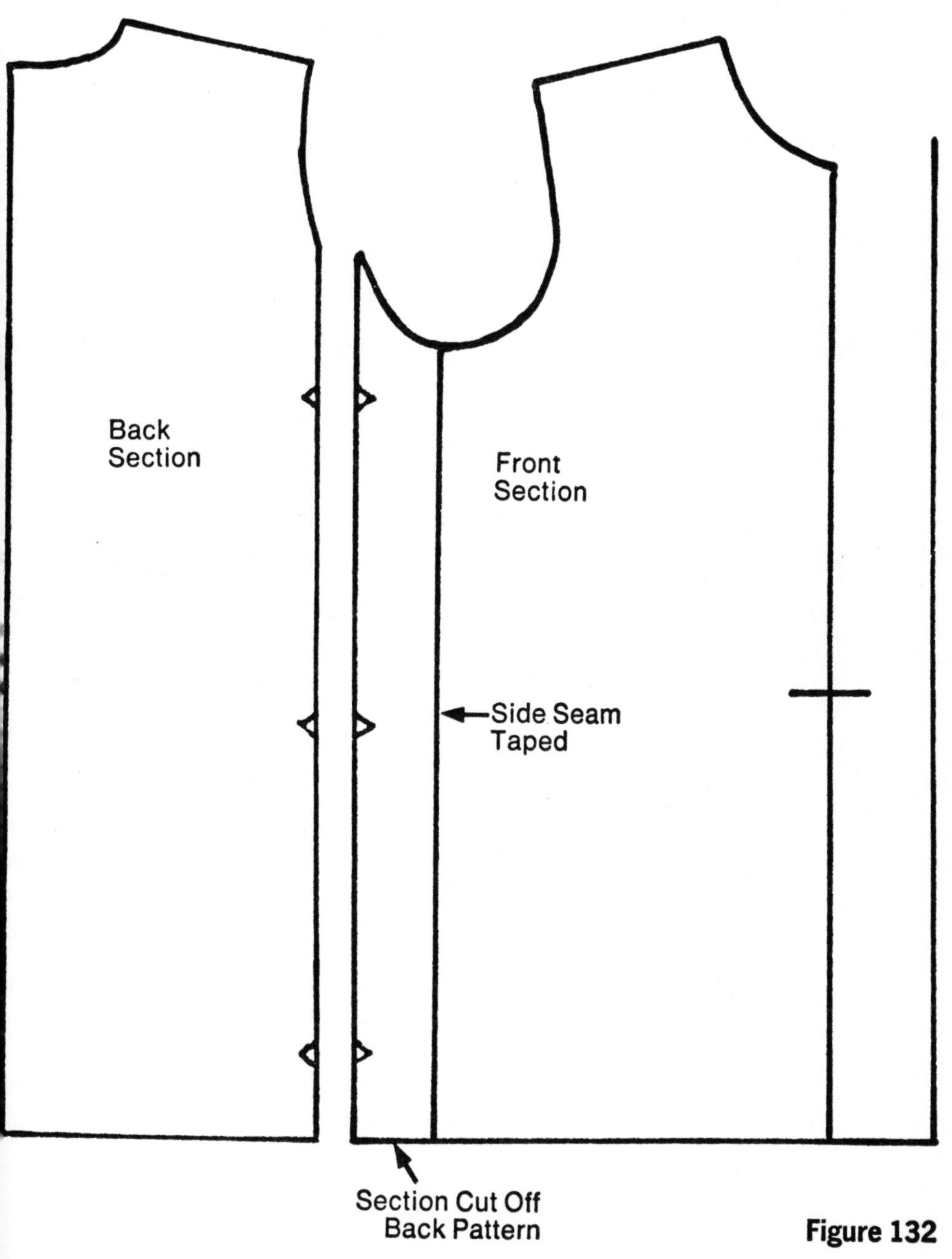

Figure 132

STEP 1. Change the Neck curve (Figure 131).

STEP 2. Redraw the Armhole curve.

STEP 3. Draw in the Center Back seam.

CHANGING THE SIDE SEAM

The Side Seam must be altered to the back of the armhole.

STEP 4. On the back pattern, draw in the Side Seam line at the point where the armhole starts to curve out to the normal Side Seam line. Mark notches on this line. (Figure 131)

STEP 5. Cut on the new seam line and tape the cut-off section to the front pattern. (See Figure 132)

DRAFTING THE LAPEL SHAPE

The lapel of any suit coat may be shaped by folding the front pattern at the Lapel Fold line. To determine the Lapel Fold line, however, the button placement must first be established.

STEP 1. The two buttons in the center row of this design are spaced 4″ apart and 1″ above the Waist line (Figure 133).

STEP 2. The buttons in the bottom row are also 4″ apart. They are approximately one-third the distance between the center buttons and the hem of the coat.

STEP 3. The top buttons are the same distance up from the center buttons as the bottom buttons are down. They are 1½″ further in on the coat.

The Lapel Fold line and the Lapel seam may now be drawn in.

STEP 4. The Lapel Fold line starts at the coat edge, at a point directly opposite the center row of buttons.

STEP 5. To locate the top point of the Lapel Fold line, extend the Shoulder Seam out ¾″ at the neck curve (See Figure 133).

DRAFTING THE LAPEL (Steps 1 to 8)

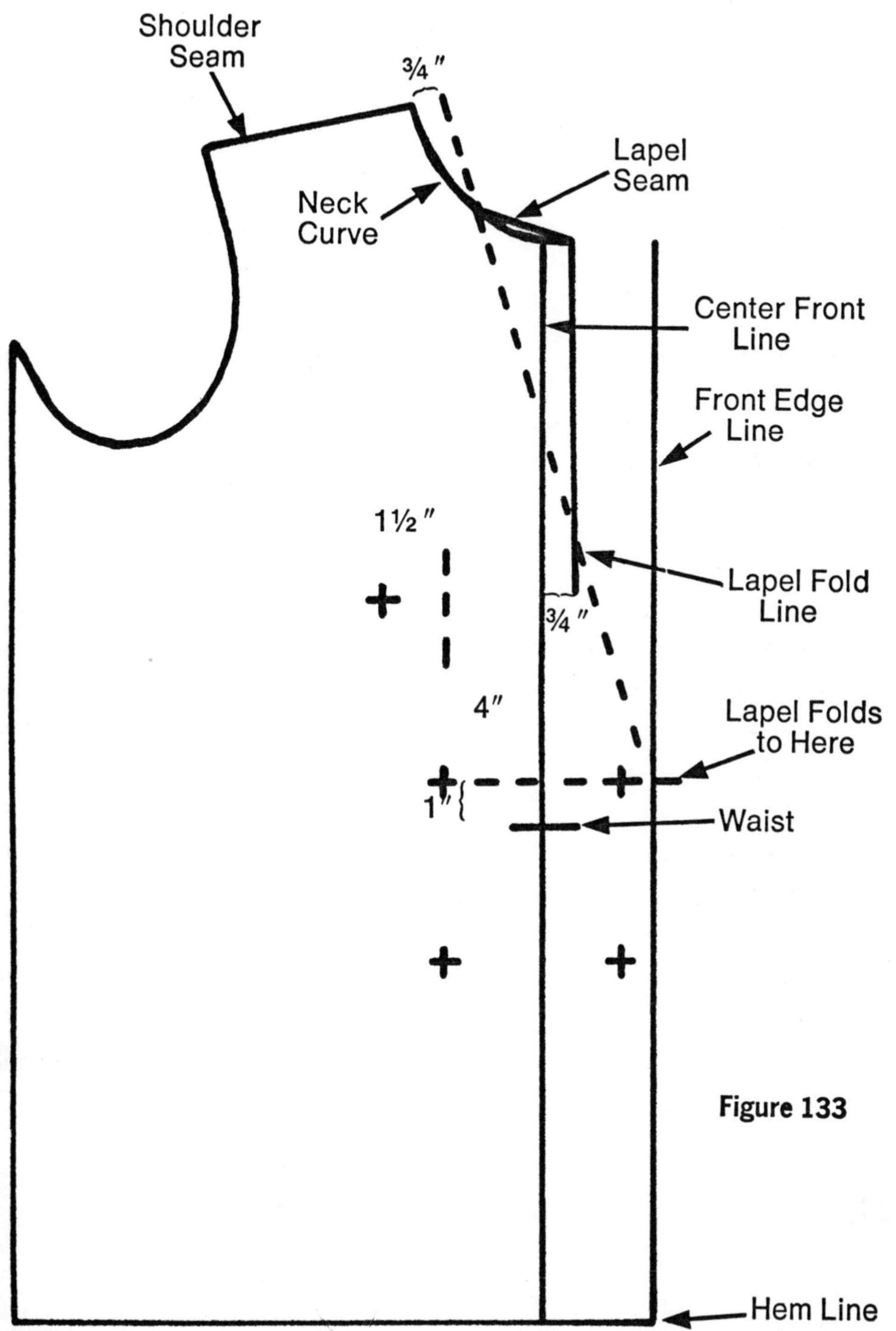

Figure 133

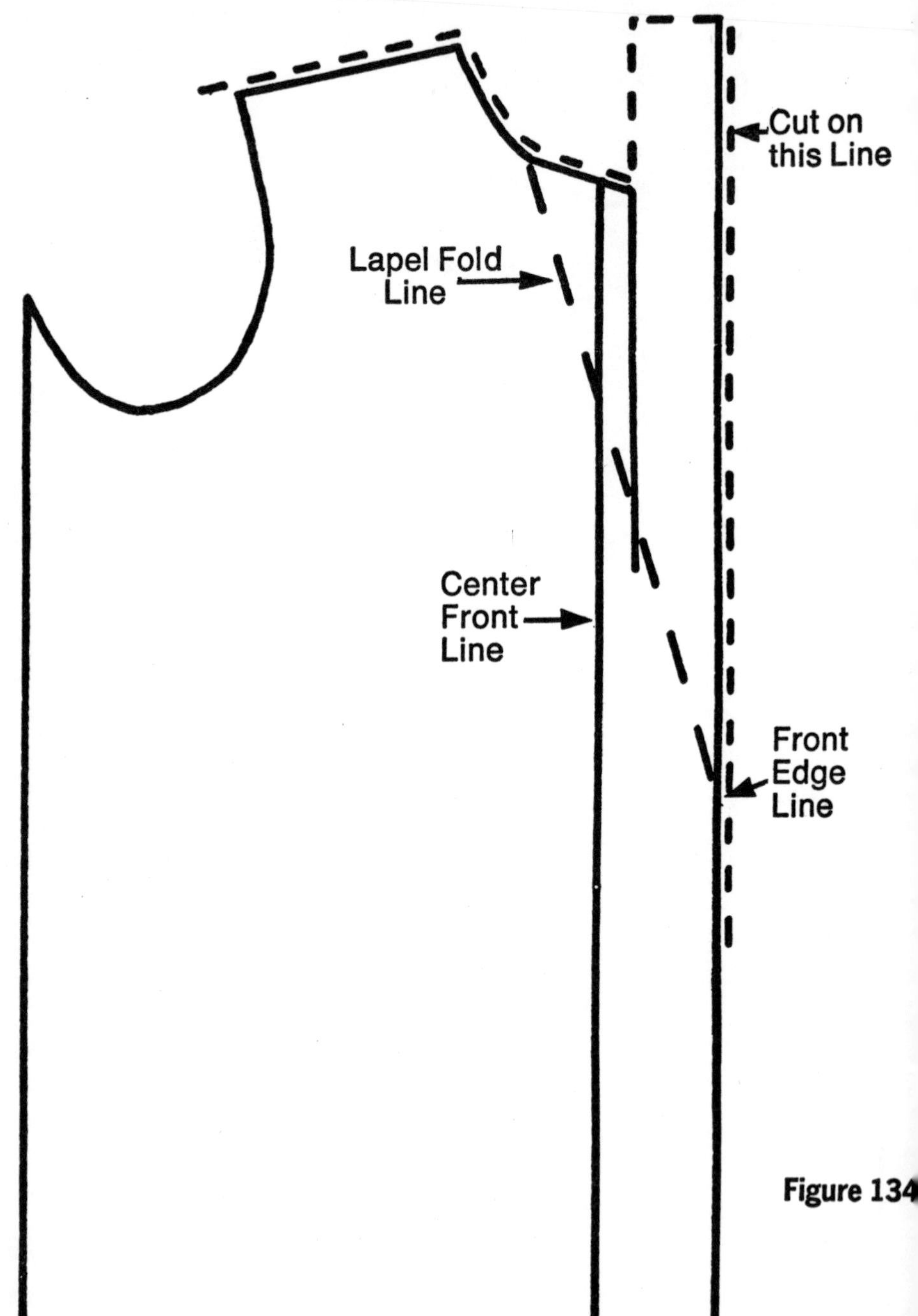
Cut on this Line
Lapel Fold Line
Center Front Line
Front Edge Line

Figure 134

STEP 6. Connect these two points and draw the Lapel Fold line.

The top of the Lapel Fold line is drawn at this point because the collar will eventually fold here.

The visible seam on lapels is derived from the center front portion of the Neck curve. For both single-breasted and double-breasted coats, the Neck curve is extended out ¾″ (or the button overlap) from the Center Front line.

STEP 7. Draw a line parallel to the Center Front line ¾″ out, towards the Front Edge line. This line should extend from the Neck curve to below the Lapel Fold line. Continue the Neck Curve to this line.

STEP 8. Draw a straight line from this new end of the neck curve to the intersection of the Neck curve and the Lapel Fold line. This will be the Lapel seam (see Figure 133).

STEP 9. If opaque paper is being used, it is easiest to cut out the pattern as it is being drafted. Seam allowances will have to be added later. Cut out the pattern as is indicated by the small dotted line in Figure 134.

STEP 10. The pattern may now be folded at the Lapel Fold line. It should be folded so that the paper to the right of the Lapel Fold is on top of the main portion of the pattern. The shape of the finished Lapel will be drawn directly onto the folded portion of the paper.

DRAFTING THE LAPEL (Step 11)
Shaping the Lapel Point

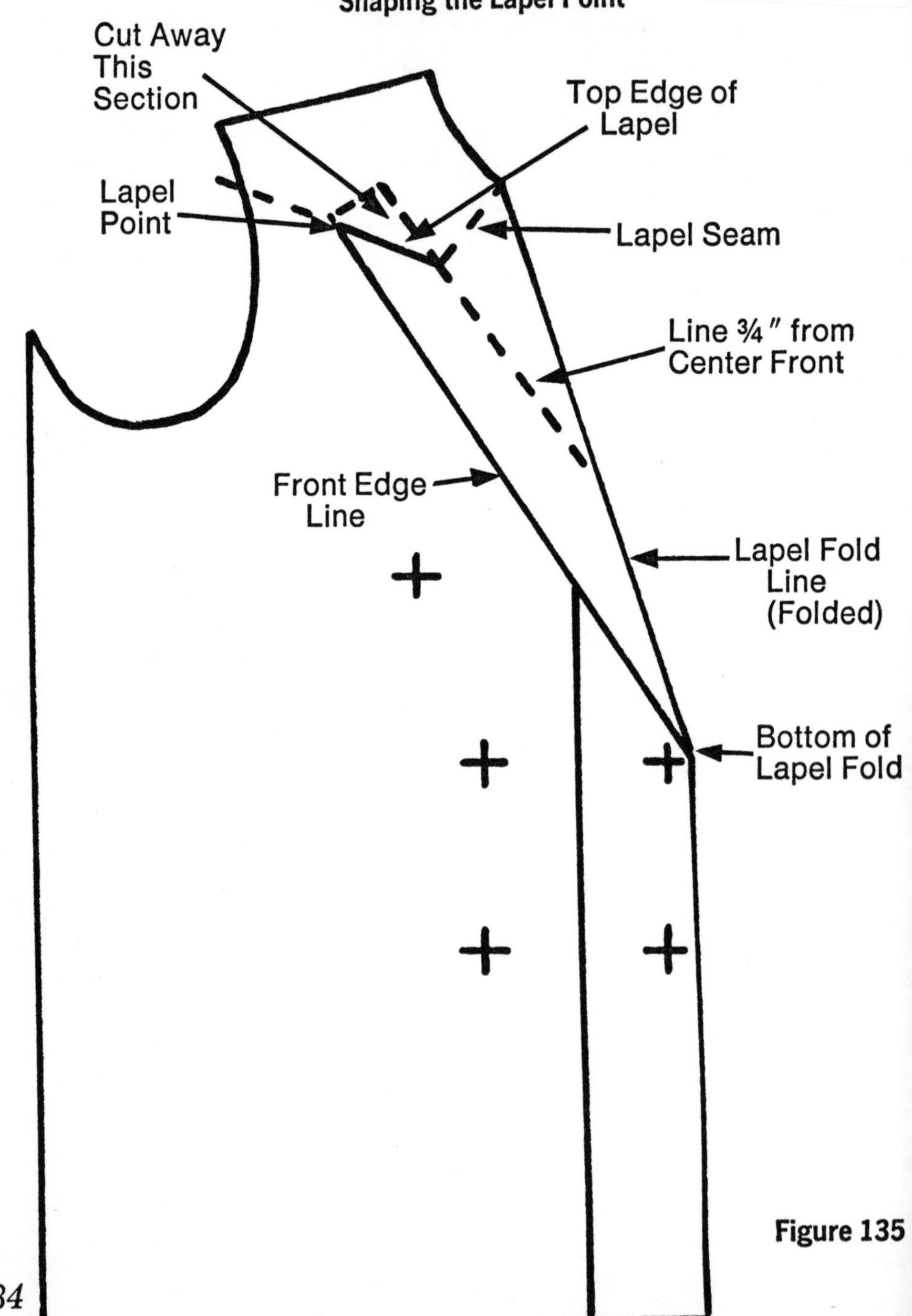

Figure 135

STEP 11. The top edge of the Lapel for this design is created by the Lapel seam and a line drawn from the end of the Lapel seam to the outer edge of the Lapel. This second line is directed to a point below the end of the Shoulder Seam line (see Figure 135). This line is 2½" long. (If opaque paper is being used, cut the lapel to the correct shape.)

This completes the shaping of the Lapel. It may be desirable or necessary to reshape the Lapel at this point to achieve the desired design.

The Collar Pattern

The collar pattern for men's suits is a variation of the Shirt Collar. The shape of the seam is basically straight. Also the collar follows up the neck, rolls over, and folds back down.

If tracing paper is being used to draft the collar, place it over the pattern so that it covers the top of the lapel and extends upward. If opaque paper is being used, insert a strip of paper about 6″ wide and 12″ long under the folded lapel of the jacket front. The long edge should be parallel to the front edge of the jacket and about 10″ of the paper should extend above the lapel seam. One edge should touch the neckline at the lapel fold front. Tape this paper in place.

The collar pattern will be drafted as follows:

Step 1. Draw in the shape of the collar at the lapel (See Figure 136).

Step 2. Starting at the left end of the collar at the lapel, draw a line that is parallel to the Center Front line. This is the Outside of the Collar line.

Step 3. Draw a second line parallel to the outside of the collar 2½″ in (or the desired width of the collar). This is the Neck Reference line.

Step 4. On the body of the coat, measure the Neck curve from the edge of the lapel to the Center Back seam. Draw a line of this length from the neck side of the Collar/Lapel seam so that it intersects with the Neck Reference line. This will be the Neck seam.

Step 5. Draw a line perpendicular to the top end of the Neck seam so that it intersects with the outside of the collar. This will be the Center Back Fold line.

COLLAR PATTERN (Steps 1 to 5)

The Dimensions

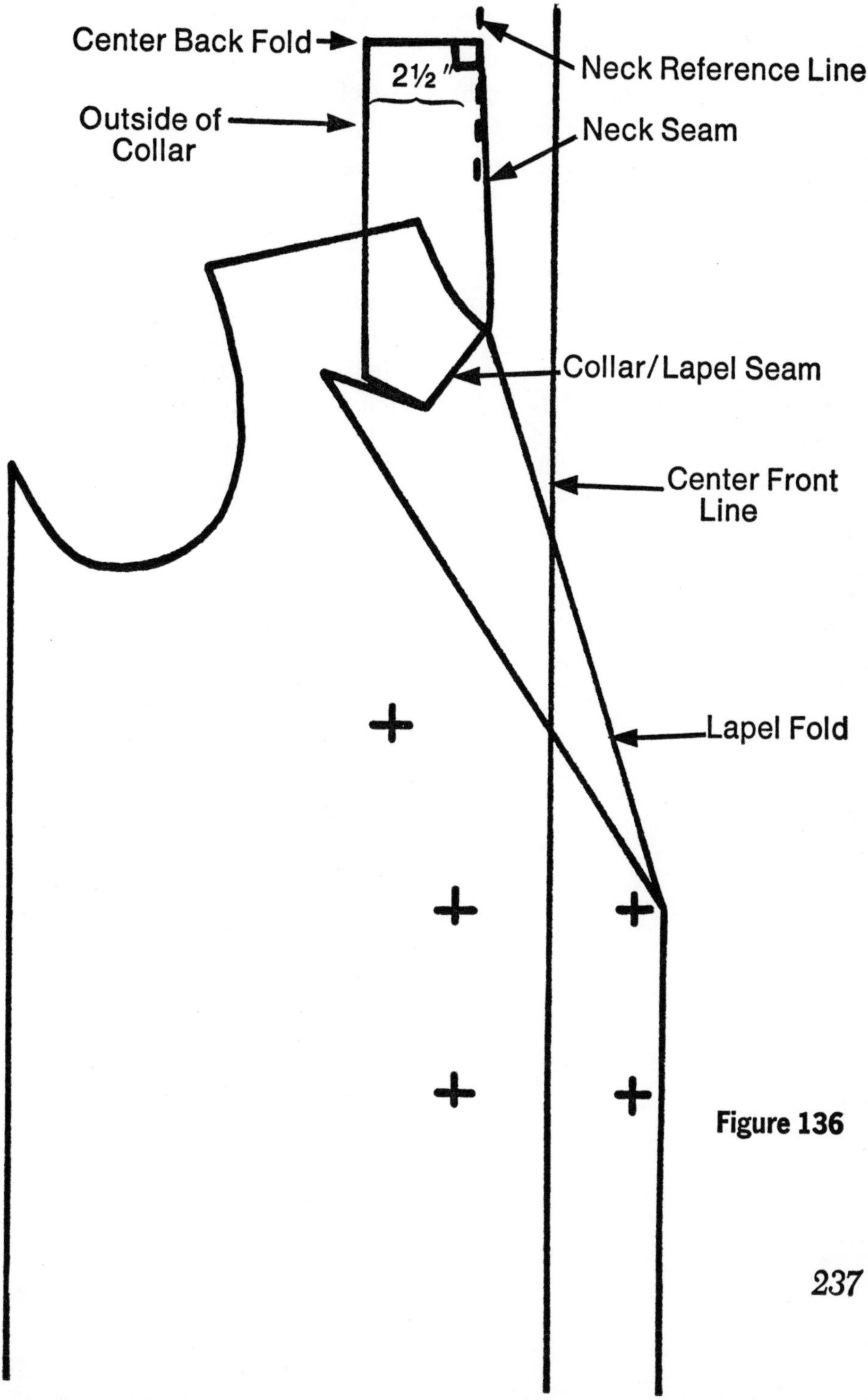

Center Back Fold

2½"

Outside of Collar

Neck Reference Line

Neck Seam

Collar/Lapel Seam

Center Front Line

Lapel Fold

Figure 136

STEP 6. Shape the Neck Seam line so that it curves gradually (see Figure 137).

The pattern for the body of the coat may now be unfolded and the lapel shape transferred to the front of the pattern.

The patterns for the body of the coat are now complete. Add seam allowances and cut.

COLLARS ON WOMEN'S SUITS

The collars on women's suits are sometimes made by the procedure described above. If, however, the collar is to be much wider than 2½″, then the collar is made by adapting the Flat Collar pattern. The following will be a description of the procedure for this adaptation.

STEP 1. Draw the fold line of the lapel so that it intersects with the Neck curve at the Shoulder Seam line (See Figure 138).

COLLAR PATTERN (Step 6)
Shaping the Neckline

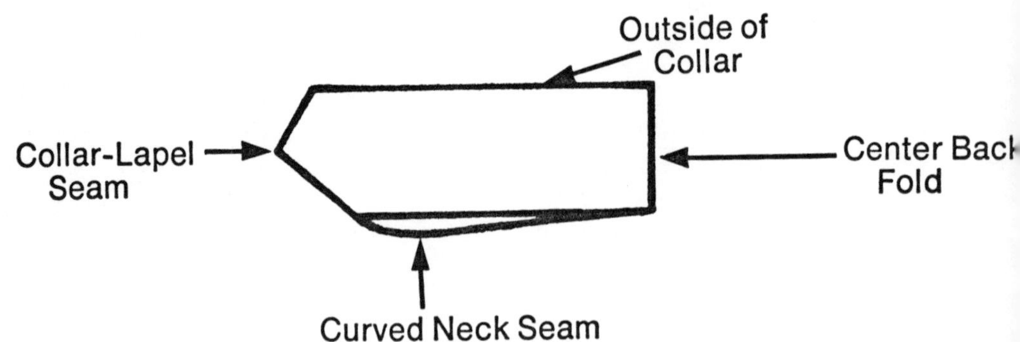

Figure 137

WOMEN'S SUIT COLLAR (Steps 1 to 3)

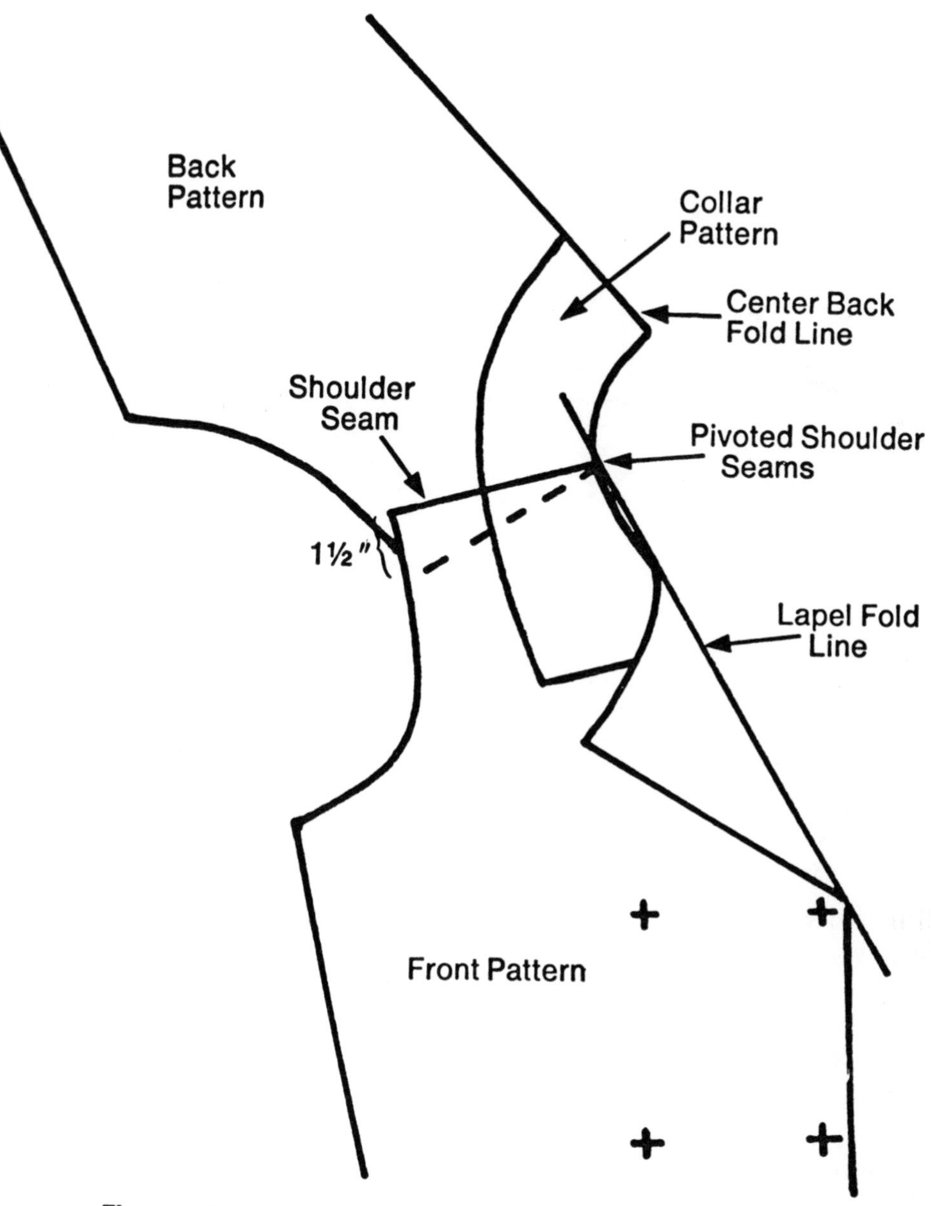

Figure 138

SLEEVE PATTERN (Steps 1 to 5)
Establishing Reference Points

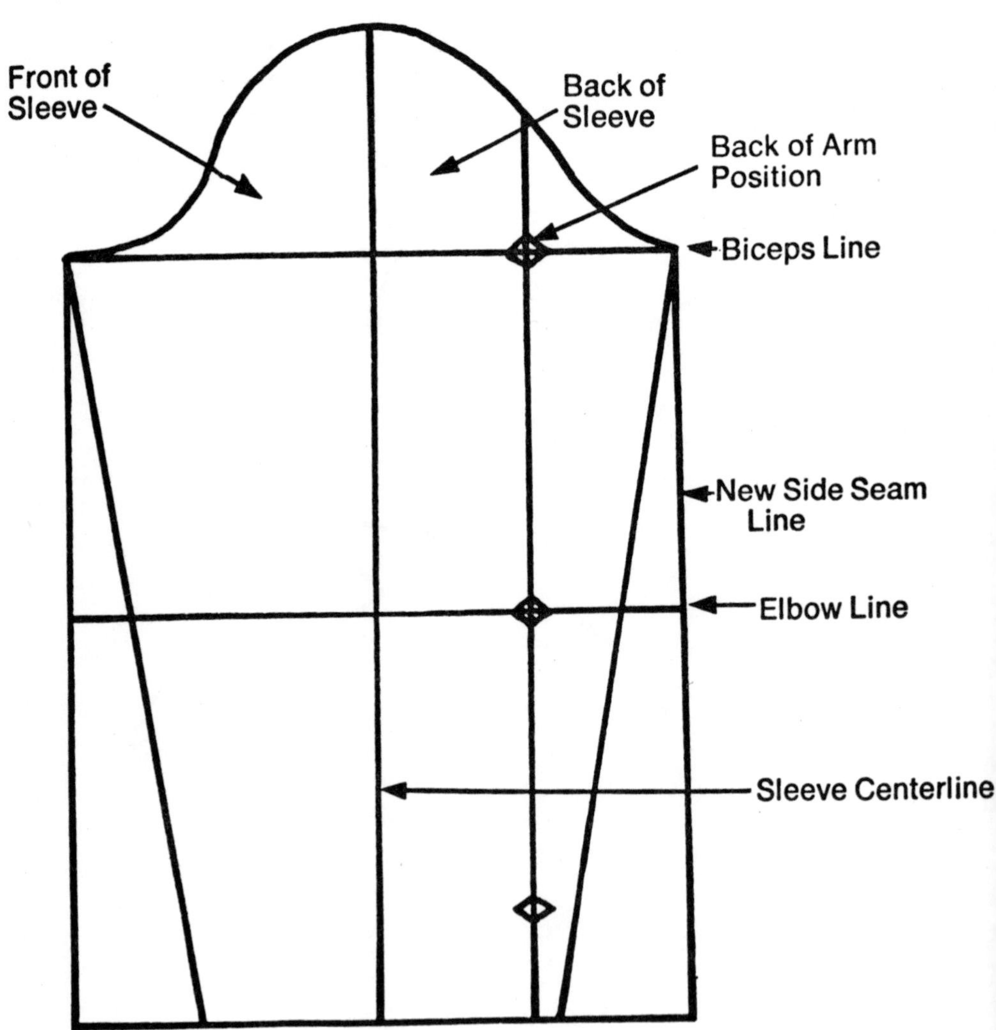

Figure 139

STEP 2. The back pattern is placed at the top of the front pattern of the bodice as if the Shoulder Seam were sewn. It is then pivoted at the Neck line as is illustrated in Figure 138.

Pivoting the back pattern in this way will cause the collar to roll at the neck. This technique may be used on any flat collar to achieve this effect.

STEP 3. The shape of the collar may be drawn directly onto the pattern and a tracing made of this.

THE SLEEVE

The sleeve on men's contemporary suits has a seam at the back of the arm and another seam approximately 1½" forward of the normal inside seam position. The sleeves are curved from the elbow to compensate for the normal angle of the arm as it hangs naturally.

STEP 1. Trace the Basic Sleeve pattern on a new sheet of paper. Draw in the sleeve Centerline. Mark the Back and Front sections of the sleeve cap.

STEP 2. Redraw the Side Seams of the sleeve pattern so that they are parallel to the Sleeve Centerline (Figure 139).

STEP 3. Measure down the Sleeve Centerline the Shoulder to Elbow length and draw a line perpendicular to the Centerline at this point. This is the Elbow line.

The seams will be relocated to the back of the arm position for one seam and 1½" forward of the inside of the arm position for the other seam, by the following procedure:

STEP 4. The back of the arm position may be found by drawing in the Biceps line and finding a spot on this line that is halfway between the Sleeve Centerline and the back edge of the sleeve. Draw a line parallel to the Sleeve Centerline from this point. This line should be the full length of the sleeve.

STEP 5. Mark notches and cut along this line.

STEP 6. Tape this section to the front edge of the redrawn sleeve pattern (Figure 140).

STEP 7. Mark a point 1½" to the right of the taped edge. Draw a line through this point parallel to the Centerline. Mark notches.

STEP 8. Cut the pattern on this line.

The two sections of the sleeve are now correctly proportioned. Next they will be shaped.

SLEEVE PATTERN (Steps 6 to 8)
Cutting the Sleeve

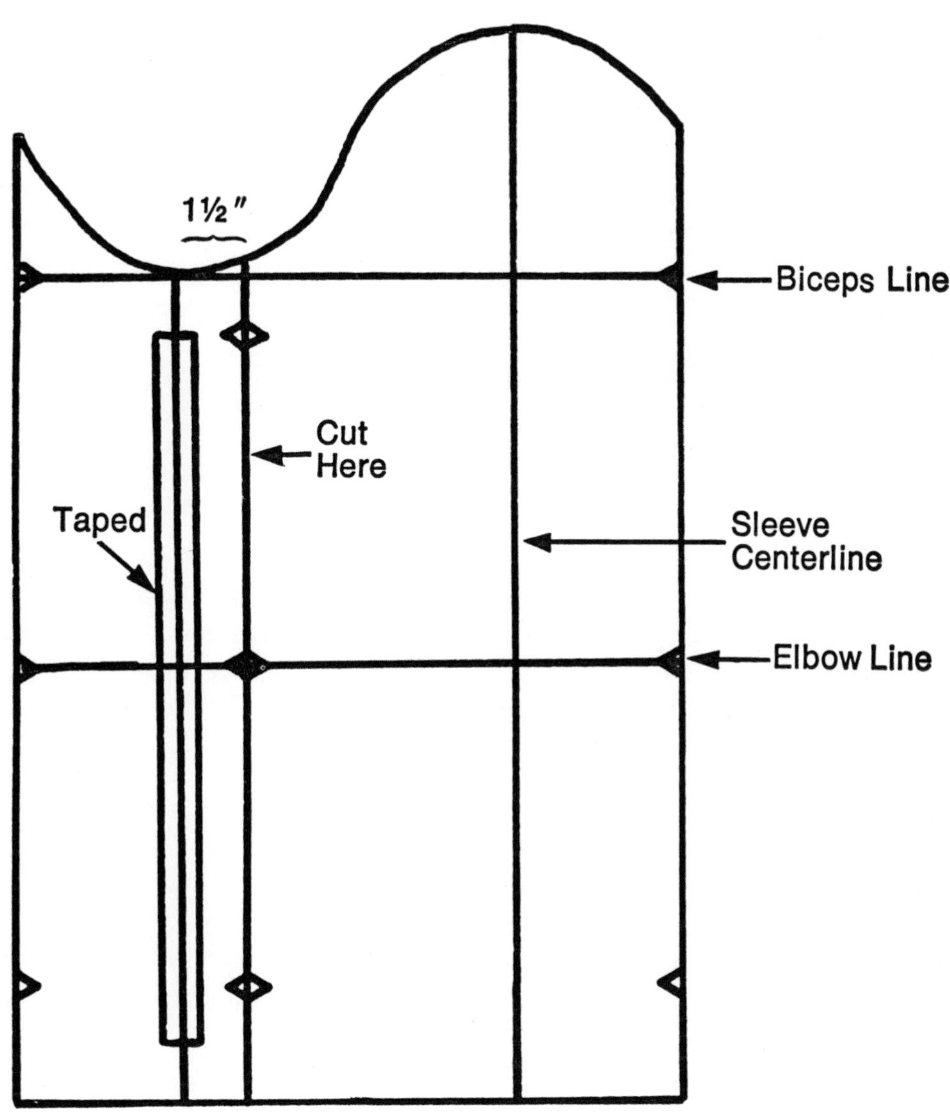

Figure 140

Step 9. Curve the back seams of both sections from the Elbow line to 2″ in on the Wrist line (see Figure 141).

Step 10. Draw new Wrist lines at right angles to the new back seams.

Step 11. Curve the front seam of the inside section slightly, as is indicated in Figure 141.

Step 12. Curve the front seam of the outside section 1″ out from the original seam line, starting at the Elbow line, as shown in Figure 141. Extend the cut pattern by taping an extra strip of paper along this edge.

Step 13. Measure the front seam of the inside section and adjust the length of the outside section to this length.

Step 14. Add seam allowances and cut.

The Fit

The major part of the fitting of the body of the coat will be done by adjusting the altered Side Seam and the Center Back seam. Additional shaping may be done by a vertical side front dart (not to exceed ½″ in width) and by a side dart where the Side Seam is normally located (not to exceed 1″ in width). The bottom of both of these darts will terminate at the pockets.

Sewing The Coat

The lapel and the collar of the coat are sewn by making a facing for the coat (approximately 4″ wide) and two copies of the collar. One of the collars is sewn to the main body of the coat and the other collar is sewn to the facing. The facing and its collar are then sewn to the coat and its collar around the outside seams. The seams are clipped and the facing is turned.

The lapel and the collar that are visible on a suit coat are actually the "facing" of the suit.

SLEEVE PATTERN (Steps 9 to 13)
Shaping the Sleeve

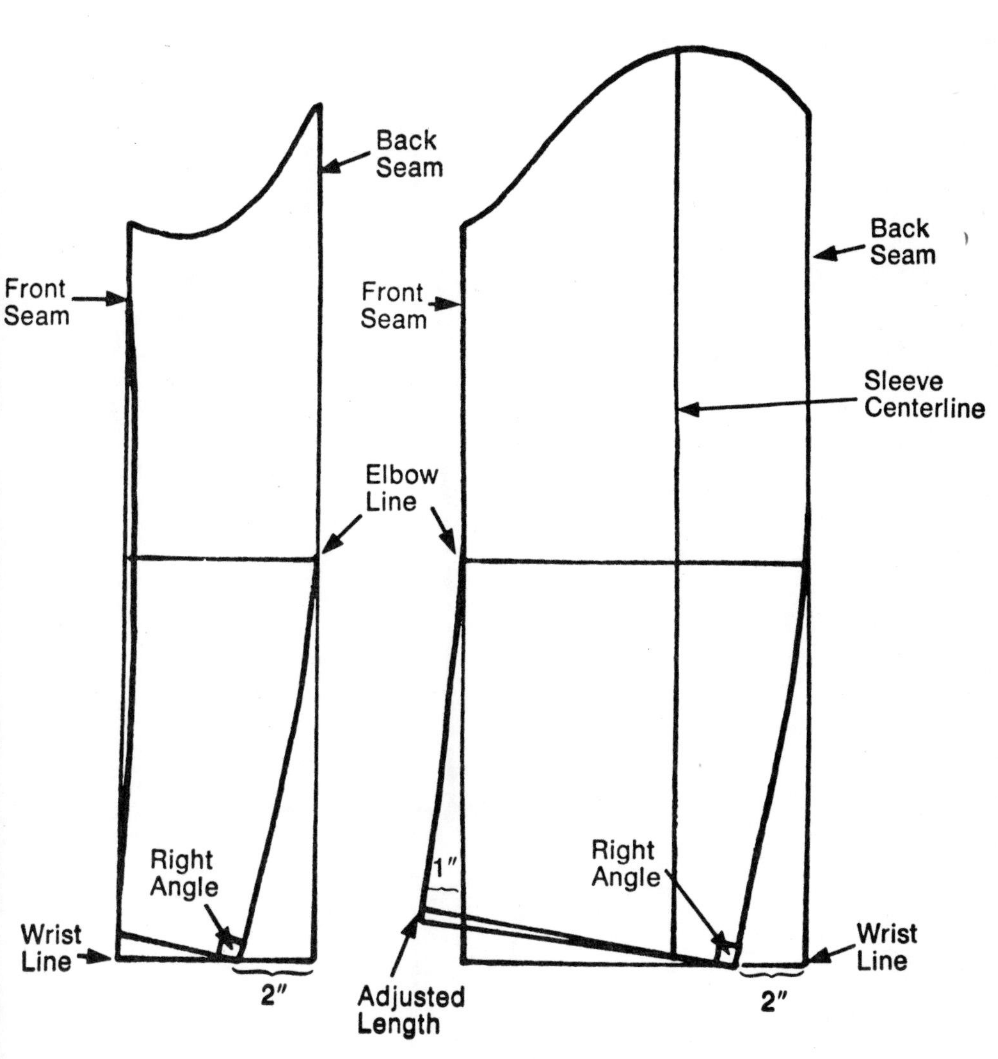

Inside Section (Pattern Reversed)

Outside Section

Figure 141

Figure 142

HISTORICAL COSTUMES FOR THE STAGE

The Drafter of Stage Costumes is given a design which must be used as the basis for creating patterns. However, there may be several possible pattern variations for this design. Two variations of the English Restoration coat illustrated in Figure 142 will be described here. First the coat will be drafted simply by altering the basic bodice.

This pattern will then be compared to the pattern of an actual Restoration coat of the same style. Through this comparison it is hoped that the value of historical sources can be appreciated.

Drafting The Coat From The Basic Patterns

To achieve the desired design of this coat, the following steps may be used.

Step 1. Extend the Center Front line of the bodice to the Above Knee measurement and draw a perpendicular line. This will be the Hem line (See Figure 143).

Step 2. Measure down from the Waist line the Waist to Hip measurement and draw a perpendicular line to the Center Front line at this point. Mark off 1″ plus one-fourth the Hip measurement to establish the Side Hip mark.

ALTERING THE BASIC PATTERN (Steps 1 to 5)
The Coat Pattern

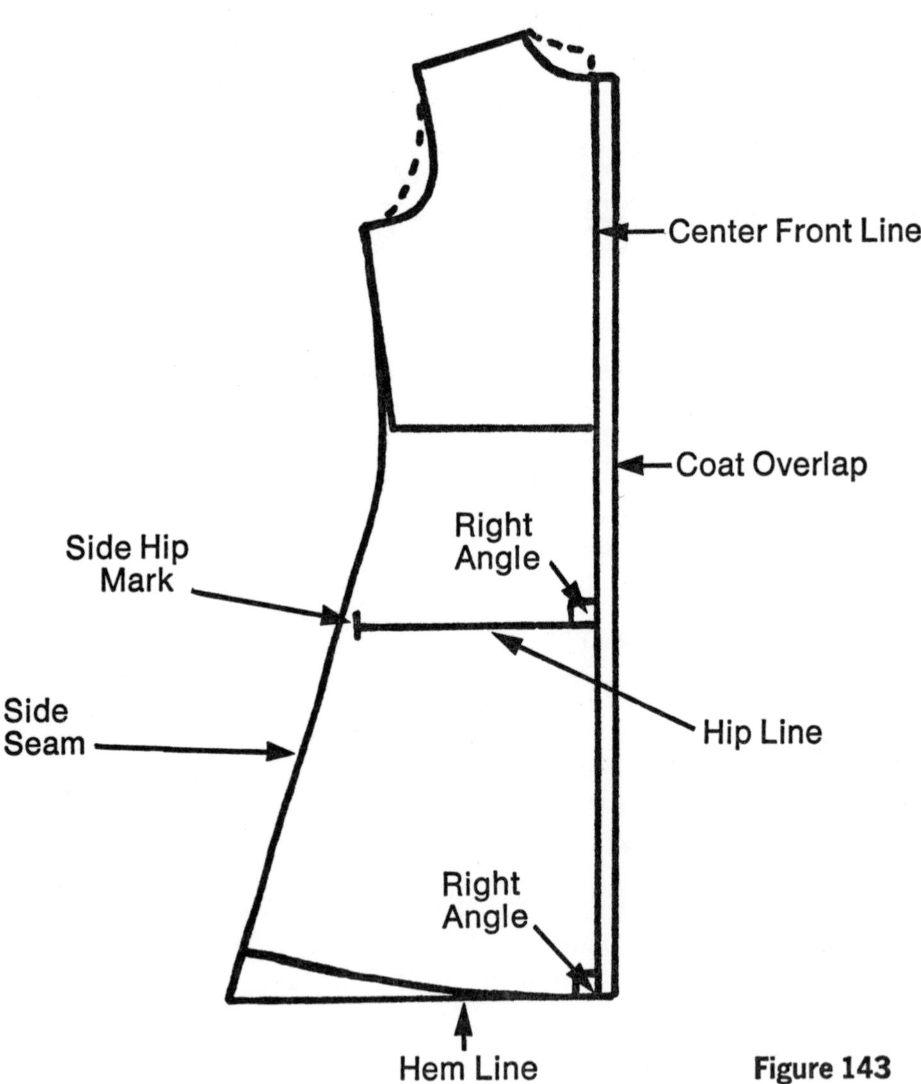

Figure 143

ALTERING THE BASIC PATTERN (Steps 6 to 9)
The Sleeve Pattern

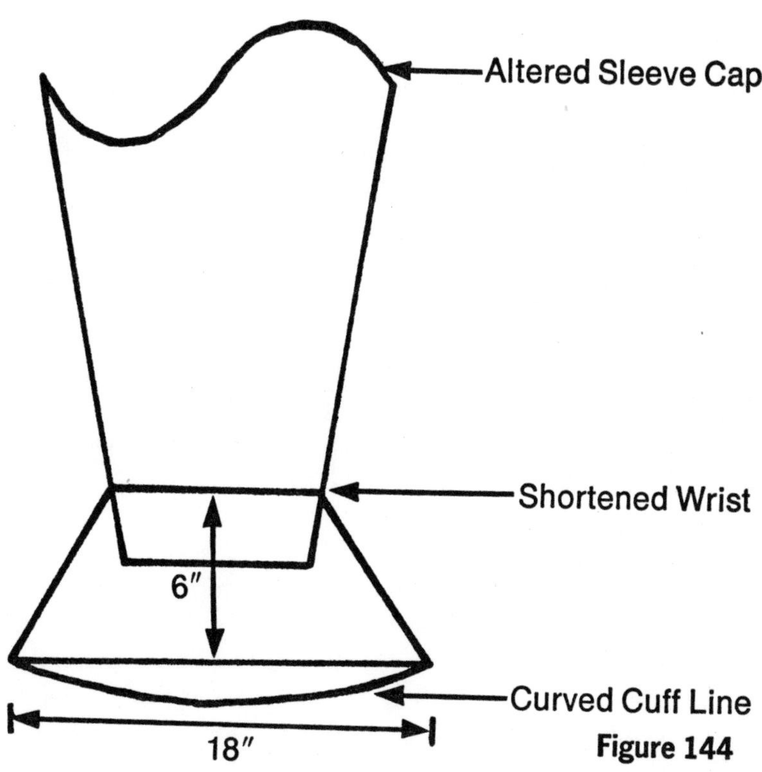

Figure 144

STEP 3. Draw a new Side Seam from the bottom of the Armhole curve past the Side Hip mark and flare it to the Hem line.

STEP 4. Draw a line ¾″ to the right of the Center Front line for the overlap of the coat.

STEP 5. Curve the Hem line by using the folding technique for the long skirt (pages 178-179).

The basic sleeve pattern is altered in the following way.

STEP 6. Change the sleeve seam from the inside position to the back of the arm (See Figure 144). (See page 76 for details.)

STEP 7. Shorten the sleeve to 3″ above the wrist.

STEP 8. Add a 6″-long cuff, flaring the sides to a finished opening of 18″.

STEP 9. Curve the end of the cuff.

STEP 10. Add seam allowances to all the patterns and cut. The basic patterns for the coat are complete.

Historical Source For The Restoration Coat

Blanche Payne in her *History of Costume* (Harper & Row, 1965, p. 522) illustrates patterns taken from an actual Restoration coat of the same design. These patterns are illustrated in Figures 145 and 146.

The principal differences in the body of the coat between the basic patterns and the historical patterns are that the side seam is moved approximately 1″ toward the back, and the shaping in the back sections is done by a center back seam rather than with two side back darts.

These two differences may not seem to be very significant, but the line of the coat and the way it hangs will be recognizably altered by these subtle changes. The alteration of the side seam is particularly important. Side seams that are at the center of the side lend themselves to being nipped at the waist. A seam that is moved further back, on the other hand, tends to make the coat hang straighter from the chest to the hips.

The difference between the two sleeve patterns is more noticeable. The first pattern is a one-piece sleeve; the historical pattern is in two pieces. The additional seam at the front of the sleeve is curved from the elbow to the fold line. This curved arm pattern suggests that the sleeve is shaped for an arm which is normally held at an angle rather than for an arm which hangs straight down to the sides. This fashion is borne out by pictures of the period which show gentlemen holding their arms at an angle. The historical sleeve pattern also has the cuff mounted differently, with the sleeve that is under the cuff being more fitted.

HISTORICAL PATTERN FOR THE COAT

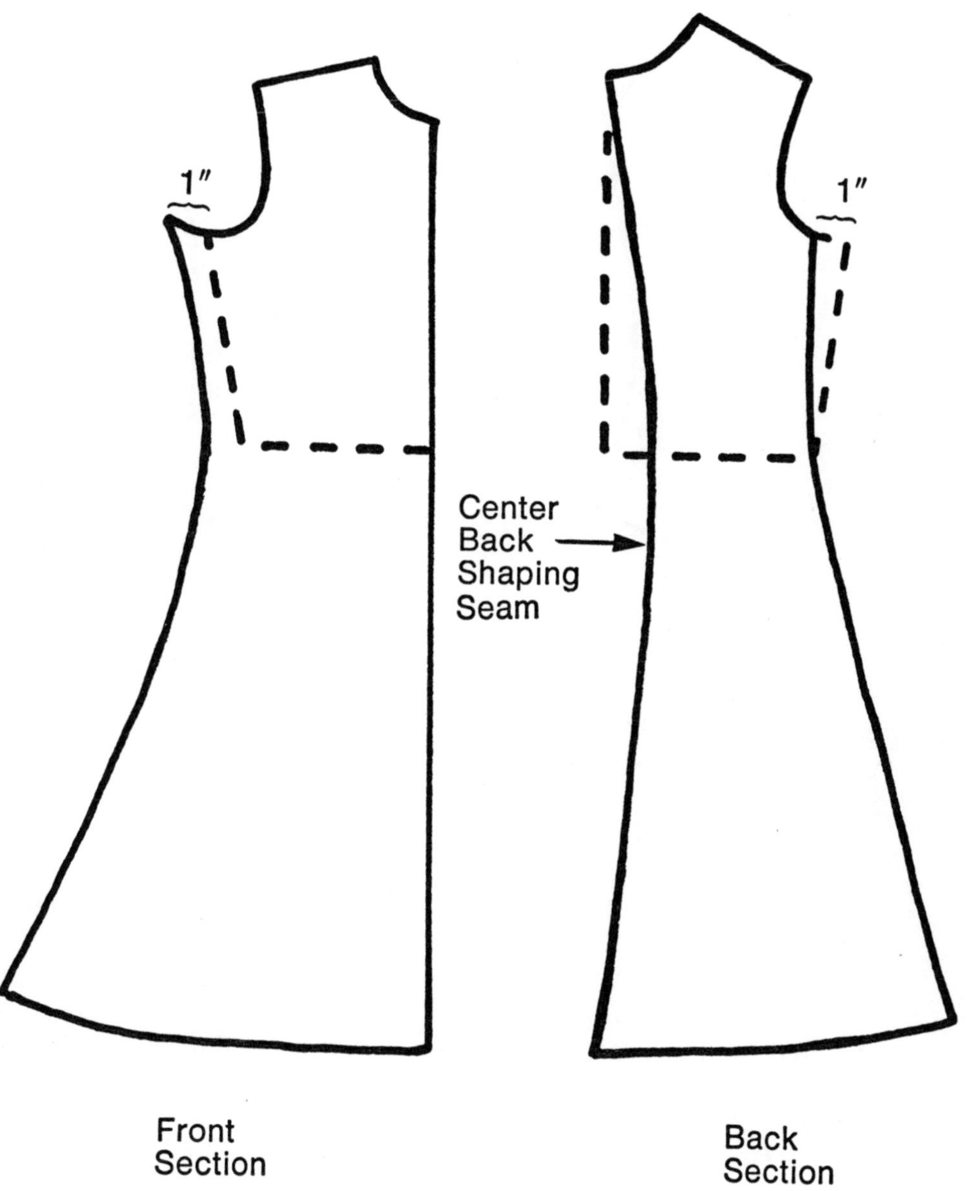

Figure 145

HISTORICAL PATTERN FOR THE SLEEVE

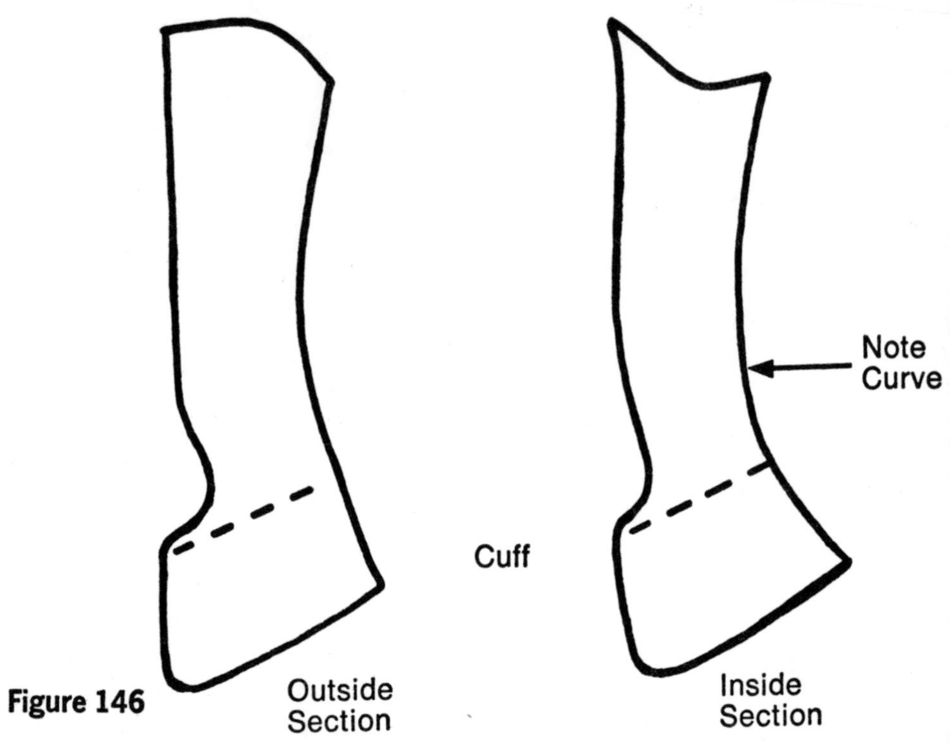

Figure 146

Reference to historical sources thus brings important factors to light. If the final costumes are based on the cut of clothes of the period from which the play evolved, they will help to enhance rather than detract from the texture of the play. To overlook these variations is to be lazy. To discover these historical differences and use them or adapt them—or even consciously ignore them—is to be exercising a creative effort.

The reading list includes four major sources for period patterns. It is highly recommended that they be consulted when a period play is being constructed.

FABRICS

THERE ARE A LARGE VARIETY of fabrics available for clothing construction. Each fabric has specific qualities which establish its character. Some of these qualities, such as color and texture, affect the design of a garment but they do not affect the way the patterns are drafted. Other qualities, such as drape, flexibility, and weight must be taken into consideration during the drafting. If these qualities are ignored, they can mar the effectiveness of the finished garment.

Understanding the drape, flexibility, and weight of a material is primarily a matter of developing a sensitive touch. There are too many different types of material and too many different end uses for each type to make any kind of specific measurement a practical consideration. The material must be aesthetically judged rather than scientifically measured.

FABRIC QUALITIES

The pattern drafter must learn how to respond to each new piece of material as though it had a personality of its own. Two different materials will respond differently to the same pattern and the pattern drafter must learn how to adjust patterns for these varying responses. Once again, time and experience are the best way to learn how to handle fabrics, but it helps to know what qualities to look for.

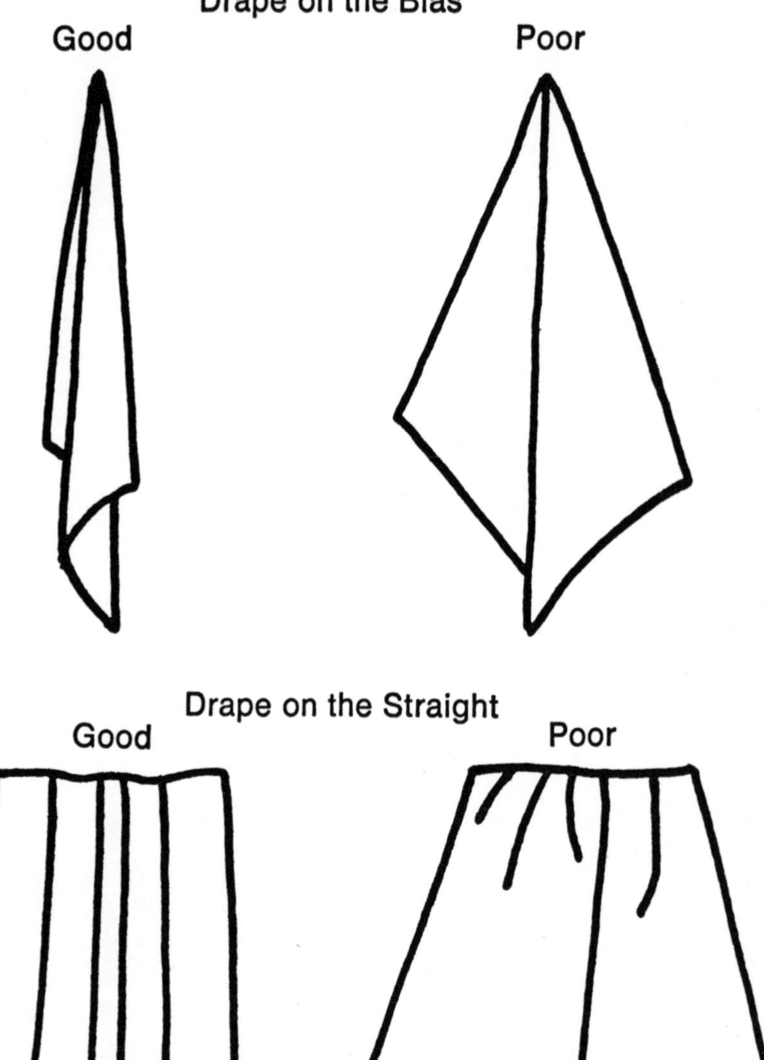

Figure 147

Drape

Drape is the ability of a fabric to fall into even and graceful folds when it is left free to hang. Any design which requires part of the garment to hang from a gathered seam should be made from material that drapes well.

A basic procedure for determining how well a fabric will drape is to pick up a corner and let the material hang on the bias. Check to see how easily the material falls into folds. Are the folds deep and do they pick up the light to accent the drape? Notice any tendency in the material toward stiffness (See Figure 147).

Normally, a fabric's ability to drape may be determined by letting it hang on the bias. However, some materials will drape well on the bias but poorly when they are hung on the straight line. To check for this quality, gather the top of the material into large pleats, or gathers and note whether the material tends to fight the gathers, or whether it falls into graceful folds.

Generally speaking, tightly woven fabrics or fabrics using tightly spun yarns will not drape as well as fabrics that are either loosely woven or loosely spun or both. Knits tend to drape well because of the looseness of their construction.

Flexibility

Examining a fabric's flexibility is another means of checking its ability to drape. Flexibility, as the term is used in this book, refers to the ability of a material to fold softly into a swag. Fabric with good flexibility will swag in smooth curves. Fabric with poor flexibility will tend to crack and be uneven when it is swagged (See Figure 148). Good flexibility is important when a design calls for material to end in gathers—such as those found at the cuff or at the waist, for example. Swag effects, such as those found in shawls or in cowl necklines, also require material with good flexibility.

The flexibility of a fabric may be determined by holding the material on the true bias at two points about 18″ apart. Move the hands together and notice whether the material drops into graceful curves or whether it tends to buckle and crack.

Some materials will drape fairly well, like no-wale corduroy, but will not have good flexibility. Other materials, such as velvets and chiffons, will drape well and have good flexibility; while still others, such as burlap, will drape poorly but have good flexibility.

Elasticity

Elasticity is usually not an essential quality for most clothing patterns, but testing the elasticity of a material is one way of learning a little more about the response of the material.

To check the elasticity of a fabric, hold it at two points approximately 18″ apart and stretch it. This check should be run in the direction of the filling threads, the warp threads, and across the bias.

Most woven fabrics will not stretch at all on the warp threads. They will stretch slightly in the filling direction, and they will stretch considerably on the bias. Knits will stretch in any direction unless they have a bonded backing.

Body And Weight

The body of a fabric is its mass or substance. The weight of a fabric is its actual weight in ounces per square yard. Normally the two are related, but some fabrics have more body than their weight would indicate. Pellon, for instance, is used to add body and stiffness to garments, but it is itself fairly lightweight. Wool will have much more body than cotton of the same weight.

A fabric with good body will hang flat. Coats must have body, so that they will hang down from the shoulders without clinging to the body. Another indication of good body is that the material does not drape into folds as the wearer moves, but remains flat and smooth.

What determines how much body will be needed in a fabric is the type of garment it is to be used for. Shirts and blouses, for instance, should be lightweight; too much body would be inappropriate for such garments, as well as uncomfortable. Pants and skirts, on the other hand, must have more body in order to fit and hang properly. Heavy outer garments, such as coats, should have the most body.

These are the basic qualities of fabrics that will affect the

FLEXIBILITY

Designs Requiring Good Flexibility

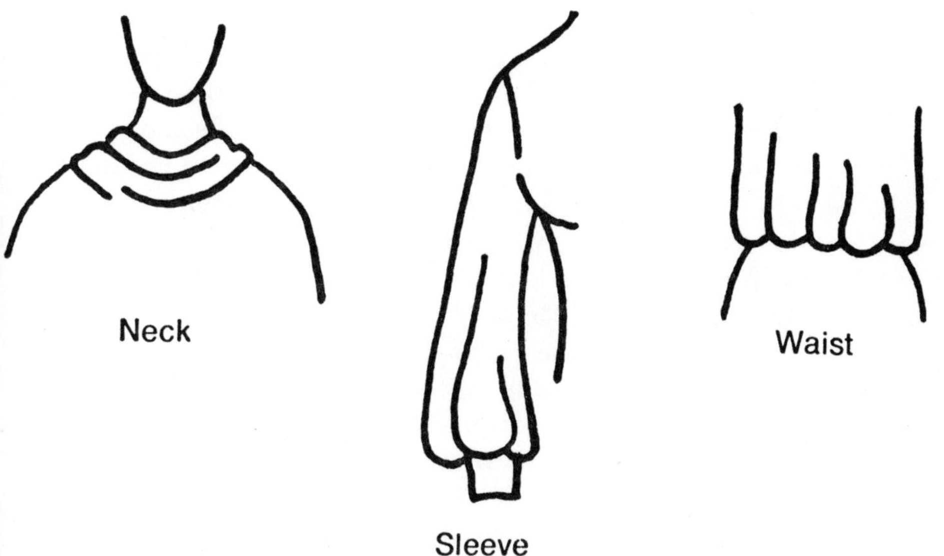

Figure 148

pattern drafter's work. A brief test for these qualities has been included in the Appendix for the reader who may wish to pursue the topic further.

FABRIC CONSTRUCTION

Basic to developing a sensitive touch for material is a knowledge of how fabrics are constructed and what to look for in a fabric. The following discussion intends to introduce the reader to these topics.

Fabrics are made up of a variety of different raw materials. Some of these materials are naturally fibrous and may be converted directly into yarn for fabrics. Other raw materials must first be converted into fibers through one of several man-made processes. These fibers are then processed in a variety of ways to achieve finished fabrics.

Natural Fibers

There are four basic types of natural fibers used in clothing: cotton, wool, flax, and silk. These fibers come in two forms: staple and filament. Staple fibers are short, from 3/4″ in the case of some cottons to up to a yard for flax. They must be twisted together to make a yarn before they can be processed into material. Filament fibers, on the other hand, are very long. Silk, which is the only natural filament fiber, measures up to two miles in length.

Cotton is the most commonly used natural fiber. It comes from the ripened seed-pod of the cotton plant. Cotton is readily available in many countries and is easily processed by machines into yarn. For these reasons, it is the most economical natural fiber. Cotton is versatile and may be made up into a variety of different types of yarn with good strength. Its main drawback is that when it is crushed it does not resume its original shape. This is called a low resilience and in practical terms means that cotton fabrics will crease easily. Cotton can, however, be processed to resist creasing.

Wool is the sheared fleece of sheep. It is not as easily processed as cotton nor is it as readily available. It is, therefore, more expensive. Wool fibers have natural air pockets, making it a very warm material. Wool also has good draping characteristics, and is very resilient when dry. Wool does, however, need special care in cleaning; it is not easily laundered, like cotton.

Flax is a very strong fiber which looks like human hair. It is made from the fibers in the stalk of the flax plant. It is the raw material from which linen is made. To process flax, the stalks must be broken open and the fibers must be degummed and separated. This process makes linen fairly expensive. Flax has a very poor resilience which causes linen fabric to wrinkle easily. New processes, however, make linen quite crease-resistant. Linen is easy to launder.

Silk filaments are made by unwinding the cocoon of the silk worm. Silk is a very strong, very fine fiber that has good luster, drape, softness, and resilience. The main disadvantage of silk is that it is very expensive to process, since most of the work must be done by hand.

Man-Made Fibers

Man-made fibers are the result of industry trying to create artificial silk. Experiments in this direction were started in the late nineteenth century. It was not until the twentieth century that man decided to use these synthetic fibers for their own properties rather than as a substitute for silk.

The basic process for manufacturing all man-made fibers is the same. It was developed from the procedure the silkworm uses. Liquid is forced through a small hole or series of holes, a spinerette. It is then solidified into a filament through one of three methods: evaporation, cooling, or chemical treatment. All man-made fibers, therefore, originate as filaments. Sometimes these filaments are cut into short lengths to make staple fibers which are in turn respun into yarns. This procedure is used to create special textures.

Rayon was the first man-made fiber. It is made by breaking down wood pulp through mechanical and chemical means into a solution of cellulose molecules. This solution is forced through the holes of the spinerette into a bath which changes the liquid into a filament of cellulose molecules. The cellulose molecules in rayon are the same as the cellulose molecules in cotton. As a result, rayon and cotton have many of the same characteristics. Both fibers are very versatile but have a low resilience. The basic difference between rayon and cotton is that—although some forms of rayon are specially reprocessed to increase their strength—rayon is not as strong as cotton.

Acetate is also made from wood pulp, but in this processing the cellulose molecules are chemically changed. The solution is liquified by the addition of a solvent. After the liquid has been forced through the spinerette the solvent evaporates, leaving the filament thread. Acetate is used for its silklike qualities. It is moderately strong, does not crease easily, has a good drape, and a pleasing luster.

Advanced technology has created a series of fibers by synthetically making long molecule chains from the atoms in oil and coal. Different characteristics are achieved by varying the exact molecular structure.

Nylon was the first synthetically created fiber. It is spun by having a molten solution forced through the spinerette. The solution, as it leaves, is cooled and thus is solidified into filaments. This process makes nylon heat-sensitive. Too hot an iron will melt it. Nylon is a very strong fiber with very good resilience. It is also elastic, which is why it is particularly suitable for stockings. It is shiny and naturally transparent but these qualities may be chemically altered.

There are other heat-sensitive synthetic fibers. Each type of fiber has been developed for particular characteristics which will make it suitable for some uses and unsuitable for others. For instance, polyesters have a very good resilience whether they are wet or dry, which makes them good for drip-dry clothes. Acrylics are valuable for their wool-like qualities.

Sometimes different fibers are combined in one fabric. If the fabric has two different types of yarn, it is called a mixture. If, however, a yarn is made up of two types of fiber it is called a blend. A mixture or blend may be created for the sake of economy, as when wool is mixed with cotton, or it may be used to combine the desirable properties of two different fibers, such as warmth with strength.

Yarns

Fibers, before they can be made into fabric, must be made into yarns, except in the case of felting. The two basic types of yarns are those made from staples and those made from filaments.

Staple yarns are spun so that the fibers of the staples will bind together through friction to form a strong, continuous, fine thread. There are two basic types of staple yarns. In the first type, the staples are aligned at more or less random angles to each other. This thread is thick and not very strong. Cotton yarns of this type are called carded yarns. Wool, when it is processed in this way, is referred to as woolen. In the other type of staple yarn, the staples are aligned during the spinning so that the fibers run parallel to each other. This results in a more compact yarn that is stronger, because the friction coefficient between the staples is higher. In cottons this is called combed cotton; wool yarns of this type are called worsted.

Filament yarns may or may not be spun together. When they are, it is for the purpose of increasing the diameter of the yarn, not for strength. Filament fibers that are used singly are called monofilament yarns. These yarns are strong, sheer, and have a very high luster. Yarns made of more than one filament are referred to as multifilament yarns. These yarns are softer and more flexible than monofilament yarns of the same diameter.

Woven Fabrics

Once the fibers have been converted into yarns, they are ready to be processed into fabric. Woven fabrics are made from a series of long threads which are held parallel to each other on the loom. These are called warp threads. Another yarn, called the weft or filling yarn, is passed at right angles to the warp yarns. The filling yarn goes over some yarns and under others. This process binds the yarns into fabric. The actual pattern of how many yarns the filling threads go over and how many they go under can be widely varied, and each variation creates its own particular type of fabric. Three basic types

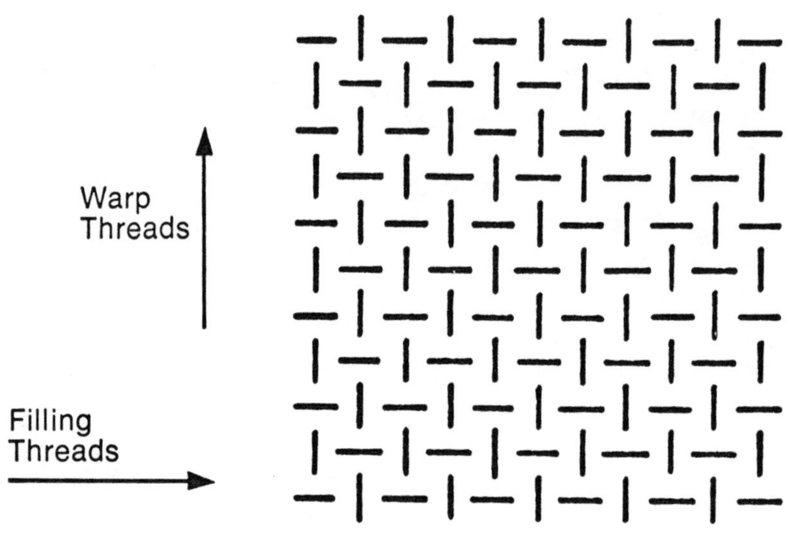

Plain Weave
Diagram A

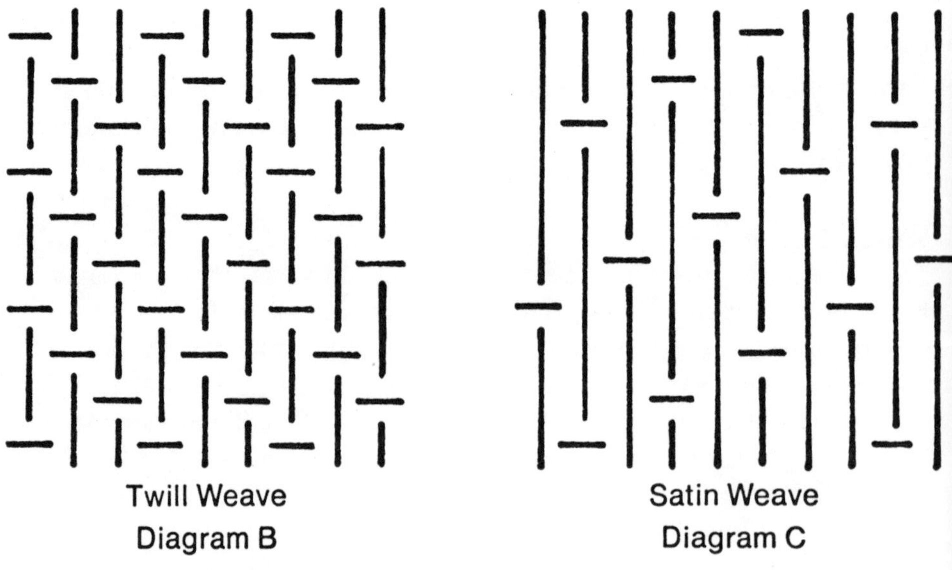

Twill Weave
Diagram B

Satin Weave
Diagram C

Figure 149

will be described here: the plain weave, the twill weave, and the satin weave.

The plain weave is the simple sequence of over one, under one with the next filling yarn alternating in the opposite manner. Plain weave is illustrated in Diagram A of Figure 149. This weave usually is made with the yarns of the fabric very close together; it makes a very strong fabric.

Twill weave is made by starting each filling thread one warp thread beyond the last filling thread. This creates a diagonal pattern in the fabric (See Diagram B of Figure 149). A variation of the twill weave is the herringbone pattern, which has filling threads that alternate to create a V-shaped design. The twill weave is used to enhance the texture and color of a fabric.

Satin weave is used to give fabrics a high sheen. It is normally used with fibers that have a high luster. To create this fabric the warp threads float over a series of filling threads (Diagram C of Figure 149). Only the warp threads are visible, which gives the fabric a very smooth finish.

Pile fabrics are a special kind of woven fabrics. They are woven with an extra set of warp or filling threads which are left in loops. These loops may be either cut or left uncut. Terrycloth is a pile fabric with uncut loops. Velvet and corduroy have cut loops. Pile is used to enhance the texture of the material. The processing of velvet and corduroy results in what is called a directional fabric. If the hand is rubbed lightly over the surface in one direction, the material will feel soft. If the direction is reversed, the material will offer resistance. This one-way feature affects the way the material reflects light from its surface. When two pieces of the same pile material are placed side by side, they will appear to be of two different colors unless the directions of the piles are matched.

A final important characteristic of woven fabrics is that they stretch on the bias of the material. The warp threads are stretched out on the loom and hold the filling threads as they pass through, so the material will not stretch or give at all in the direction of the warp threads. Similarly, there is little if any give in the direction of the filling threads, particularly if the material has been tightly woven. But when the material is pulled at a diagonal to the warp threads it will stretch. This diagonal is referred to as the bias of the material (See Figure 150). True bias runs at a forty-five-degree angle to the warp threads. The straight of the goods is the direction of the fabric which runs parallel to the warp or to the filling threads. For most garments the material normally hangs straight, so that there will be no sagging. Sometimes, however, a pattern will be deliberately cut on the bias in order to achieve a particular effect. When this is done, the fabric must be handled very carefully in the sewing, so that the garment does not stretch out of shape.

BIAS

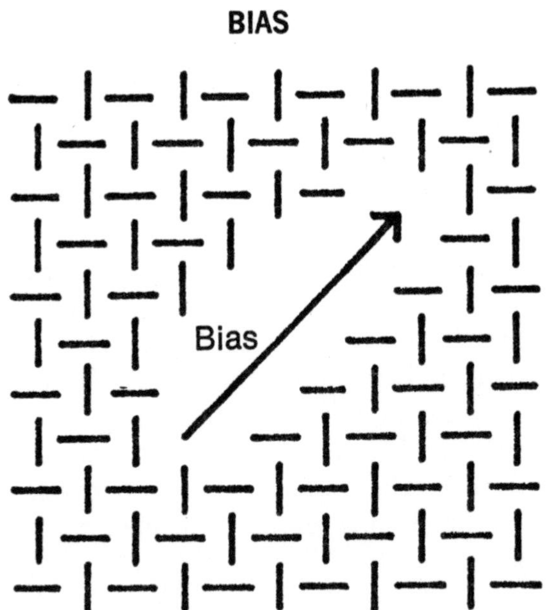

Figure 150

Knitted Fabrics

Knitted fabrics are formed by rows of single yarns connected by a series of interlocking loops to each other. There are two basic types of knits: filling knit and warp knit. The two types are illustrated in Figure 151.

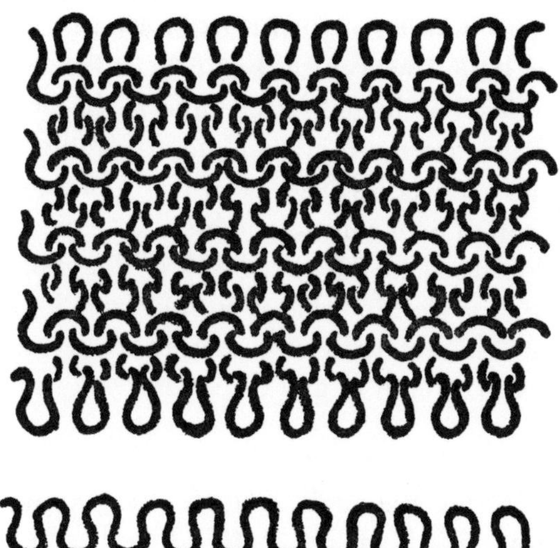

Filling Knit

Diagram A

Figure 151

Warp Knit

Diagram B

In the filling knit the yarn runs in a horizontal direction (Diagram A, Figure 151). This type of knit is most frequently used in stockings and sweaters. Its chief disadvantage is that it runs easily.

Warp knits are more convenient to produce than filling knits because a series of needles may be used to create the vertical warp rows rather than the one needle which is required by filling knits (Diagram B, Figure 151). This type of knit does not ravel and is therefore appropriate for clothing that is cut out from a pattern.

The chief characteristic of knits is that—because they are formed of loops—they will stretch in any direction.

Felted Fabrics

Felted fabrics are made from fibers that have not been converted into yarns. The fibers are matted together in a random order by a combination of heat, pressure, and moisture. Felted fabrics have no particular direction as knitted and woven fabrics do. They may be cut in any way and they will not ravel. They will also stretch only slightly, if at all, in any direction. Wool is the only natural fiber which may be felted and when it is, it is called felt. Pellon is one of the felted fabrics that is made from synthetic fibers. The chief disadvantage of felted fabrics is that their shape may become distorted in the presence of heat, moisture, and pressure.

CREATING ORIGINAL DESIGNS

THE READER, by now, should be able to draft patterns for original designs. The final concern is to understand what pattern variations are possible so that the widest range of creativity may be achieved.

It would be futile to try to describe or illustrate all the different contemporary and historic styles of clothing that are possible, because records of historical clothing already fill hundreds of volumes, and contemporary fashions are constantly changing from decade to decade, from year to year, and even from month to month. This chapter will point to sources where the reader can obtain fresh inspiration and new ideas.

The problems of pattern variation are different for the home sewer than they are for the pattern drafter of stage costumes. The stage costumer is given the design he is to execute by the designer and he must adhere to this design. But within this requirement, there are possible pattern variations which can enhance the final product. Section Five discussed the importance of consulting historical sources for these variations.

The home sewer, on the other hand, is not handed a specific design to execute. The design may come from a garment catalog, a window display, a newspaper ad, or from the sewer's own imagination. In any case, the home sewer is free to change the collar style or sleeve style when such a change is desired.

There are a large number of contemporary sources for clothing designs. Some of these sources are garment ads in newspapers and magazines, clothing catalogs for ready-made clothes, and pattern catalogs. Other designs may be picked up from actual garments seen in clothing stores, on the street, at parties, or in shop windows. Finally, the designs may also be derived from the imagination of the sewer.

The multitude of different possible designs may seem to be staggering. Even when the designs are limited to those which are suited to the personal taste of the sewer, the large variety of choices can be overwhelming. At the same time, however, the possible variations of the basic patterns may seem to be limited. To resolve these problems, the following discussion will describe a technique for analyzing designs that will make pattern drafting a practical consideration for many different styles.

The first step in drafting any design is to look at a sketch of the garment to be constructed. This sketch may be created by the drafter, traced from a picture, or borrowed from a catalog. The sketch must be looked at with two questions in mind: First, "How does it look?", then, "How is it made?"

When a sketch is looked at from a distance, the entire picture is taken in at a glance. This viewpoint can be used to check the design to see if the elements of the design are in harmony or discord. This distance-viewing results in a subjective reaction to the design which says "I like it," or "I don't like it." From this viewpoint, most designs will appear to be unique. The implication for the drafter is that the design may present problems which have never been encountered.

Looking at a design from up close is the second way of looking at a sketch. It is a more objective view which analyzes each individual element as a separate entity without trying to take in the entire design. This viewpoint may focus on a seam or a dart, a collar or a part of a sleeve. It is the way the drafter analyzes how the patterns are to be executed. It may also be used to alter a design by adding details and making modifications and adaptations to the design. However, after the design has been altered, the sewer must look at the sketch from a distance to see the effect of the change.

When analyzed from a close viewpoint, the large selection of different designs may be classified into a number of basic variations. The following illustrated checklist shows basic variations for dresses.

CHECKLIST

These basic variations are combined to create the wide range of different dress designs. The techniques for achieving these variations have all been described in this book or can be easily inferred by applying the basic principles and techniques described here.

The procedure for developing patterns for a design is to look at each element separately. If the succeeding steps are followed, the reader should have no difficulty in drafting almost any dress pattern.

1) Look at the body of the dress. Is there fullness, or is it fitted?

2) Where are the darts located and what direction do they take?

3) Where are the seams? What is their shape? Do the seams shape the dress or are they decorative?

4) Where is the waistline?

5) How does the garment open and close?

6) Is the skirt sewn separately or is it cut with the body?

7) What is the shape of the skirt?

8) Is there a collar? If so, what type is it?

9) What is the shape of the neckline?

10) Is there a sleeve? If so, what kind of sleeve is it?

11) How is the sleeve shaped?

12) Is there a cuff? If so, what kind?

This same type of analysis may be applied to other garments, such as shirts, coats, and pants.

This, then, is a technique for analyzing designs. It reduces most designs to an almost disappointingly few variations. It quickly singles out any new and distinctive pattern variations. But, most important of all, it makes the rendering of patterns a practical consideration for anyone who has mastered the basic drafting skills.

After the technique of looking at designs and visualizing patterns for them has been mastered, the drafter will want to discover different variations. The simplest means of discovering variations is to go back over the checklist and look for something different. Other variations may be found in pattern catalogs. These are a particularly good source for new ideas because if there is a problem in executing the desired variation the actual pattern may be consulted. Frequently, the pattern layouts on the back of a pattern envelope will be a sufficient indication of the pattern shape to resolve any difficulty in execution.

Another good way to get "new" ideas is to look at books on the history of clothing. Frequently an old line will have a new look when it is adapted to contemporary usage.

The more pattern variations the drafter attempts, the better will be his ability to develop new and unique designs. Not only does the repertoire of basic variations increase, but original ideas will also be stimulated by this broadened background.

CHECKLIST OF DRESS VARIATIONS

BODY

I. Shape

Fitted__________ or Full__________

Amount of Fullness__________

Fullness Controlled By__________

Type of Fullness: Gathered__________, Pleated__________,

Tucked__________, or Shirred__________.

Gathered Fullness

Pleated Fullness

Tucked Fullness

Figure 152

Front Dart: None________, Straight________, or Curved________.
Dart Direction: Waist________, Side Waist________,
Side Seam________, Armhole________, Shoulder Seam________,
Neck Line________, or Center Front________.
Back Dart: Yes________, No________
Dart Direction: Waist________, Shoulder________, or Neck________.

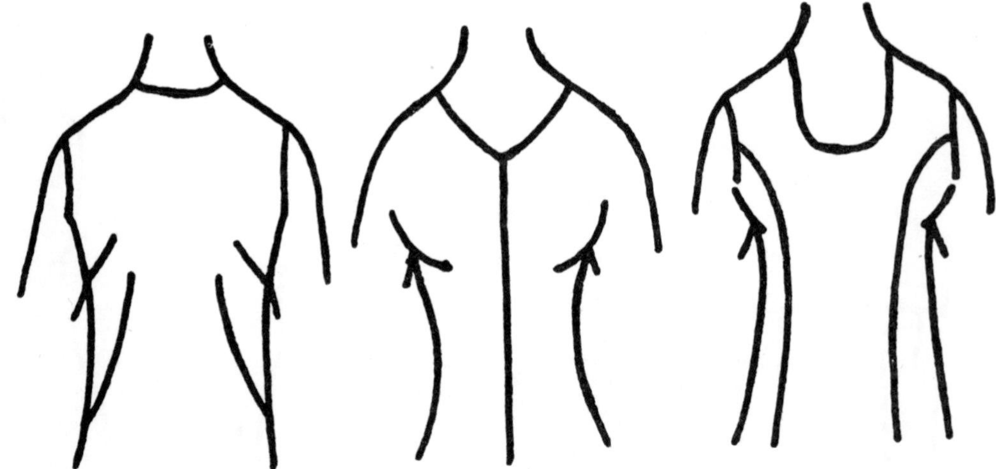

Side Waist and Side Dart

Center Front Seam

Side Front Seams

Figure 153

Seams: Center Front________, Center Back________, Side________,
Side Front________, Side Back________, Special________.

Waistline: None________, High________, Natural________,
Low________.

No Waist

Natural Waist (Gathered Skirt)

High Waist (Gored Skirt)

Figure 154

II. The Skirt

Cut with Body________ or Cut Separately________

Fitted________ or Full________

Gored________, Gathered________, Pleated________.

III. The Line

Neckline: V________, U________, Square________

High________, Medium________, Low________

High V Neck  Medium U Neck 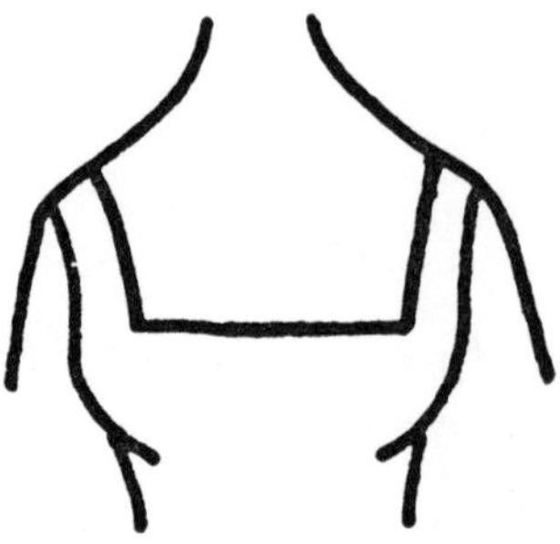 Low Square Neck

Hemline: Very High________, Above Knee________,

Knee Length________, Below Knee________,

Mid-Calf________, Ankle-Length________,

Floor Length________

Decorative Seams________ Yoke________

Pockets________

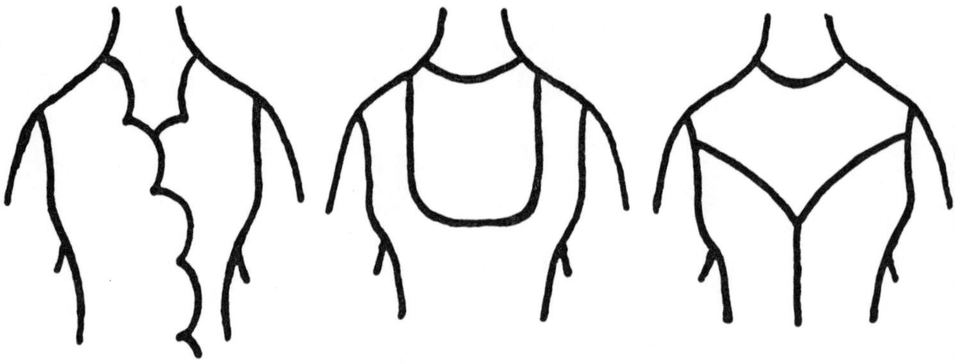

Decorative Seams

Figure 155

IV. Closure

Location: Center Back________, Center Front________,

Side Seam________, Wrap Around________

Type: Zipper______, Buttons___ __, Hook and Eyes______,

Placket________

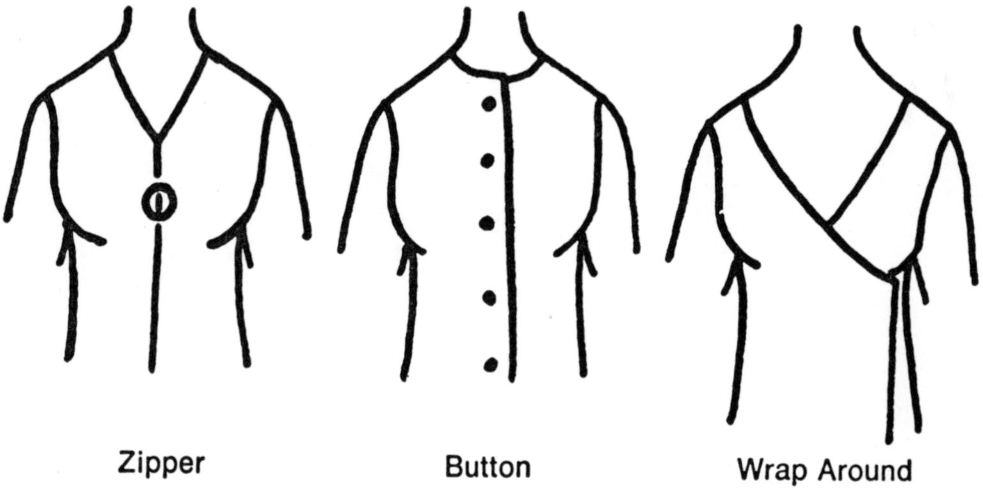

Zipper

Button

Wrap Around

Figure 156

COLLAR

I. Type

None________, Flat Collar________, Shirt Collar________,

Mandarin Collar________, Suit Collar________.

II. Shape________

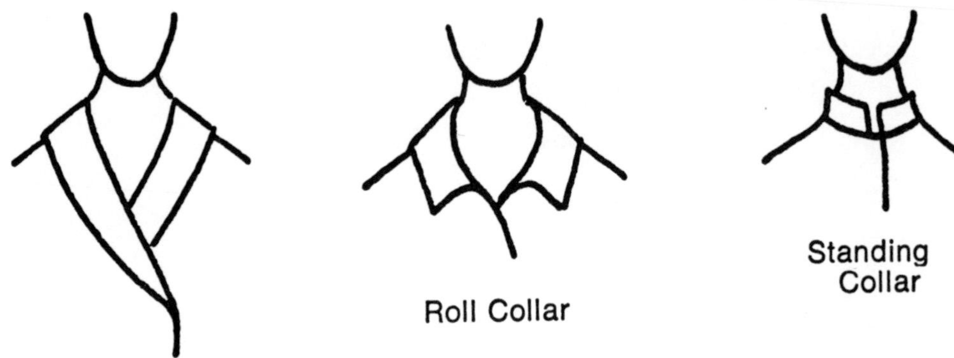

Figure 157

SLEEVE

I. Type

None______, Set in______, Raglan______, Peasant______,
Tunic______.

II. Length

Short______, To Elbow______, Three-Quarter______,
Full Length______.

III. Shape

Top: Fitted______, Gathered______.

Shoulder to Elbow: Fitted______, Full______:
Gathered______, Loose______.

Elbow to Wrist: Fitted______, Full______:
Gathered______, Loose______.

Bottom of Sleeve: Fitted______, Gathered______,
Flared______

Cuff: None______, Small______, Decorative______

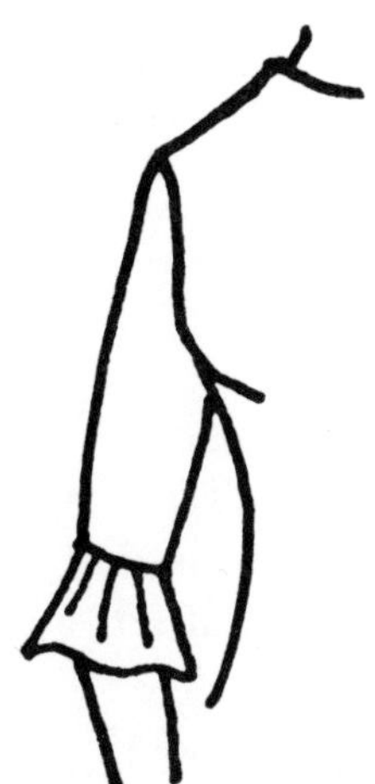

¾ Length Set-in Sleeve
Fitted to Elbow, Full from
Elbow to Bottom

Full Length Set-in Sleeve
Gathered at Top and
Fitted to the Rest of Arm

Raglan Sleeve
Gathered into Cuff

Short Peasant
Sleeve, Full

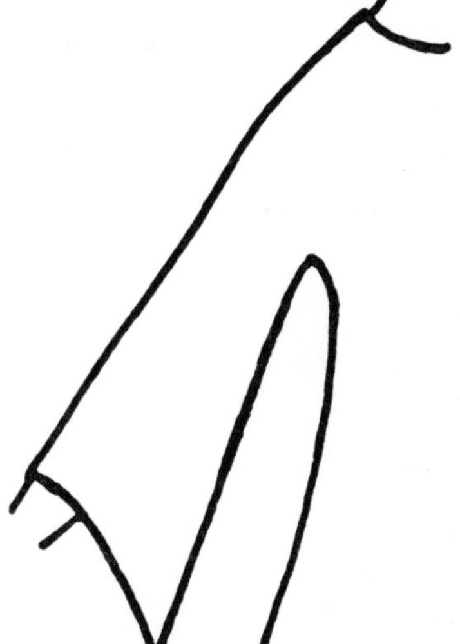

Tunic Sleeve
Flared at Bottom

Figure 158

CONCLUSION

The Art of Pattern Drafting is like any other art. Part of the process is to develop an eye for the work. The drafter's eye will tell him: 1) what techniques to use to achieve a particular design, 2) whether or not a pattern looks right as it is being drafted, and 3) how to get the optimum shape in a fitting session.

There is only one way this eye can be developed and that is by drafting original patterns; making mistakes (but not more than necessary); and by learning from these mistakes. The first creations will not be masterpieces. It takes time and practice and, above all, patience.

APPENDIX

FABRIC TESTING

The following tests are not meant to be accurate scientific tests. They are simply intended to give the reader a way of comparing various fabrics with some basic measurements.

All of the tests described are based on using an 18″ by 18″ sample of the material to be tested.

Draping Test

Take one edge of the 18″ by 18″ sample and gather it to 6″. Measure the bottom edge of the material while allowing it to hang freely. Record the results. Now gather the material to 9″ and measure the bottom edge, once again recording the results.

This test should be run with the material hanging in both the filling and the warp direction. (To gather the material, it is not necessary to sew it. It may be pinned to the edge of a board with push pins. This procedure will save considerable time.)

The following table will provide a means of evaluating the draping qualities of the material.

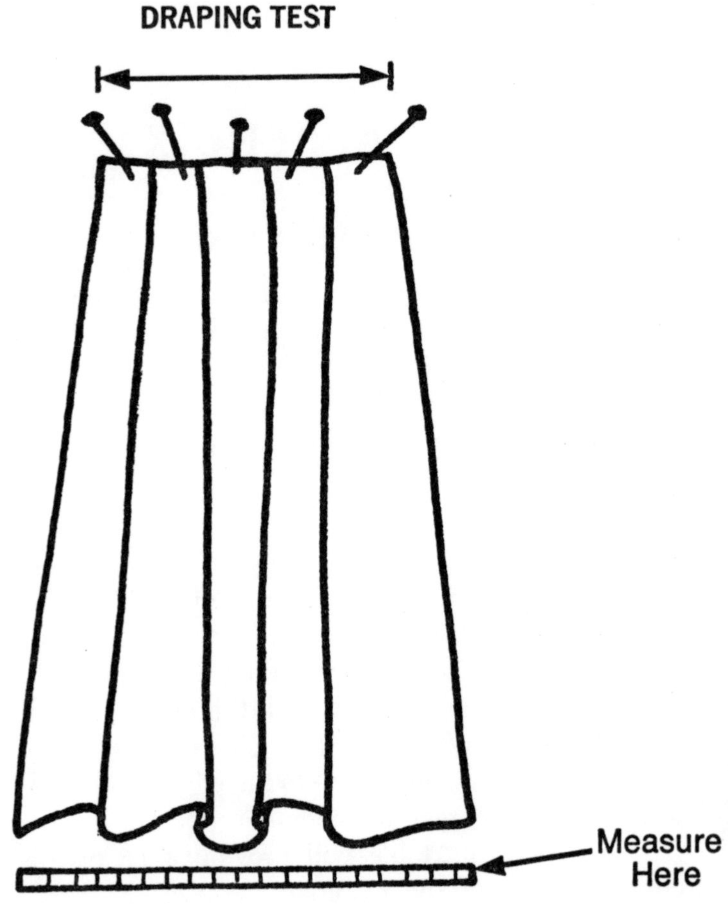

Figure 159

CHART I

DRAPING QUALITIES

	Material Gathered to 9″	6″	Quality of Drape
Bottom Edge Measures	9″ to 12″	6″ to 9″	*Very Good*
	13″	10″ to 11″	*Good*
	14″ to 16″	12″ to 14″	*Passable*
	17″ to 18″	15″ to 18″	*Poor*

Flexibility Test

Hold the sample material at diagonally opposite corners; allow the material to hang freely. Bring the corners slowly together until the material starts to crack, as described on page 255. Measure the distance from where the material is being held to the top of the swag (See Figure 160). Record this measurement.

The flexibility of the material may be appraised by comparing it to Chart II.

FLEXIBILITY TEST

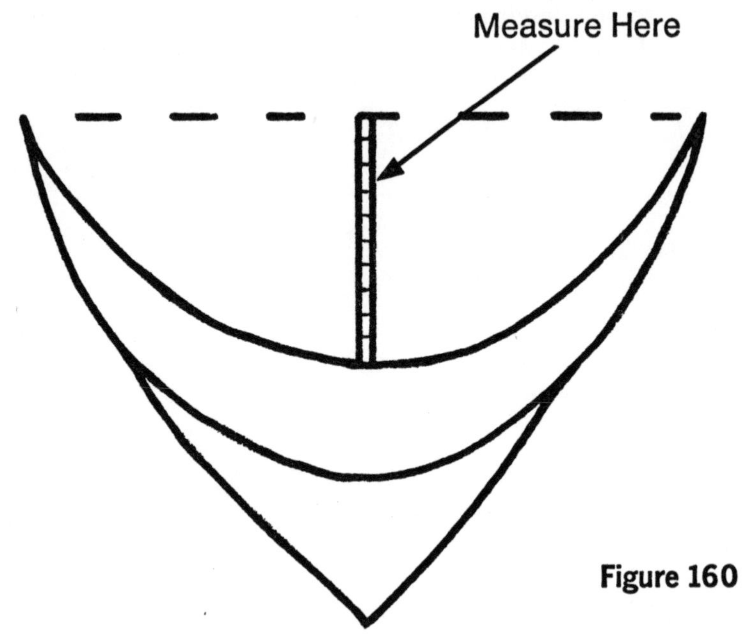

Figure 160

CHART II

FLEXIBILITY QUALITIES

Swag Dips To	Quality of Flexibility
10″ to 9″	*Very Good*
8″ to 6″	*Good*
5″ to 3″	*Fair*
2″ to 0″	*Poor*

Elasticity Test

Take the opposite corners of one edge of the material and stretch it. Measure the increased length and record it. This should be done in both the warp and filling direction. To test the bias direc tion, hold two diagonally opposite corners and stretch it. Measure the increased length and record it.

Chart III gives the normal elasticity for woven fabrics.

CHART III

ELASTICITY OF WOVEN FABRICS

Amount of Stretch			Standard of
Warp	Filling	Bias	Elasticity
over 1″	over 1″	over 6″	*Above Average*
0″ to 1″	0″ to 1″	3″ to 6″	*Average*
		0″ to 2″	*Below Average*

Weight

The weight of a fabric is normally measured in ounces per square yard. The sample fabric 18″ by 18″ may be weighed on a postal scale and this figure may be multiplied by four to get the appropriate weight.

Chart IV gives a standard for comparing the weights of fabric.

CHART IV

WEIGHT

Weight	Standard
under 3 ozs.	*Light*
3 to 5 ozs.	*Medium*
over 5 ozs.	*Heavy*

Chart V is a combined comparison of all the qualities for a selected group of fabrics. The fabrics are grouped by fiber content.

CHART V

FABRIC QUALITIES

	Drape	Flexibility	Elasticity	Weight
Cotton				
Muslin	**	*	**	*
Corduroy	**	*	**	***
No-Wale Corduroy	***	*	**	***
Wool				
Herringbone Weave	***	***	***	**
Felt	*	*	*	**
Hemp				
Burlap	*	***	***	***
Rayon				
Velvet	****	****	**	**
Plain Weave	**	**	**	***
Cupronium	**	***	**	*
Acetate				
Satin	**	**	**	*
Lining	**	**	**	*
Nylon				
Chiffon	****	****	***	*
Polyester				
Knit	****	**	***	***
Rayon/Nylon				
Pellon (Heavy)	*	*	*	*

**** Very Good
*** Good
** Fair
* Poor

*** Above Av.
** Average
* Below Av.

* Light
** Med.
*** Heavy

SUGGESTED READING

THE FOLLOWING BOOKS are suggested as supplemental reading for those who want to pursue specific topics further.

Basic Sewing Skills

Margolis, Adele P. *The Dressmaking Book.* New York: Doubleday and Company, 1967.

This is a good book for the beginning sewer and a handy reference for the advanced sewer. It covers many of the basic sewing problems and is written in a very readable style.

Pattern Alteration

Hollen, Norma R. *Flat Pattern Methods.* Minneapolis: Burgess Publishing Company, 1965..

An excellent book on pattern alteration which treats the subject with considerable detail and has easy to follow directions.

Pattern Drafting. Tokyo: Kamakura-Shobo Publishing Co. Ltd., 1969.

This is a very good book for ideas for pattern alteration techniques. It gives specific designs and shows how to alter the basic bodice to achieve this. Some analysis will be required to correlate their procedure for drafting with the one described in this book.

Fabric

Miller, Edward. *Textiles.* New York: Theatre Arts, 1968.

This is written so that the average lay reader can understand it. The details of fabric construction are described in non-technical terms and the complex chemical formulas sometimes found in books on fabrics are excluded.

Historical Sources

Edson, Doris and Barton, Lucy. *Period Patterns.* Boston: Walter H. Baker Company, 1942.

This is a supplement to Lucy Barton's *Historic Costume for the Stage.* The patterns are scaled to 1/16th the actual size.

Kohler, Carl. *A History of Costume.* New York: Dover Publications, Inc., 1963.

The patterns in this book are illustrated, with the measurements of critical points given in centimeters from an axis line.

Payne, Blanche. *History of Costume.* New York: Harper and Row Publishers, 1965.

The back of this book contains pattern drafts for 43 different costumes. They are scaled to 1/8th the actual size.

Waugh, Norah. *Corsets and Crinolines.* London: Batsford, 1954.

This book contains patterns for various undergarments from 1630 to 1925. They are illustrated to scale.

ACKNOWLEDGMENTS

A BOOK SUCH AS THIS is never the work of one person. It is an accumulation of the thoughts, ideas, and knowledge of many people channeled onto the written page by the author.

I learned the basic system of drafting described in this book from Dr. Paul D. Reinhardt of the Drama Department at the University of Texas. Much of what is written here is an echo of his teaching, and my thanks must therefore start with him. Since then, the system has been expanded and revised. Many people I have worked with and taught have added their contribution to the final product. Unfortunately, it would be impossible to list all their names.

Since the book has been in manuscript form, I have had the help of many people in editing, proofreading and trying out the patterns. In particular, I wish to give thanks to Pam Ashton, Carol Holben, Teddi Jean McCunn, Helen Paul, to Gertrude, and to my wife. I would also like to thank Dr. William Reardon for his encouragement and advice.

Last but not least, I would like to thank Mrs. Judith Klugmann, the editor of this book. She has spent many hours working on the book and trying out the patterns. Her resulting suggestions have been very useful.

INDEX

B

C

D

E

G

H

I

J

K

L

M

N

O

P

S

T

U

V

Y

Z